Y0-BRC-390

WHAT IS THE
PURPOSE OF CREATION?

WHAT IS THE PURPOSE OF CREATION?

A Jewish Anthology

Michael J. Alter

JASON ARONSON INC.
Northvale, New Jersey
London

For credits, see pp. 313–316.

10 9 8 7 6 5 4 3 2 1

Library of Congress Cataloging-in-Publication Data

Alter, Michael J.
    What is the purpose of creation? : a Jewish anthology / Michael J. Alter.
       p. cm.
    Includes bibliographical references and index.
    ISBN 0-87668-769-9
    1. Creation—History of doctrines. 2. Cosmology, Biblical.
  3. Man (Jewish theology). I. Title.
    BS680.C69A57 1991
    296.3'4—dc20   90-48734

Manufactured in the United States of America. Jason Aronson Inc. offers books and cassettes. For information and catalog write to Jason Aronson Inc., 230 Livingston Street, Northvale, New Jersey 07647.

CONTENTS

PREFACE

The primary purpose of writing this book was to fulfill my own curiosity on the subject of creation and the purpose of life. During the years of research I found that while an abundance of writing is available on the subject, several problems would confront the layperson attempting to locate this information. Many of the works are written in Hebrew, and the translations are scattered over a vast area of literature (e.g., general religion, theology, kabbalah, philosophy, psychology). Many of these sources may also be unavailable to individuals and groups, due to a lack of resources in their communities. This book is an attempt to bring together in one volume representative selections from Jewish sources that address the cosmic question: What is the Purpose of Creation and Life?

The book may be used in several different ways: as a textbook, either alone or with other readings; as source materials for a fellowship (e.g., *havurot*); as a guide to independent study for the reader; and as a springboard to facilitate one's reflections on a subject that is profound, esoteric, and perhaps of great personal significance.

The book is divided into six parts. Part 1 is the Introduction, which presents the themes of the cosmic question. Parts 2-5 present, in chronological order, excerpts from the Tanakh, the Oral Law (i.e., Mishnah and Talmud), the Apocrypha, the Midrash, and the writings of over sixty commentators, spanning a 2,000-year period. Part 6 is the Epilogue. This brief section discusses the central topic as it relates to three critical contemporary issues: cults, drugs, and suicide.

This work is an anthology of works, many of which are translations. No matter how meticulously prepared, translations cannot do justice to the original. Idiomatic terms and expressions, for example, often lose nuances of meaning in translation. Also, the precise meaning of an original text may suffer in the translator's attempt to preserve the author's original style. Hence, the reader is forewarned to take this into account.

Contemporary readers, both Jewish (specifically reform or secular) and non-Jewish, may take exception to many of the statements propounded in this book. Claims that the Jews are the "chosen people" and Israel is "the purpose of creation" may be viewed as obsolete, ethnocentric, and possibly offensive. The sources from which these excerpts are derived cover vast areas of geography and history, and are thus the products of many different cultures, societies, environments, and times. The interpretations of such statements change over time and across cultures, and it is hoped that the presentation of this breadth of views will be of use to readers in expanding their own interpretations.

The library of traditional Jewish writings on religion, theology, and philosophy is voluminous, and many interpretations exist regarding the purposes of creation and life. Nonetheless, according to tradition, there is only one truth. The solution to this seeming contradiction, however, is found in the Mishnah: "Provide yourself with a teacher and avoid doubt" (Pirke Avoth 1:16).

ACKNOWLEDGMENT

Foremost, I wish to thank Rabbi Mitchell Chefitz of Havurah of South Florida and all its members for ten inspiring years of study.

Also, I'd like to express my gratitude to the many who made this work possible. My thanks go to individual authors, translators, and publishers, all of whom generously gave me permission to reprint parts of their publications and works.

I am also grateful to Jason Aronson Inc., who made this project possible. In particular, I wish to thank Arthur Kurzweil, the vice-president, for his initial and enthusiastic interest in the proposed project. Lastly, I acknowledge Jane Andrassi, my senior production editor; Nancy Berliner, my copy editor; and all the other members of the Jason Aronson staff for their assistance throughout the production of this book.

INTRODUCTION

What is the purpose of creation and life? Before the answer to this cosmic question can be approached, the question itself must be examined. The term "purpose" has two distinct meanings or uses. It can refer to an *end* or *goal* of an action. For example, the purpose of a saw is to cut wood, the purpose of a typewriter is to print type, and the purpose of a car is to transport passengers. *Purpose* may also refer to the will or intention to achieve some end or goal. Thus, perhaps, your purpose in going to college is to get an education, your purpose in working is to acquire income to support yourself, and the purpose of God's creation is such-and-such. And thus it is the objective of this anthology to examine the purpose of creation and life.

In further analyzing the cosmic question, three positions need to be addressed. At one extreme, there are those who contend that the universe, and life in particular, is purposeless. This view is based on the theory that the universe has always existed (i.e., the eternity of the universe), that mankind is a product of a long evolutionary process, and that God does not exist. At the opposite extreme are those who have perfect faith in the existence of a Creator. Accordingly, these believers hold as a fundamental truth that God exists and that the universe and mankind are planned and purposeful. To support this position, they point to passages taken from the Scriptures and other sacred works.

Between these extremes are those who are confused, in doubt, and/or undecided. Those who have doubts generally contend that science has not and cannot answer such fundamental questions as: What is the origin of the universe and mankind? Why is there something rather than nothing? If God is the Creator, and if God is perfect, why should He need to create? This latter question implies that God is lacking in something and is therefore imperfect. The argument is refuted by those with faith that Creation was the Creator's most perfect act of altruism and loving-kindness.

Many commentators, philosophers, and sages have written on and addressed the question, "What is the purpose of creation and life?" In many instances, these individuals cite Scripture. However, many others merely elaborate upon what they believe to be the ultimate purpose or what they believe are God's ultimate purposes. Commonly cited meanings (both Jewish and non-Jewish) include but are not limited to the following list of the purposes of the creation and life.

1. Materialism–a philosophy preoccupied with or stressing material things.
2. Hedonism–a philosophy that accepts the pursuit of pleasure as the important and lasting concern of human life.
3. Aestheticism–a philosophy devoted to beauty or the cultivation of the arts.
4. Epicureanism–a philosophy that considers attainment of an imperturbable emotional calm the highest good.

5. Intellectualism–a philosophy that accepts the pursuit of the intellect as the important and lasting concern of human life.

6. Transcendentalism–a philosophy that asserts the primacy of the spiritual and transcendent over the material.

7. Mysticism–a philosophy postulating the possibility of direct and intuitive acquisition of ineffable knowledge and power, that direct knowledge of God or ultimate reality can be attained.

However, our primary concern here is, "What is our purpose in terms of the intention or will of the Creator?" In other words, Why did God create the universe and, more important, mankind?

I

THE CLASSICAL
SOURCES

The Tanakh

The Tanakh is the Hebrew name given to the Jewish Bible. In the non-Jewish community it is commonly referred to as the Old Testament. However, knowledgeable Jews do not use this expression, since the term "old" implies that there is a "new" testament.

The Tanakh is divided into three main parts:

1. The Torah, the Hebrew word for "teaching" or "instruction."
2. The Nebiim, the Hebrew word for "prophets."
3. The Ketubim, the Hebrew word for "writings."

The word TaNaKh is derived from the first letter of each of these words, with vowels added between them.

The three main parts of the Tanakh are further subdivided into twenty-four sacred canonical books, according to tradition (*Baba Bathra* 14b–15a; *Taanith* 8a). However, counting each title separately, the total number of books in the Tanakh is thirty-nine (Table 1–1).

TABLE 1-1

The Three Main Parts of the Tanakh	Canonical Books

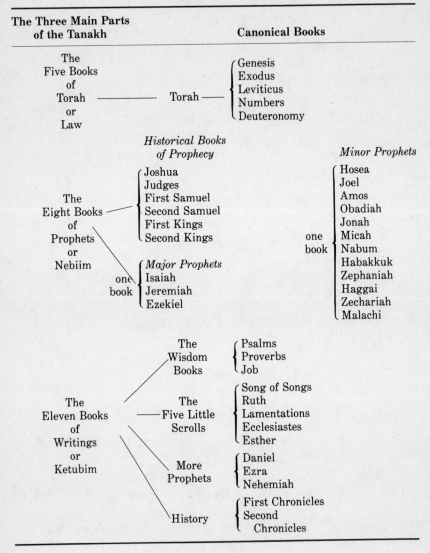

The
Five Books
of
Torah ——————— Torah ——
or
Law

Genesis
Exodus
Leviticus
Numbers
Deuteronomy

Historical Books of Prophecy

The
Eight Books
of
Prophets
or
Nebiim

Joshua
Judges
First Samuel
Second Samuel
First Kings
Second Kings

one book

Major Prophets
Isaiah
Jeremiah
Ezekiel

Minor Prophets

one book

Hosea
Joel
Amos
Obadiah
Jonah
Micah
Nabum
Habakkuk
Zephaniah
Haggai
Zechariah
Malachi

The
Eleven Books
of
Writings
or
Ketubim

The
Wisdom
Books

Psalms
Proverbs
Job

The
Five Little
Scrolls

Song of Songs
Ruth
Lamentations
Ecclesiastes
Esther

More
Prophets

Daniel
Ezra
Nehemiah

History

First Chronicles
Second
   Chronicles

The Torah is comprised of five books:

Hebrew	Translation	Greek	Translation
Bereshit	In the beginning	Genesis	Creation
Shemot	Names	Exodus	Departure
VaYikra	And He called	Leviticus	Priestly
Bamidbar	In the Wilderness	Numbers	Numbers
Devarim	Words	Deuteronomy	Repetition

According to tradition, the Torah was received by Moses at Mount Sinai and is the actual words of God. These five books contain the 613 commandments upon which Halacha (i.e., traditional Jewish law) is based. This is known as the Written Law as distinct from the Oral Law. Other names for the Torah are

> The Five Books of Moses
> The Chumash (in Hebrew literally "fifth")
> Sefer Ha-Brith (the Book of the Covenant)
> Sefer Moshe (the Book of Moses)
> Sefer Torah (the Book of the Law)
> Torah Shel Moshe (the Torah of Moses)
> The Pentateuch (from the Greek, "consisting of five parts")

The second part of the Tanakh is the Nebiim or the Prophets. This section has eight books and is commonly divided into two parts. In the Hebrew Bible the title Nebiim Rishonim or "Former Prophets" applies to the four historical books of Joshua, Judges, Samuel, and Kings. The Nebiim Aharonim or "Latter Prophets" is also made up of four books: Isaiah, Jeremiah, Ezekiel, and the twelve minor Prophets.

The Ketubim, the third and last part of the Tanakh, comprises those writings that in Greek are called the Hagiographa. The eleven books of the Ketubim are usually in the order of Psalms, Proverbs, Job, Song of Songs, Ruth, Lamentations, Ecclesiastes, Esther, Daniel, Ezra-Nehemiah, and Chronicles.

Eight major themes emerge from the Tanakh that are related to the purpose of creation and life:

1. God created everything.
   Isaiah 45:7,
   Isaiah 45:18,
   Nehemiah 9:6

2. Everything has a Purpose and nothing is Purposeless.
   Proverbs 16:4
   Ecclesiastes 3:1
   Ecclesiastes 3:17
   Ecclesiastes 8:6

3. Man is God's partner in creation.
   Genesis 1:26–28
   Genesis 2:15

4. Man was created to propagate and inhabit the earth.
   Genesis 1:28
   Isaiah 45:18

5. Creation was for the sake of Abraham and the nation and people of Israel.
   Genesis 12:3
   Genesis 17:5
   Genesis 22:18
   Deuteronomy 10:15
   Deuteronomy 14:2
   Isaiah 42:6
   Nehemiah 9:6–7

6. Creation was an act of altruistic and perfect lov-
   ing-kindness.
   > Psalm 89:3
   > Psalm 145:9
   > Isaiah 48:17

7. Creation was for God's own Glory.
   > Isaiah 43:7
   > Zechariah 14:9

8. Man and Israel were created to either fear God,
   love God, keep God's commandments, recognize
   God, and/or keep holy. (Note that a similar justi-
   fication is stated in the Koran, *Sura* 51:55–58; see
   page 304.)
   > Leviticus 19:3
   > Deuteronomy 8:6
   > Deuteronomy 11:3
   > Micah 6:8
   > Zechariah 14:9
   > Psalm 145:12
   > Ecclesiastes 12:13

Following are passages from the Tanakh representing the
above interpretations.

When God began to create the heaven and the earth.

> Genesis 1:1

And God said, Let us make man in our image, after our
likeness. They shall rule the fish of the sea, the birds of the
sky, the cattle, the whole earth, and all the creeping things
that creep on earth.

> Genesis 1:26

And God created man in His image, in the image of God He
created him; male and female He created them.

> Genesis 1:27

God blessed them and God said to them, Be fertile and increase, fill the earth and master it; and rule the fish of the sea, the birds of the sky, and all living thing that creep on earth.

Genesis 1:28

Such is the story of heaven and earth when they were created.

Genesis 2:4

The Lord God took the man and placed him in the garden of Eden, to till it and to tend it.

Genesis 2:15

The Lord God said, It is not good for man to be alone; I will make a fitting helper for him.

Genesis 2:18

I will bless those who bless you, And curse him that curses you; And all the families of the earth shall bless themselves by you.

Genesis 12:3

And you shall no longer be Abram, but your name shall be Abraham, for I make you the father of a multitude of nations.

Genesis 17:5

All the nations of the earth shall bless themselves by your descendants, because you have obeyed My command.

Genesis 22:18

The Lord spoke to Moses, saying: Speak to the whole Israelite community and say to them: You shall be holy, for I, the Lord your God, am Holy.

Leviticus 19:2

Therefore keep the commandments of the Lord your God: walk in His ways and revere Him.

Deuteronomy 8:6

Yet it was to your fathers that the Lord was drawn in His love for them, so that He chose you, their lineal descendants, from among all peoples—as is now the case.

Deuteronomy 10:15

For you are a people consecrated to the Lord your God: the Lord your God chose you from among all other peoples on earth to be His treasured people.

Deuteronomy 14:2

The secret things belong unto the Lord our God: but those things which are revealed belong unto us and to our children for ever, that we may do all the words of this law.

Deuteronomy 29:28

I the Lord, in My grace, have summoned you, and I have grasped you by the hand. I created you, and appointed you a covenant people, a light of nations . . . .

Isaiah 42:6

All who are linked to My name, when I have created, formed, and made for My glory—

Isaiah 43:7

For thus said the Lord, the Creator of heaven who alone is God, Who formed the earth and made it, Who alone established it—He did not create it a waste, but formed it for habitation: I am the Lord, and there is none else.

Isaiah 45:18

For He has said: It is too little that you should be My servant in that I raise up the tribes of Israel and restore the survivors of Israel: I will also make you a light of nations, that My salvation may reach the ends of the earth.

Isaiah 49:6

Indeed, my Lord God does nothing, without having revealed His purpose to His servants the prophets.

Amos 3:7

He has told you, O man, what is good; and what the Lord requires of you: only to do justice and to love goodness, and to walk modestly with your God.

Micah 6:8

And the Lord shall shall be king over all the earth: in that day there shall be one Lord with one name.

Zechariah 14:9

The Lord is good to all, and His mercy is upon all His works.

Psalm 145:9

The Lord hath made everything for a purpose, even the wicked for an evil day.

Proverbs 16:4

God thunders marvelously with His voice; He works wonders that we cannot understand.

Job 37:5

To everything there is a season, and a time to every purpose under the heaven. . . .

Ecclesiastes 3:1

I know that, whatsoever God doeth, it shall be for ever: nothing can be put in it, nor any thing taken away from it: and God doeth it, that men should fear before him.

Ecclesiastes 3:14

I said in mine heart, God shall judge the righteous and the wicked: for there is a time for every purpose and for every work.

Ecclesiastes 3:17

Because to every purpose there is time and judgment, and the evils coming upon a man are many.

Ecclesiastes 8:6

Let us hear the conclusion of the whole matter: Fear God and keep His commandments: for this is the whole duty of man.

Ecclesiastes 12:13

Thou, even thou, art Lord alone; thou hast made heaven, the heaven of heavens, with all things that are therein, the seas, and all that is therein, and thou preservest them all; and the host of heaven worshipeth thee. Thou art the Lord the God, who didst choose Abram, and broughtest him forth out of Ur of the Chaldeans, and gavest him the name Abraham.

Nehemiah 9:6–7

The Oral Law

The second source of Jewish literature to be explored is the Oral Law or "Torah she-be-al Peh." According to Jewish tradition, Moses also received an Oral Law at Mount Sinai. This he transmitted to Joshua, who passed it to the elders, who in turn gave it to the prophets, and the prophets to the men of the Great Assembly. The Mishnah is the legal codification of the Oral Law, and it was accomplished in the early third century. The Oral Law complemented the Written Law and explained it according to the different requirements of each generation. Later, the Mishnah was incorporated into two great compilations: the Babylonian Talmud and the Jerusalem (or Palestinian) Talmud. These also contained the comprehensive collection of the discussions on a wide range of topics by generations of scholars and jurists from many academies and in more than one country during several centuries. The Babylonian Talmud contains about 2½ million words and is approximately three times as long as the Palestinian Talmud.

THE MISHNAH

Aboth

The tractate *Aboth* belongs to the first of six divisions of the Mishnah (Nezikin). *Aboth* contains the sayings and religioethical teachings of the sages from about 300 B.C.E. to 300 C.E. This tractate contains no Talmud commentary.

Aboth 2:9

Rabban Johanan ben Zaccai received from Hillel and from Shammai. He used to say: If thou hast learned much Torah, take no credit for thyself, for to this end wast thou created.

Aboth 6:11

All which the Holy One, blessed be He, created in His world He created not except for His glory as it is said (Isaiah 43:7):—'Every thing that is called by my name, and that I have created for my glory, I have formed it, yea I have made it.' And it says (Exodus 15:18):—'The Lord shall reign for ever and ever'.

THE TALMUD

Berakoth

The tractate *Berakoth* belongs to the Mishnah order of Zeraim. *Berakoth* consists of nine chapters. It deals with the recitation of the *Shema*, the treating of benedictions and prayers, and prayer in general.

Berakoth 6b

R. Helbo further said in the name of R. Huna: If one is filled with the fear of God his words are listened to. For it is said:

The end of the matter, all having been heard: fear God, and keep his commandments, for this is the whole man.[1] What means, *'For this is the whole man'?*—R. Eleazar says: The Holy One, blessed be He, says: The whole world was created for his sake only. R. Abba b. Kahana says: He is equal in value to the whole world. R. Simeon b. Azzai says (some say, R. Simon b. Zoma says): The whole world was created as a satellite for him.

Berakoth 61b

It has been taught: R. Jose the Galilean says, The righteous are swayed[2] by their good inclination, as it says, *My heart*[3] *is slain within me.*[4] The wicked are swayed by their evil inclination, as it says, *Transgression speaketh to the wicked, methinks, there is no fear of God before his eyes.*[5] Average people are swayed by both inclinations, as it says, *Because He standeth at the right hand of the needy,*[6] *to save him from them that judge his soul.*[7] Raba said: People such as we are of the average. Said Abaye to him: The Master gives no one a chance to live![8] Raba further said: The world was created only for either the totally wicked or the totally righteous.[9] Raba said: Let a man know concerning himself whether he is completely righteous or not! Rab said: The world was created only for Ahab son of Omri and for R. Hanina b. Dosa; for Ahab son of Omri this world, and for R. Hanina b. Dosa the future world.

---

[1]Ecclesiastes 12:13. He interprets: 'Everything is heard, if you fear God'.
[2]Lit., 'judged'.
[3]I.e., evil promptings.
[4]Psalm 109:22. E.V. [English version of the Bible] *'wounded'*.
[5]Ibid. 36:2.
[6]I.e., in good deeds.
[7]I.e., his two inclinations. Ibid. 109:31.
[8]If Raba is only average, what must other people be?
[9]I.e., this world for the wicked and the next for the righteous.

Shabbath

The tractate *Shabbath* is in the order of Moed. *Shabbath*
is comprised of twenty-four chapters. It is concerned with
rules and regulations of observing the Sabbath.

Shabbath 31a–b

Rabbah b. R. Huna said: Every man who possesses learning
without [31*b*] the fear of Heaven is like a treasurer who is
entrusted with the inner keys but not with the outer: how is
he to enter? R. Jannai proclaimed: Woe to him who has no
courtyard yet makes a gate for same![4] Rab Judah said, The
Holy One, blessed be He, created His world only that men
should fear Him,[5] for it is said, *and God hath done it, that
men should fear before Him.*[6]

---

[4]Learning is a gate whereby one enters the court of piety. Woe to him who
prepares the entry without the court itself!
[5]By 'fear' not dread but awe and reverence is to be understood, proceeding
out of man's realization of God's essential perfection. This reverence, and
the attempt to attain something of that perfection which it inculcates, is
man's highest aim in life, and that is probably the meaning of this dictum;
cf. Maimonides *Guide*, 3:52.
[6]Ecclesiastes 3:14.

Shabbath 77b

Honey, sufficient to place on a scab. A Tanna taught: As
much as is required for putting on the opening of a scab. R.
Ashi asked: 'On a scab': [does that mean] on the whole opening of the scab,[2] or perhaps [it means] on the top of the scab,[3]
thus excluding [sufficient for] going all round the sore,
which is not required?[4] The question stands over.

Rab Judah said in Rab's name: Of all that the Holy One,
blessed be He, created in His world, He did not create a

---

[2]The entire surface being referred to as the opening.
[3]Lit., "the first projecting point."
[4]Before a penalty is incurred.

single thing without purpose. [Thus] He created the snail as a remedy for a scab; the fly as an antidote to the hornet['s sting];[5] the mosquito [crushed] for a serpent['s bite]; a serpent as a remedy for an eruption, and a [crushed] spider as a remedy for a scorpion['s bite]. 'A serpent as a remedy for an eruption':[6] what is the treatment? One black and one white [serpent] are brought, boiled [to a pulp] and rubbed in.

[5]A crushed fly applied to the affected part is a remedy.
[6]This phrase is added in the text by BaH.

Hagigah

The tractate *Hagigah* belongs to the Mishnah order of Moed. It consists of three chapters. *Hagigah* deals with the Temple sacrificial obligations of the individual during the three pilgrim festivals.

Hagigah 2a–b

As He comes to see, so He comes to be seen: just as [He comes] to see with both eyes, so also to be seen with both eyes. Alternatively, I could answer: Actually, it is as I said at first;[4] and as for your objection [arising] from the statement of Rabina, it is not a [valid] objection: the one [teaching][5] is according to the earlier Mishnah,[6] and the other[7] is accord-

[4]I.e., that the world *all* comes to include a half-slave.
[5]I.e., the statement that unfreed slaves are exempt from visiting the Temple, which Rabina interprets as inferring such as are half free.
[6]I.e., the Mishnah as it was formulated before the School of Hillel (whose ruling was authoritative against that of the Shammaite School cf. Ber. 36*b* and Grätz, vol. IV, p. 424, n. 4; Heb. edn. vol. II, p. 172, n. 1) came over to the view of the School of Shammai. משנה ראשונה (rendered, 'the earlier Mishnah') may refer either (*a*) to a single previous ruling later revised, or (*b*) to an entire compilation of the Mishnah, in which case it may be rendered, 'the first Mishnah'; cf. *J.E.* vol. VIII, p. 610f, and refs.
[7]V. note 4.

ing to the later Mishnah.[8] For we have learnt: One who is half a slave and half a freedman serves his master one day and himself the other day: this is the view of Beth Hillel. Said Beth Shammai to them: [2b] You have made it right for his master,[9] but you have not made it right for himself.[10]

---

[8]I.e., representing the later opinion of the School of Hillel. Though this second opinion contradicts the first, the earlier ruling was not erased from the Mishnah, on the principle that a Mishnah (ruling) which had once been taught was not to be removed from its place; cf. Yeb. 30a *et passim*.

[9]I.e., he gets the full benefit of his half-ownership.

[10]R. Meshullam (in Tosaf.) prefers the opposite reading. 'You have made it right for himself, but you have not made it right at all for his master'; because the latter loses any possible share of the offspring.

He may not marry a bondwoman, nor may he marry a freewoman.[1] Should he abstain [from marriage]? But then was not the world created only for propagation?[2] as it is said:[3] *'He created it not a waste, He formed it to be inhabited'*. For the sake of the social order,[4] therefore, his master must be compelled to set him free, and the latter must give him a bond for the half of his value. Thereupon Beth Hillel retracted and gave their ruling in accordance with the view of Beth Shammai.

Sanhedrin

Sanhedrin is a part of the Mishnah division Nezikin. This tractate consists of eleven chapters, primarily concerned with courts of justice and judicial procedures.

---

[1]Being partly a freedman he may not marry a slave; being partly a slave he may not marry a freewoman; v. Deuteronomy 23:18 and Targum Onklos a.l.

[2]Lit., 'for fruitfulness and multiplication', cf. Genesis 1:28.

[3]Isaiah 45:18.

[4]Lit., 'for the sake of the establishment (or improvement) of the world'; cf. Gittin IV, 2, 3, where Danby renders; 'as a precaution for the general good'.

Sanhedrin 98b

Rab said: The world was created only on David's account.[7] Samuel said: On Moses' account;[8] R. Johanan said: For the sake of the Messiah. What is his [the Messiah's] name?—The School of R. Shila said: His name is Shiloh, for it is written, *until Shiloh come.*[9] The School of R. Yannai said: His name is Yinnon, for it is written, *His name shall endure for ever:*[10] *e'er the sun was, his name is Yinnon.*[11] The School of R. Haninah maintained: His name is Haninah, as it is written, *Where I will not give you Haninah.*[12] Others say: His name is Menahem the son of Hezekiah, for it is written, *Because Menahem* ['the comforter'], *that would relieve my soul,* . . .

The Apocrypha

The Apocrypha contains those books that were not canonized into the Tanakh. Literally, the term means "the hidden books." The Talmud refers to them as the Sefarim Hitzonim ("outside books") and Kethuvin Aharonim ("latter writings") because they were produced when direct revelation had ceased. Some writers refer to these books as the Pseudepigrapha. This is because they are attributed to someone who was not really the author. These books were written during the period of the Second Temple and for some time after its destruction (i.e., approximately 135 C.E.).

---

[7]That he might sing hymns and psalms to God.
[8]That he might receive the Torah.
[9]Genesis 49: 10
[10]E.V. *'shall be continued'.*
[11]Psalms 72:17.
[12]Jeremiah 16:13. Thus each School evinced intense admiration of its teacher in naming the Messiah after him by a play on words.

Generally, Jews do not study these works. There are two explanations for this. First, these works were suspected of having arisen from Christian doctrine and later interpolations. Second, Rabbi Akiva stated in the Mishnah (*Sanhedrin* 10:1) that those who study such works would have no share in the world to come (Birnbaum 1975). However, for scholars, the Apocrypha is important because it can be used for reference and contains ideas such as resurrection, reward and punishment, messianism, and the Last Judgment.

THE BOOK OF ENOCH

There are two versions of the *Book of Enoch*. Much of the work deals with apocalyptic visions, messianic yearnings, and moral discourses. The original is lost and is extant only in Greek.

Book of Enoch 69:1–25

69: The Names and Functions of the (Fallen Angels and) Satans: the Secret Oath.

1   And after this judgement they shall terrify and make them to tremble because they have shown this to those who dwell on the earth.

2   And behold the names of those angels [and these are their names: the first of them is Samjâzâ, the second Artâqîfâ, and the third Armên, the fourth Kôkabêl, the fifth Tûrâêl, the sixth Rûmjâl, the seventh Dânjâl, the eighth Nêqâêl, the ninth Barâqêl, the tenth Azâzêl, the eleventh Armârôs, the twelfth Batarjâl, the thirteenth Busasêjal, the fourteenth Hanânêl, the fifteenth Tûrêl, and the sixteenth Sîmâpêsîêl, the seventeenth Jetrêl, the eighteenth Tûmâêl, the nineteenth Tûrêl, the twentieth

3 Rûmâêl, the twenty-first Azâzêl. And these are the chiefs
  of their angels and their names, and their chief ones over
  hundreds and over fifties and over tens].
4   The name of the first Jeqôn: that is, the one who led
  astray [all] the sons of God, and brought them down to the
5 earth, and led them astray through the daughters of men.
  And the second was named Asbeêl: he imparted to the
  holy sons of God evil counsel, and led them astray so that
6 they defiled their bodies with the daughters of men. And
  the third was named Gâdreêl: he it is who showed the
  children of men all the blows of death, and he led astray
  Eve, and showed [the weapons of death to the sons of
  men] the shield and the coat of mail, and the sword for
  battle, and all the weapons of death to the children of
7 men. And from his hand they have proceeded against
8 those who dwell on the earth from that day and for ever-
  more. And the fourth was named Pênêmûe: he taught the
9 children of men the bitter and the sweet, and he taught
  them all the secrets of their wisdom. And he instructed
  mankind in writing with ink and paper, and thereby
  many sinned from eternity to eternity and until this day.
10 For men were not created for such a purpose, to give
11 confirmation to their good faith with pen and ink. For
  men were created exactly like the angels, to the intent
  that they should continue pure and righteous, and death,
  which destroys everything, could not have taken hold of
  them, but through this their knowledge they are perishing, and through this power it is consuming me. And the
12 fifth was named Kâsdejâ: this is he who showed the children of men all the wicked smitings of spirits and de-
  mons, and the smitings of the embryo in the womb, that it
  may pass away, and [the smitings of the soul] the bites of
13 the serpent, and the smitings which befall through the
  noontide heat, the son of the serpent named Tabâ'ĕt. And
  this is the task of Kâsbeêl, the chief of the oath which he
  showed to the holy ones when he dwelt high above in
14 glory, and its name is Bîqâ. This (angel) requested Mi-

chael to show him the hidden name, that he might enun-
ciate it in the oath, so that those might quake before that
15 name and oath who revealed all that was in secret to the
children of men. And this is the power of this oath, for it
is powerful and strong, and he placed this oath Akâe in
the hand of Michael.

16   And these are the secrets of this oath . . .
And they are strong through his oath:
And the heaven was suspended before the world was
created,
And for ever.

17   And through it the earth was founded upon the water,
And from the secret recesses of the mountains come
beautiful waters,
From the creation of the world and unto eternity.

18   And through that oath the sea was created,
And as its foundation He set for it the sand against the
time of (its) anger,
And it dare not pass beyond it from the creation of the
world unto eternity.

19   And through that oath are the depths made fast,
And abide and stir not from their place from eternity
to eternity.

20   And through that oath the sun and moon complete
their course,
And deviate not from their ordinance from eternity to
eternity.

21   And through that oath the stars complete their course,
And He calls them by their names,
And they answer Him from eternity to eternity.

22   [And in like manner the spirits of the water, and of the
winds, and of all zephyrs, and (their) paths from all the
23 quarters of the winds. And there are preserved the voices
of the thunder and the light of the lightnings: and there
are preserved the chambers of the hail and the chambers
24 of the hoarfrost, and the chambers of the mist, and the
chambers of the rain and the dew. And all these believe

and give thanks before the Lord of Spirits, and glorify
(Him) with all their power, and their food is in every act
of thanksgiving: they thank and glorify and extol the
name of the Lord of Spirits for ever and ever.]
25   And this oath is mighty over them,
     And through it [they are preserved and] their paths
are preserved,
     And their course is not destroyed.

THE ASSUMPTION OF MOSES

This apocryphal work, *The Assumption of Moses*, is
essentially prophetic in character. It consists of predic-
tions delivered by Moses to Joshua. *The Assumption of
Moses* foretells in brief outline the history of Israel down
to the time of Herod, forecasting the messianic era. It is
extant in Greek.

The Assumption of Moses 1:1–18

1   The Testament of Moses *even* the things which he
    commanded in the one hundred and twentieth year of
2 his life, that is the two thousand five hundredth year
    from the creation of the world: [But according to
3 oriental reckoning the two thousand and seven hun-
    dredth, and the four hundredth after the departure
4 from Phoenicia], when the people had gone forth after
    the Exodus that was made by Moses to Amman
5 beyond the Jordan, in the prophecy that was made by
    Moses in the book Deuteronomy: and he called to him
6,7 Joshua the son of Nun, a man approved of the Lord,
8 that he might be the minister of the people and of the
    tabernacle of the testimony with all its holy things,
9 and that he might bring the people into the land given
    to their fathers, that it should be given to them accord-

ing to the covenant and the oath, which He spake in
the tabernacle to give (it) by Joshua: saying to Joshua
10 these words: '(Be strong) and of a good courage so as to
do with thy might all that has been commanded that
11,12 thou mayst be blameless unto God.' So saith the Lord
13 of the world. For He hath created the world on behalf
of His people. But He was not pleased to manifest this
purpose of creation from the foundation of the world,
in order that the Gentiles might thereby be convicted,
14 yea to their own humiliation might by (their) arguments convict one another. Accordingly He designed
and devised me, and He prepared me before the foundation of the world, that I should be the mediator of
15 His covenant. And now I declare unto thee that the
time of the years of my life is fulfilled and I am pass-
16 ing away to sleep with my fathers even in the presence
of all the people. And receive thou this writing that
17 thou mayst know how to preserve the books which I
shall deliver unto thee: and thou shalt set these in
order and anoint them with oil of cedar and put them
away in earthen vessels in the place which He made
18 from the beginning of the creation of the world, that
His name should be called upon until the day of repentance in the visitation wherewith the Lord will
visit them in the consummation of the end of the days.

THE BOOK OF BARUCH

Like other works, the original Hebrew text of the *Book
of Baruch* (Apocalypse of Baruch) has been lost. However, a sixth-century Syriac version exists in its entirety.
Essentially, this work deals with the destruction of Jerusalem, the Messiah, and theological problems. Charles
(1913) contends that it was written by Pharisaic Jews as
an apology for Judaism, and is in part an implicit polemic
against Christianity.

2 Baruch 14:1-19

1 And I answered and said: 'Lo! Thou hast shown me the method of the times, and that which shall be after these things, and Thou hast said unto me, that the retribution, which has been spoken of by Thee, shall come upon 2 the nations. And now I know that those who have sinned are many, and they have lived in prosperity, and departed from the world, but that few nations will be left in those times, to whom those words shall be said which Thou didst say. 3 For what advantage is there in this, or what (evil), worse than what we have seen befall us, are we to expect to see?

(23-25) 14. I. And I answered and said: 'Behold, thou hast shown me the methods of the times, and that which shall be.

(25-27) And thou hast said unto me that the retribution which was spoken of by thee shall be endured by the nations.

(27-32) 2. And now I know that those who have sinned are many, and they have lived . . ., and departed from the world, but that few nations will be left in those times to whom . . . the words (which) thou didst say.

(32-33) 3. And what advantage (is there) in this or what worse than (these?) . . .

4,5 But again I will speak in Thy presence: What have they profited who had knowledge before Thee, and have not walked in vanity as the rest of the nations, and have not said to the dead: "Give us life," but al-
6 ways feared Thee, and have not left Thy ways? And lo!
7 they have been carried off, nor on their account hast

Thou had mercy on Zion. And if others did evil, it was due to Zion, that on account of the works of those who wrought good works she should be forgiven, and
8 should not be overwhelmed on account of the works of those who wrought unrighteousness. But who, O LORD, my Lord, will comprehend Thy judgement,
Or who will search out the profoundness of Thy way?
Or who will think out the weight of Thy path?
9 Or who will be able to think out Thy incomprehensible counsel?
Or who of those that are born has ever found
The beginning or end of Thy wisdom?
10,11 For we have all been made like a breath. For as the breath ascends involuntarily, and again dies, so it is with the nature of men, who depart not according to their own will, and know not what will befall them in
12 the end. For the righteous justly hope for the end, and without fear depart from this habitation, because they have with Thee a store of works preserved in treasur-
13 ies. On this account also these without fear leave this world, and trusting with joy they hope to receive the
14 world which Thou hast promised them. But as for us—
15 woe to us, who also are now shamefully entreated, and at that time look forward (only) to evils. But Thou knowest accurately what Thou hast done, by means of Thy servants; for we are not able to understand that
16 which is good as Thou art, our Creator. But again, I will speak in Thy presence, O LORD, my Lord. When of
17 old there was no world with its inhabitants, Thou didst
18 devise and speak with a word, and forthwith the works of creation stood before Thee. And Thou didst say that Thou wouldst make for Thy world man as the administrator of Thy works, that it might be known that he was by no means made on account of the world,
19 but the world on account of him. And now I see that as for the world which was made on account of us, lo! it

abides, but we, on account of whom it was made, depart.'

EZRA

Ezra (or 2 Esdras) is extant in a number of translations. *Ezra* is considered one of the most profound
books in apocalyptic literature. Its subject matter deals
with the problem of human suffering, a vindication of
God's actions, and especially the fate of Israel and the
advent of the Messiah. The book was probably written
after the destruction of the Second Temple.

4 Ezra 6:38–59

II. The Problem propounded in its Final Form:
If the World was created for Israel's Sake
why is Israel deprived of its Inheritance?

38 And I said: O Lord, of a truth thou didst speak at the
     beginning of the creation upon the first day, saying: Let
39 heaven and earth be made! and thy word perfected the
     work. Then was the spirit hovering; darkness and silence
     were on every side; the sound of man's voice was not yet
40 before thee. Then thou didst command a ray of light to be
     brought forth out of thy treasuries, that then thy works
     might become visible.
41 Upon the second day again thou didst create the spirit
     of the firmament, and didst command it to make a divi-
     sion between (the waters and) the waters that the one
     part might go up, the other remain beneath.
42 On the third day thou didst command the waters to be
     gathered together in the seventh part of the earth; six
     parts thou didst dry up and preserve, in order that (issu-

ing) from them there might serve before thee those who
both plough and sow.

43   But as soon as thy word went forth the work was done.
44   For immediately there came forth
  Fruits in endless abundance,
   in pleasure of taste exquisitely varied,
  Flowers of inimitable colour
   (trees infinitely varied in form)
  and odours of scent indefinable
This was done the third day.

45   But on the fourth day thou didst command that there
should come into being the brightness of the sun, the
46 light of the moon and the order of the stars; and didst
command them that they should do service unto man,
47 who was about to be formed. Upon the fifth day thou
didst bid the seventh part, where the water was gathered
together, to bring forth living creatures, birds, and
48 fishes; and so it came to pass. The dumb and lifeless
water produced living creatures that for this the nations
49 might declare thy wondrous works. Then didst thou preserve two living creatures; the name of the one thou didst
50 call Behemoth and the name of the other thou didst call
Leviathan. And thou didst separate the one from the
other; for the seventh part, where the water was ga-
51 thered together, was unable to hold them (both). And
thou didst give Behemoth one of the parts which had
52 been dried up on the third day to dwell in, (that namely)
where are a thousand hills: but unto Leviathan thou gavest the seventh part, namely the moist: and thou hast
reserved them to be devoured by whom thou wilt and
when.

53   But upon the sixth day thou didst command the earth
that it should bring forth before thee cattle, beasts, and
54 creeping things; and over these Adam, whom thou didst
ordain lord over all the works that thou didst create
before him: of him we are all sprung, whom thou hast
chosen (to be) (thy) people.

55   All this have I spoken before thee, O Lord, because

thou hast said that for our sakes thou hast created this
56 world. But as for the other nations, which are descended
from Adam, thou hast said that they are nothing, and
that they are like unto spittle; and thou has likened the
57 abundance of them to a drop on a bucket. And now, O
Lord, behold these nations which are reputed as nothing
58 lord it over us and crush us. But we, thy people whom
thou hast called thy first-born, thy only-begotten, thy
59 beloved [most dear], are given up into their hands. If the
world has indeed been created for our sakes why do we
not enter into possession of our world? How long shall
this endure?

The Midrash

According to Weissman (1980), the usual English rendition
of the term Midrash or Midrashim as legends, fables, or
tales is not only inadequate but in fact misleading. Tradi-
tionally, the Midrashic literature is seen as an exegesis that
delves deeply into the spirit of the Scriptures, examining the
text from all sides and deriving interpretations that are not
immediately obvious. Thus, the goal of the Midrash is to
search for the true inner meaning of each phrase, word, or
even letter of the Tanakh.

Midrash is classified into two categories. The Midrash
Halakhah deals with the derivation of laws from scriptural
passages as proof of its authenticity. The Midrash Hag-
gadah is concerned with interpretations, illustrations, or
expansion of nonlegal portions of the Tanakh from a moral,
ethical, or devotional point of view.

GENESIS RABBAH

Genesis *Rabbah* is an aggadic Midrash on the Book of
Genesis. This work presents a consecutive exposition of

the Book of Genesis, chapter by chapter, verse by verse, and often even word by word. It is thought to be the product of Palestinian *amoraim* and was arranged no later than 425 C.E.

Bereshith

Genesis 1:4-7
Midrash *Rabbah*

In the beginning God created. Six things preceded the creation of the world; some of them were actually created, while the creation of the others was already contemplated. The Torah and the Throne of Glory were created. The Torah, for it is written, *The Lord made me as the beginning of His way, prior to His works of old* (Proverbs 8:22). The Throne of Glory, as it is written, *Thy throne is established of old*, etc. (Psalm 93:2). The creation of the Patriarchs was contemplated, for it is written, *I saw your fathers as the first-ripe in the fig tree at her first season* (Hosea 9:10). [The creation of] Israel was contemplated, as it is written, *Remember Thy congregation, which Thou hast gotten aforetime* (Psalm 74:2). [The creation of] the Temple was contemplated, for it is written, *Thou throne of glory, on high from the beginning, the place of our sanctuary* (Jeremiah 17:12). The name of Messiah was contemplated, for it is written, *His name existeth ere the sun* (Psalm 72:17). R. Ahabah b. R. Ze'ira said: Repentance too, as it is written, *Before the mountains were brought forth*, etc. (Psalm 90:2), and from that very moment, *Thou turnest man to contrition, and sayest: Repent, ye children of men* (Psalm 90:3). I still do not know which was first, whether the Torah preceded the Throne of Glory or the Throne of Glory preceded the Torah. Said R. Abba b. Kahana: The Torah preceded the Throne of Glory, for it says, *'The Lord made me as the beginning of His way, ere His works of old,'* which means, ere that whereof it is written, *'Thy throne is established of old.'*

R. Huna, reporting R. Jeremiah in the name of R. Samuel b. R. Isaac, said: The intention to create Israel preceded everything else. This may be illustrated thus: A king was married to a certain lady, and had no son by her. On one occasion the king was found going through the marketplace and giving orders: 'Take this ink, inkwell, and pen for my son,' at which people remarked: 'He has no son: what does he want with ink and pen? Strange indeed!' Subsequently they concluded: 'The king is an astrologer, and has actually foreseen that he is destined to beget a son!' Thus, had not the Holy One, blessed be He, foreseen that after twenty-six generations Israel would receive the Torah, He would not have written therein, *Command the children of Israel!*

R. Banayah said: The world and the fullness thereof were created only for the sake of the Torah: *The Lord for the sake of wisdom* [i.e., the Torah] *founded the earth* (Proverbs 3:19). R. Berekiah said: For the sake of Moses: *And He saw the beginning* [i.e., the Creation] *for Himself, for there a portion of a ruler* [sc. Moses] *was reserved* (Deuteronomy 33:21).

R. Huna said in R. Mattenah's name: The world was created for the sake of three things: *ḥallah*, tithes, and first-fruits, as it is said, IN THE BEGINNING (BERESHITH) GOD CREATED. Now *reshith* alludes to *ḥallah*, for it is written, *Of the first* (reshith) *of your dough* (Numbers 15:20); again, *reshith* alludes to tithes, for it is written, *The first-fruits* (reshith) *of thy corn* (Deuteronomy 18:4); and finally, *reshith* alludes to first-fruits, for it is written, *The choicest* (reshith) *first-fruits of thy land*, etc. (Exodus 23:19).

For all these things hath My hand made (Isaiah 66:2). R. Berekiah objected in the name of R. Judah b. R. Simon: Not with labour or wearying toil did the Holy One, blessed be He, create His world, yet you actually say, *'For all these things hath My hand made'!* R. Judah said: [It means that God created the world] for the sake of the Torah [which is referred to as 'these' in the verse,] *These are the statutes and ordinances and laws*—toroth (Leviticus 26:46). R. Joshua b. R. Nehemiah said: For the sake of the tribes, [as it is written,] *Now these are the names of the tribes* (Ezekiel 48:1). *And*

so all these things came to be, saith the Lord (Isaiah *loc. cit.*):
hence, These are the generations of the heaven.

EXODUS RABBAH

Exodus *Rabbah* is an aggadic Midrash on the Book of
Exodus. It consists of two different Midrashim and is
divided into fifty-two sections. These works were redacted and arranged as early as the ninth century C.E.

Va'era

Exodus 10:1

*And the Lord spoke unto Moses: Go in unto Pharaoh . . . and
if thou refuse to let them go, behold, I will smite all thy borders
with frogs* (Exodus 7:26, 27). Thus it is written: *But the profit
of a land every way is a king that maketh himself servant to
the field* (Ecclesiastes 5:8). (The entire Midrash thereof is
given in Leviticus Rabbah and in 'This is the Statute of the
law'.) Our Rabbis explained the words *'But the profit of a
land every way is'* thus: Even those creatures you deem
redundant in this world, like flies, bugs, and gnats, nevertheless have their allotted task in the scheme of creation, as
it says: *And God saw every thing that He had made, and,
behold, it was very good* (Genesis 1:31). R. Aha b. Hanina
explained thus: Even those creatures deemed by you superfluous in the world, like serpents and scorpions, still have
their definite place in the scheme of creation. For God said
to His prophets: 'Do you think that if you refuse to fulfil My
message I have none else to send? Oh no; *"The superfluity of
a land every way is"* means that My message will be fulfilled
even by a serpent, scorpion, or frog.' The proof is this: had it
not been for the hornet, how would God have exacted retribution from the Amorites? Had it not been for the frog, how

would He have punished the Egyptians? Hence it says:
BEHOLD, I WILL SMITE ALL THY BORDERS WITH FROGS.

Bo

Exodus 17:1

And ye shall take a bunch of hyssop (Exodus 12:22). It is
written: *The Lord hath made every thing for His own purpose*
(Proverbs 16:4). You will find that everything which God
created during the six days of creation was created for His
glory and for the fulfillment of His will. On the first day, He
created the heavens and the earth; they also were created for
His glory, for it says: *Thus saith the Lord: The heaven is My
throne, and the earth is My footstool* (Isaiah 66:1); and also:
The heavens declare the glory of God (Psalm 19:2). The light
also was created for His glory, for it is written: *Who coverest
Thyself with light as with a garment* (*ib.* 104:2). What was
created on the second day? The firmament—also for His
glory, that the angels might stand there and praise Him, as
it says: *Praise Him in the firmament of His power* (*ib.* 150:1).
What was created on the third day? The herbs and the
trees—and the herbs, also we find, offer up praises to the
Lord, for it says: *They shout for joy, yea, they sing* (*ib.* 65:14).
And the trees? Because it says: *Then shall the trees of the
wood sing for joy, before the Lord* (1 Chronicles 16:33). You
find that God commanded certain precepts to be performed
with material from the trees: in the case of the Red Heifer,
He commanded that cedar wood and hyssop should be
thrown in. He also commanded that the sprinkling of the
waters of lustration should be performed with hyssop, and
the purification of the leper was likewise to be carried out
with cedar wood and hyssop; likewise in Egypt did He command to strike the lintel and the two side-posts with the
blood and the bunch of hyssop, as it says: AND YE SHALL TAKE
A BUNCH OF HYSSOP. The seas too He created on the third day,

when He gathered them together from off the earth; and from them His praise ascends, as it says: *Above the voices of many waters, the mighty breakers of the sea, the Lord on high is mighty* (Psalm 93:4). What was created on the fourth day? The luminaries—also for His glory, as it says: *Praise ye Him, sun and moon (ib.* 148:3). On the fifth day, He created the fowl of heaven for His honour, wherewith to offer up a sacrifice, as it says: *And if his offering to the Lord be a burnt-offering of fowls* (Leviticus 1:14). What was created on the sixth day? The cattle, also for His honour; for He commanded sacrifices to be offered from them, as it says: *When any man of you bringeth an offering unto the Lord, ye shall bring your offering of the cattle, even of the herd or of the flock (ib.* 2). Man likewise He created on that day for His glory, for it says: *Praise the Lord from the earth, ye sea-monsters, and all deeps . . . kings of the earth and all peoples,* etc. (Psalm 148:7, 11 *seq.*). A proof that: *'The Lord hath made everything for His own purpose.'*

Did I not hearken unto them in the days of Samuel through prayer, as it says, *And Samuel cried unto the Lord for Israel; and the Lord answered him* (1 Samuel 7:9)? And thus although the people of Jerusalem provoked Me to anger, yet had I mercy on them too because they wept unto Me, as it says, *For thus saith the Lord: Sing with gladness for Jacob . . . announce ye, praise ye, and say: O Lord, save Thy people* (Jeremiah 31:6)—all this is a decisive proof that I do not seek at your hands either sacrifices or offerings, only *"words"*; as it says, *'Take with you words, and return unto the Lord.'* This is why David said: *'I will wash my hands in innocency'* (Psalm 26:6); he does not say, in order to offer up sacrifices unto Thee, but *'That I may make the voice of thanksgiving to be heard'* (*ib.*7),—namely, I will thank Thee for Thy words of Law. Another explanation of *'Take with you words'.* Moses said: *The eternal God is a dwelling-place, and underneath are the everlasting arms* (Deuteronomy 33:27). This refers to Israel for whose sake the world was created and upon whom it stands. Rabbi said: *And He thrust out the* enemy *from before Thee* (Deuteronomy 33:27); this refers to Haman, as it says, *An adversary and an* enemy, *even this wicked Haman* (Esther 7:6). Why does it say '*an adversary and an enemy*'? Because he was an adversary of God and an enemy of Israel; he was an adversary of their ancestors and an enemy of their offspring; he is an adversary to me and an enemy to me. *And he said: Destroy* (Deuteronomy *loc. cit.*); this refers to his children. *And Israel dwelleth in safety, . . .*

ECCLESIASTES RABBAH

Ecclesiastes *Rabbah* is an aggadic Midrash on the Book of Ecclesiastes. Its exposition is given chapter by chapter and verse by verse. This work is thought to date from no earlier than the eighth century C.E.

Ecclesiastes 7:1

CONSIDER THE WORK OF GOD; FOR WHO CAN MAKE THAT STRAIGHT WHICH HE HATH MADE CROOKED (7:13)? When the Holy One, blessed be He, created the first man, He took him and led him round all the trees of the Garden of Eden, and said to him, 'Behold My works, how beautiful and commendable they are! All that I have created, for your sake I created it. Pay heed that you do not corrupt and destroy My universe; for if you corrupt it there is no one to repair it after you. Not only that, but you will cause death to befall that righteous man [Moses].'

SHOHER TOV

Shoher Tov is the commonly used name for the Midrash on the Book of Proverbs. Essentially, it is a collection of homilies. The work is thought to have been redacted and arranged between 600–900 C.E.

Shoher Tov 34

David said to God: "Thou hast created all things in wisdom, and the greatest thing Thou hast created is the capacity of a human brain to acquire and retain wisdom. But when I behold a witless man on the street with torn shirt and bare chest, with children running after him to torment him, I wonder why Thou hast permitted a human being to become insane. Why is there insanity in the Universe?"

God answered: "David, I created nothing without a purpose. A time will come when thou wilt see the uses of insanity itself."

When David escaped to Achish (1 Samuel 21:14), and Achish, the King of Gath wished to slay him, David prayed to God: "Teach me the madness which Thou hast created." God instructed him in feigning madness, and David beheld then that even madness has a purpose.

II

THE COMMENTATORS

Philo Judaeus of Alexandria
(c. 20 B.C.E.–50 C.E.)

Philo was an Alexandrian philosopher. Few details are
known of his life. He wrote on a number of topics
including metaphysics, ethics, and history, and also produced a Bible commentary. The following extract is from
Philo's *Questions and Answers on Genesis*, translated by
Ralph Marcus.

QUESTIONS AND ANSWERS ON GENESIS

Genesis, Book I

6. (Genesis 2:8) Why is God said to have "planted Paradise"
and for whom? And what is Paradise?

Of Paradise, so far as the literal meaning is concerned,
there is no need to give an explicit interpretation. For it is a
dense place full of all kinds of trees. Symbolically, however,
it is wisdom or knowledge of the divine and human and of
their causes. For it was fitting, after the coming into being

37

of the world, to establish the contemplative life in order that through a vision of the world and the things in it praise of the Father might also be attained. For it is not possible for nature to see nor is it possible without wisdom to praise the creator of all things. And His ideas the Creator planted like trees in the most sovereign thing, the rational soul. But as for the tree of life in the midst (of the garden), it is the knowledge, not only of things on the earth, but also of the eldest and highest cause of all things. For if anyone is able to obtain a clear impression of this, he will be fortunate and blessed and truly immortal. But after the world wisdom came into being, since after the creation of the world Paradise was made in the same manner as the poets say the chorus of Muses (was formed), in order to praise the Creator and His work. For just as Plato said, the Creator is the greatest and best of causes, while the world is the most beautiful of created things.

*

Isaac ben Solomon Israeli
(c. 855–955)

Israeli was a native of Egypt and is considered to be one of the first Jewish medieval philosophers. He was a court physician to the caliphs, and a medical writer and Bible commentator. The following selection is from Israeli's *Book of Definitions*, translated by A. Altmann and S. M. Stern.

BOOK OF DEFINITIONS

Texts

2. When the philosophers understood this and it became clear to them that definition can be composed only from

genera and substantial differentiae, and found for philosophy no genus from which its definition could be composed,
they made a subtle investigation according to their superior
deliberation and cogitation and described it by three de-
scriptions: (i) one derived from its name, (ii) another from
its property, (iii) and a third from its traces and actions.

(i) The description taken from its name is as follows:
Philosophy is the love of wisdom. This is deduced from the
name of 'philosopher': philosopher is composed of *phila* and
sophia, and in Greek *phila* means lover and *sophia* wisdom;
thus it is clear that 'philosopher' means 'the lover of wisdom',
and if 'philosopher' means 'the lover of wisdom', 'philosophy'
must mean 'love of wisdom'.

(ii) The description of philosophy taken from its property
is as follows: Philosophy is the assimilation to the works of
the Creator, may He be exalted, according to human capacity. By the words 'assimilation to the works of the Creator' is
meant the understanding of the truth of things, viz. acquiring true knowledge of them and doing what corresponds to
the truth; by the words 'understanding the truth of things'
is meant understanding them from their four natural
causes, which are the (1) material, (2) formal, (3) efficient,
and (4) final causes.

(1) The material cause can be either spiritual or corporeal. A case of a spiritual material cause is that of the genera
which are divided into their species and are the substratum
for their forms which complete their speciality, as for instance 'living being', which is the genus of man and horse
and other species, and is the substratum for their forms
which constitute their essence. A case of a corporeal material cause is silver, which is the matter of the *dirham* and
the ring and the substratum for their forms, or gold, which
is the matter of the *dīnār* and the bracelet and the substratum for their forms.

(2) The formal cause can also be either spiritual or corporeal. A case of a spiritual formal cause is that of the substantial forms which are predicated of the genus and constitute
the essence of the species. For instance rationality, which is

predicated of the living being and thus constitutes the essence of man, and the faculty of neighing, which is predicated of the living being and thus constitutes the essence of
the horse. A case of the corporeal formal cause is the form of
the brick, the sandal, the bell, and suchlike.

(3) The efficient cause can also be either spiritual or corporeal. A case of the spiritual efficient cause is the power of
the sphere which was appointed by the Creator, may He be
exalted, in nature, and ordained in it over the effects which
take place in the corporeal microcosm, viz. coming-to-be and
passing-away, growth and decrease, newness and oldness,
health and illness, and other natural actions. A case of a
corporeal efficient cause is the craft of the goldsmith in
making a ring, the form of a picture made on the wall, and
the work of the builder of a house.

(4) The final cause can also be either spiritual or corporeal. A case of a corporeal final cause is the form of a house
and its completion which is necessary in order to make it
suitable for habitation and protection, and the form of a ring
in order that it should have a seal and be suitable for sealing.
A case of a spiritual final cause is the union of soul and body
to the end that the truths of the subject of science may
become clear to man; that he may distinguish between good
and evil, between what is laudable and what is not; that he
may do what corresponds to truth, in justice and rectitude;
that he may sanctify, praise, and exalt the Creator, and
recognize His dominion; that he may avoid beastly and unclean actions in order thereby to obtain the reward of his
Creator, blessed be He, which is the union with the upper
soul, and the illumination by the light of intellect and by the
beauty and splendour of wisdom. When attaining this rank,
he becomes spiritual, and will be joined in union to the light
which is created, without mediator, by the power of God,
and will become one that exalts and praises the Creator for
ever and in all eternity. This then will be his paradise and
the goodness of his reward, and the bliss of his rest, his
perfect rank and unsullied beauty. For this reason Plato
said that philosophy is a zeal, a striving, an effort, and

concern for death. Says Isaac: This is a description of great profundity and elevated meaning. For in saying 'concern for death' the sage meant it to be understood in the sense of the killing of beastly desires and lusts, for in their mortification and avoidance is the highest rank, the supernal splendour and the entry into the realm of truth. And by vivifying beastly desires and lusts and by strengthening them, men of intellect are drawn away from that which is due to God in the way of obedience, purity, and attention to prayer at the prescribed hours. The saying of the philosopher means this, and intellect testifies to its truth. He said: God has intellectual precepts which He reveals to the elect among His creatures, meaning thereby the prophets and messengers and the true teachers who guide His creatures towards the truth, and who prescribe justice and rectitude and the acceptance of things permissible; the pursuit of goodness, loving-kindness, and mildness, the shunning of evil, injustice, and injury; and the refusal of things unlawful. He who does not attach himself to the intellectual precepts which God has revealed to the elect among his creatures, his priests, and teachers, and perseveres in his own injustice, sinfulness, coarseness, and in the evil of his ways, will be rendered unclean by his impurities, and they will weigh him down and prevent him from ascending to the world of truth. He will not attain the light of intellect and the beauty of wisdom, but remain contained under the sphere, sorrowful, in pain without measure, revolving with the revolution of the sphere in the great fire and the torturing flame. This will be his hell and the fire of his torture which God has prepared for the wicked and sinners who rebel against the precepts of the intellect.

(iii) The description of philosophy from its effect is as follows: Philosophy is man's knowledge of himself. This also is a description of great profundity and elevated intelligence, for the following reason. Man, if he acquires a true knowledge of himself, viz. of his own spirituality and corporeality, comprises the knowledge of everything, viz. of the spiritual and corporeal substance, as in man are joined substance and accident. Substance is twofold, spiritual and corporeal; spiritual, as for instance soul and intellect; corporeal, as for instance the long and broad and deep body. Accident is also twofold, spiritual and corporeal; spiritual, as for instance mildness, knowledge, and similar spiritual accidents which are predicated of the soul; corporeal, as for instance blackness, whiteness, yellowness, redness, thickness, variety, and the other corporeal accidents which are predicated of the body. This being so, it is clear that man, if he knows himself in both his spirituality and corporeality, comprises the knowledge of all, and knows both the spiritual and the corporeal substance, and also knows the first substance which is created from the power of the Creator without mediator, which is appropriated to serve as substratum for diversity; as well as the first generic accident, which is divided into quantity, quality, and relation, together with the remaining six compound accidents which derive from the composition of substance with the three accidents. If man comprises all these, he comprises the knowledge of everything and is worthy to be called a philosopher.

*

Saadiah ben Joseph, the Gaon (882–942)

Saadiah lived in Egypt and traveled extensively through Palestine and other countries. Between 928 and 930, he was appointed gaon of the academy of Sura. Saadiah was a philosopher, talmudist, translator, commentator, author, grammarian, educator, and Jewish leader. He was the greatest sage of his time. The following excerpts are from two sections of his work *Emunot ve-Deot* (*Beliefs and Opinions*), translated by Samuel Rosenblatt.

EMUNOT VE-DEOT

Treatise I
Concerning the Belief that All Existing Things Have Been Created

... Perhaps again someone will wonder: "For what reason did the Creator create all these beings?" To this question there are three answers. The first would be to say that He had created them without any motive, and yet it could not be considered a wanton act, because only man acts wantonly when he does anything without a motive, inasmuch as he would thereby be neglecting his own benefit. But such a thing is far removed from the Creator. The second answer is that God intended thereby to reveal and make manifest His wisdom, as Scripture says: *To make known to the sons of man His mighty acts and the glory of the majesty of His kingdom* (Psalm 145:12). The third is that His intention therein was to benefit His creatures by their use of all these things so that they might obey Him, as He says: *I am the Lord thy God, who teacheth thee for thy profit, who leadeth thee by the way that thou shouldest go* (Isaiah 48:17).

If, again, that individual were to ask, "Then why did He not create them before this time?" our reply would be: "There was no time in existence as yet that one could ask about, and furthermore it is of the very nature of him that acts by free choice to do what he wants when he wants."

The first treatise is hereby completed.

Treatise IV
Concerning Obedience and Rebellion and Predestination and (Divine) Justice

Exordium

I shall open this treatise with the introductory remark that, even though we see that the creatures are many in number, nevertheless, we need not be confused in regard to which of them constitutes the goal of creation. For there exists a natural criterion by means of which we can determine which one of all the creatures is the end. When, then, we make our investigation with this criterion [as a guide], we find that the goal is man.

We arrive at this conclusion in the following manner: Habit and nature place whatever is most highly prized in the center of things which are themselves not so highly prized. Beginning with the smallest things, therefore, we say that it is noted that the kernel lodges inside of <146> all the leaves. That is due to the fact that the kernel is more precious than the leaves, because the growth of the plant and its very existence depend upon it. Similarly does the seed from which trees grow, if edible, lodge in the center of the fruit, as happens in the case of the nut. But even if [a tree grows] from an inedible kernel, this kernel is located in the center of the fruit, no attention being paid to the edible portion, which is left on the outside to preserve the kernel. In the same way is the yolk of the egg in the center, because from it springs the young bird and the chicken. Likewise also is the heart of man in the middle of his breast, owing to the fact that it is the seat of the soul and of the natural heat of the body. So, too, is the power of vision located in the center of the eye because it is by means of it that one is able to see.

When, therefore, we see that this situation appertains to many things and then find the earth in the center of the heaven with the heavenly spheres surrounding it on all sides, it becomes clear to us that the thing which was the object of creation must be on the earth. Upon further investigation of all its parts we note that the earth and the water are both inanimate, whereas we find that the beasts are irrational. Hence only man is left, which gives us the certainty that he must unquestionably have been the intended purpose of creation.

When we examine the Scriptures, we likewise find in them a statement by God to the effect that *I, even I, have made the earth, and created man upon it* (Isaiah 45:12). In fact, at the very beginning of the Torah God listed all classes of creatures. Then, when He had completed them all, He said: *Let us make man* (Genesis 1:26), like a person who builds a palace and, after having furnished and decorated it, brings its owner into it.

*

Solomon ben Judah ibn Gabirol (c. 1021–c. 1057)

Gabirol was a Spanish poet and philosopher. He was orphaned at an early age and supported by philanthropy, and few details are known of his life. His most famous works are *Tikkun Middot ha-Nephesh* (*Improvement of the Moral Quality*), *Keter Malkhut* (*Crown of Divine Kingship*), and *Mekkor Hayyim* (*Fountain/Source of Life*). It is from this latter work that the following extract, translated by Rabbi Yakov Fellig, is taken.

MEKKOR HAYYIM

From all said above, it is clear to me that knowledge is the purpose of man's existence. But, I also see that we should search the character of the soul as it is alone and the changes that occur to it by knowledge that it acquires. It is also for us to know what knowledge does the soul retain after it departs from the body. These questions are not of interest to me now since I have dealt with them when we delved into the soul. Now, I would like to concentrate on the knowledge for which man was created.

The knowledge that is the purpose of man's creation is to what everything is and in particular the knowledge of the first existence from which everything comes.

There are no ways to know the first existence.

This knowledge is not impossible, but not in all cases.

So, what is impossible and what is possible?

It is impossible to know the character of the first existence without being able to meditate on the creation He created. But, one can understand Him from the acts that He has done.

*

Solomon Yitzhak ben Isaac—Rashi (1040-1105)

Rashi was a French rabbinical scholar who is considered one of the greatest biblical and talmudic commentators. His style is simple and concise, and stresses the direct rational meaning of the text. The following extract is from the first page of The Pentateuch and Rashi's Commentary: A Linear Translation into English by Abraham ben Isaiah and Benjamin Sharfmal.

RASHI'S COMMENTARY

| God created | בָּרָא אֱלֹהִים | 1. In the beginning | 1 בְּרֵאשִׁית |

ב' רבתי.

Rashi — רש"י

1 1 **בְּרֵאשִׁית.**

Rabbi Isaac said: — אָמַר רַבִּי יִצְחָק:

It was not necessary to begin the Torah, [whose main object is to teach commandments, mitzvoth, with this verse] — לֹא הָיָה צָרִיךְ לְהַתְחִיל אֶת הַתּוֹרָה

but — אֶלָּא

from "This month shall be unto you" [the beginning of months] (Ex. 12.2), — מֵהַחֹדֶשׁ הַזֶּה לָכֶם,

since this is the first mitzvah [commandment] — שֶׁהִיא מִצְוָה רִאשׁוֹנָה

that Israel was commanded [to observe]. — שֶׁנִּצְטַוּוּ בָּהּ יִשְׂרָאֵל,

And what is the reason that it begins with Genesis? — וּמַה טַּעַם פָּתַח בְּרֵאשִׁית?

Because of [the verse] — מִשּׁוּם

"The power of His works — כֹּחַ מַעֲשָׂיו

He hath declared to His people — הִגִּיד לְעַמּוֹ

in giving them — לָתֵת לָהֶם

the heritage of the nations (Ps. 111.6). — נַחֲלַת גּוֹיִם, (תְּהִלִּים קי"א):

For if the nations of the world should say to Israel: — שֶׁאִם יֹאמְרוּ אֻמּוֹת הָעוֹלָם לְיִשְׂרָאֵל:—

"You are robbers, — לִסְטִים אַתֶּם,

because you have seized by force — שֶׁכְּבַשְׁתֶּם

the lands of the seven nations" [of Canaan], — אַרְצוֹת שִׁבְעָה גּוֹיִם,

they [Israel] could say to them, — הֵם אוֹמְרִים לָהֶם:—

"The entire world belongs to the Holy One, Blessed Be He, — כָּל הָאָרֶץ שֶׁל הַקָּבָּ"ה הִיא,

He created it — הוּא בְּרָאָהּ

and gave it to whomever it was right in His eyes. — וּנְתָנָהּ לַאֲשֶׁר יָשָׁר בְּעֵינָיו,

Of His own will He gave it to them — בִּרְצוֹנוֹ נְתָנָהּ לָהֶם

and of His own will He took it from them — וּבִרְצוֹנוֹ נְטָלָהּ מֵהֶם

and gave it to us." (Yalkut, Ex. 12.2). — וּנְתָנָהּ לָנוּ:

In the beginning He created — בְּרֵאשִׁית בָּרָא.

This passage calls for a midrashic interpretation, — אֵין הַמִּקְרָא הַזֶּה אוֹמֵר אֶלָּא דָּרְשֵׁנִי,

as our Rabbis have interpreted it: — כְּמוֹ שֶׁדְּרָשׁוּהוּ רַבּוֹתֵינוּ:—

"[God created the world] for the sake of the Torah" — בִּשְׁבִיל הַתּוֹרָה

since it is called (Prov. 8.22), — שֶׁנִּקְרֵאת (מִשְׁלֵי ח)

"The beginning (ראשית), of His way" — רֵאשִׁית דַּרְכּוֹ,

and for the sake of Israel — וּבִשְׁבִיל יִשְׂרָאֵל

since they are called (Jer. 2.3), — שֶׁנִּקְרְאוּ (יִרְמְיָ' ב)

"The beginning (ראשית) of His crops." — רֵאשִׁית תְּבוּאָתֹה:

*

Bahya ben Joseph ibn Paquda (1050–1120)

Very little is known about Bahya's life. He lived in Muslim Spain and was a dayyan (judge of a rabbinical court) at Saragossa in Spain. His main work is *Hovot ha-Levavot* or *Duties of the Heart*. The following two excerpts are from a translation of this work by Moses Hyamson.

HOVOT LEVAVOT

Second Treatise
On the examination of created things and God's abounding goodness towards them.

Introduction

As we began, in the first treatise, with a discussion of the various modes in which the Unity of God can be demonstrated so that it shall be wholeheartedly accepted, and found that examination of the wisdom manifested in the Universe which the Creator called into being, is the most direct and surest road to a realization of His existence and reality, we deem it our duty to deal immediately with this theme so that to each treatise the one most nearly resembling it should be joined, and each topic should be followed by what is appropriate to it—this being among the subjects which we have to deal with in regard to the Almighty's service, the purpose for which we were created, as the wise man said (Ecclesiastes 3:14) "And God hath so made it that man should fear before Him". First we have to note that though the benefits God bestows upon His creatures are all-embracing, as Scripture saith (Psalm 145:9) "The Lord is good to all", the majority of mankind are too blind to recognize these benefits or comprehend their high excellence.

Duties of the Heart

Chapter II

Both methods of calling attention to the service of God are necessary because the innate urge is deficient in three respects; and we are therefore obliged to strengthen it by religious instruction. First, man is made up of diverse entities, natures conflicting and mutually antagonistic. These entities are his soul and his body. The Creator has implanted in his soul qualities and forces which make him yearn for things, the use of which will promote his physical wellbeing, so that he will develop vigour to populate the earth, in order that the race may continue while individuals perish. This quality is the desire for bodily pleasures common to all living creatures that propagate their species. The Creator has also engrafted in the human soul other qualities and forces, which, if he uses them, will make him loathe his position in this world and yearn to separate himself from it. This is the desire for perfect wisdom. Since, however, bodily pleasures come to a man's soul first, already in early youth, and the attachment to them is, from the outset, strong, great and extremely urgent, the desire for sensual pleasure overcomes his other faculties, and even predominates over the intellect, for the sake of which man was created. And so his spiritual sight fails and the indications of his desirable qualities disappear. Man therefore needs external means, by the aid of which he may resist his despicable instinct—the lust for animal enjoyments—and revitalize the marks of his noblest endowment—the intellect. These aids are the contents of the Torah, whereby God, through His messengers and prophets, taught His creatures the way to serve Him. Secondly, the intellect is a spiritual entity, originating in the higher, spiritual world. It is a stranger in this world of gross material bodies. Sensual lust in man is the product of natural forces and of a combination of his physical elements. Its foundation and root are in this world. Food gives it strength. Physical pleasures add to its vigour, while the intellect, because it is a stranger here, stands without support or ally, and all are against it. Hence it follows that it must become weak and that it needs an external means to repel the mighty power of lust and overcome it. The Torah is the remedy for such spiritual maladies and moral diseases. The Torah therefore prohibits many kinds of food, apparel, sexual relations, certain acquisitions and practices, all of which strengthen sensual lust; it also exhorts us to use those means which will resist lust and are its opposites. These are prayer, fasting, alms-giving, kindness; by which the intellectual faculties are revived and man is aided in this world and for the world to come, as David said: "Thy word is a lamp to my feet and a light to my path" (Psalm 119:105); "For the commandment is a lamp and the law is light" (Proverbs 6:23); "I saw that wisdom is preferable to folly as light is preferable to darkness" (Ecclesiastes 2:13).

Third, the sensual desire, constantly enforced by bodily nourishment, never ceases working by day or night. The intellect, on the other hand, is only called into activity to help one gratify his passions. Now it is well known that organs which are constantly exercised in accordance with their nature, improve and become more efficient, while those that are less frequently used deteriorate and become inefficient. It logically follows therefore that the sensual desire would become stronger because it is continually exercised, while the intellectual faculty would weaken, because it is so seldom used, and so little for its proper purpose. Hence the need of something, the acquisition of whose truth demands neither the use of man's physical organs nor the indulgence of his passions but only the exercise of his intellect, freed from the predominance of lusts. This aid is the Torah, the study of which will make the intellect stronger, purer, more luminous, and will drive away from man the folly that masters his soul and keeps him from seeing things as they really are and placing them in their proper relations. As the Psalmist says, "The law of the Lord is perfect, restoring the soul; the testimony of the Lord is faithful, making wise the simple; the ordinances of the Lord are right, rejoicing the heart; the commandment of the Lord is pure, enlightening the eyes" (Psalm 19:8–9).

From what has been said, it is clearly established how necessary it is that a human being should be aroused to the service of God by the Torah, which includes rational precepts as well as those accepted on authority, so that through these we may rise to the service of God which, our reason demonstrates, is man's duty and the main purpose for which the human species has been called into existence in this world.

*

Joseph ben Jacob ibn Zaddik
(?–1146)

Little is known of the Zaddik's life. He was a philosopher, poet, and dayyan (in Cordoba). His most famous work is the *Sefer ha-Olam ha-Katan* or *Microcosm*. Following are several excerpts from this work. The translation is by Jacob Haberman, undertaken as part of his 1954 dissertation at Columbia University.

SEFER HA-OLAM HA-KATAN

Since man, however, is an intelligent being and possesses a heart [of wisdom] he will not attain his purpose unless he studies and practices. All this is in order that he should perceive and understand that he has to practice all these things, for man was created only to learn since we see that in

all other things he has a true affinity with the beasts. When
he does not exercise the intellectual faculty which he possesses, and by virtue of which he is superior to all animals,
and does not attempt to unravel the fundamental principles
of existent things, then there is no difference between him
and the animals.

A Discussion to Prove that God
Is Not in Need of Anything,
and That He Is Self-Sufficient

Know you, unto whom the Creator may be gracious, that if
He needed anything He first of all would need the one who
created Him and gave Him the appearance of an existent
thing, for every existent thing must have its own particular
existence and a characteristic by which it can be described.
For example, the figure and shape of an image requires the
work of a smelter to cast it and a designer to design it, and as
long as this form does not exist there can be no image.
Similarly, it [every existent thing] is in need of a place which
it fills, and time in which it moves; but the Eternal does not
need any of these. The prophet similarly said: "To whom will
you liken God, or what likeness will you compare unto Him?
The image perchance which the craftsman hath melted, and
the goldsmith spread over with gold?" But if someone should
say: "We do not maintain that He needed someone to create
Him, but perhaps He created it [the world] for His own
benefit, as we make things by which we are helped in our
purposes; and He did not create the world for nought and in
vain." We shall say to him: "If He needed something which
He created there would be a defect in His essence, and He
could not create it. In this there is a great difference between us and Him, for we prepare food but we cannot bring
it forth into being from non-being, as He, may He be blessed,
produces His works; we weave a garment but we cannot
bring forth its raw materials when it is non-existent."

If He created the world for His own benefit, then inevitably He was always in need of it, or the need arose then [at the time of creation]. If He was always in need of it, it is impossible that the world should not exist with Him from eternity, but this leads to a belief in the eternity of the world and that it is not created. But if He created it in the midst of His need, and not before then, this would indicate impotence in Him before that time, and what He was impotent to create at any given time, He could not create at any other time. However, if the need newly arose in Him, then inevitably it either arose in Him as heat arises in a body after cold, or motion after rest; if so, however, He is like a created thing and whoever is like created things is [himself] created, as we have explained; or some other being created it [the need] in Him, but then He could in no way be eternal. It is thus proven that the eternal does not need anything, that He is essentially self-sufficient. He alone is worthy of being worshipped among all the beings that are worshipped, for He is truly self-sufficient, but all need Him since they need a Creator to create them and a Leader to lead them. Therefore, praise and song, adoration and purity of heart is due to God alone, may His name be praised. For the true meaning of purity of heart is that nothing is truly worthy of being worshipped except Him; neither is there anyone righteous except Him, inasmuch as He is truly self-sufficient, but everything else is truly needy, destitute and indigent; He is veritably honorable, but everything else is despicable. Therefore, the hearts of all beings are cleansed before Him, as Plato says in his *Laws*: "Praised be Thy name, Oh God, for before Thee all cleanse and purify their hearts, and none of them indicates inertia or inutility." Inasmuch as it has been proven that He is self-sufficient, it follows that He created the world because of His generosity and lovingkindness, and not for any other reason. But if someone should say: "Why did He refrain from creating the created things until the time that He [actually] did create them, He having always been benevolent, desiring goodness and kindness?" We shall

say to him: "The answer to your question will be explained
in the next chapter, according to our ability." (May He who
helps me, be blessed; for it is the function of God to help
man.)

. . .

But the Creator, may He be blessed, knows our inclination, our secret thoughts, and our occupation much more
than we know, as the Scripture says: "I the Lord search the
heart, I try the reins" (Jeremiah 17:10). He sees that we
provoke Him more than we worship Him. Moreover, we do
not worship Him in truth. Still He does not remove His
loving-kindness from us, as it is said: "[The Lord is] . . . long-
suffering and abundant in goodness" (Exodus 34:6).

Now that we have first prefaced this, and explained what
we wished to explain, namely, that the abandonment of
divine service is a premeditated sin or at least a transgression, we shall add to this what is pertinent to it.

But before I begin, I shall pose this question: What necessity did the Creator, may He be blessed, have to give us
Commandments? Someone might object: "Since you think
that the Creator is self-sufficient and not in need of anything, and neither deficiency nor any other needs will over-
take Him, then why was it necessary for Him to give us His
Commandments and His Statutes, some of which lie beyond
the capacity of reason: as for example, to honor one part of
the parts of time—such as the Sabbath and the festivals; also
to honor one place more than other places—such as the Holy
Land and the Holy Temple; also to honor some people more
than other people—such as Moses, our teacher, peace be
upon him, and the other prophets and pious people; and also
to prefer certain foods and to reject other foods—such as
eating the meat of cattle and sheep, but abstaining from
swine, the hare, and similar kinds?" His answer is: "As
regards your first question, 'What was the intent and need of
the Creator, may He be blessed, in giving us Commandments,' I will answer you that if we knew why He has

created man, we would know why He gave him admonitions
and commandments."

Now the creation of mankind must inevitably be con-
strued in one of four ways: (1) either the Creator, may He be
blessed, created people for their own good; or (2) He created
them for their own evil; (3) or He created them for both their
own good and their own evil; or (4) He created them neither
for their own good nor for their own evil. This has already
been made clear by proofs and arguments in the third treatise, in the chapter proving that God has absolutely no needs
and that He is self-sufficient. Otherwise, He would not be a
Creator, and conversely if He is a Creator, He is free from
need, weakness and defeat. Now if He created the people for
their own evil, he must have been able at the same time to
create them for their own good or not; or He could only have
created them more for their own evil than for their own
good. But if he could not create them for their own good, He
is not the Creator. For the true Creator could create anything and its opposite. And if He were more able to create
them for their own evil than for their own good, He would
not be a creator because He would then have obstacles that
prevent Him from doing part of His work.

Should someone object: "He is a Creator and could have
equally created them either for their own good or for their
own evil," we shall reply: "Their creation for their own evil
was an evil act; but one who does evil would not prefer the
evil act over a good act, if he were able to do the good act,
unless He did not know about the good act or He had some
necessity and use for the bad act, such as to derive a benefit
from it or to ward off some injury therewith. But He is self-
sufficient and free from need, and He is a wise being, free
from ignorance; it therefore follows that He did not create
mankind for their own evil."

But if you will say: "He created them for their own good
and for their own evil, equally and at the same time," we
shall reply: "This is untenable, just as it is impossible for a
body to stand and sit at the same time, because of the contradiction of the two attributes: for if He created them for their

own good, then there cannot be any evil present, and if He created them for their own evil, then there cannot be any good present."

If someone should say: "He created them partly for their own good and partly for their own evil," we shall reply to him: "If there is some evil present, then He did not perfect the good and this is not the work of a wise being."

The refutation of this hypothesis entails also the refutation of the hypothesis that He created them neither for their own good nor for their own evil. For such a creation would be in vain. But the All-Wise would not create something waste and void.

Thus, with the elimination of the three alternatives, only the fourth alternative, which is true, remains, namely, that He created them for their own good and not for any need He had in them.

This having been explained, it follows that the Commandments which He gave to the people were also for their own good in order that they may attain true goodness and enjoy blissfulness in the future world. It was also brought out in this exposition that He created man so that he would abide by His commandments, and that He wants him to keep his commandments in order to give him a good reward. This was the desire of the Creator when He created man, and this is what He asked of him. This too was the intent in the creation of man, and because of this the corporeal world as it exists at present was created for him. And He gave him great dominion over all the existing things, according to the dictation of the wisdom of the Creator, may He be blessed. Man was created after all other things in order to make known that all of them were created for his sake. He created his body corresponding to the whole creation so that this fact would bestir him to think and seek knowledge which would be a source of help and salvation for him, as we shall presently explain, with the help of the Creator, may He be blessed.

If you will ask: "Is it possible to receive the good reward without [observing] commandments?" I shall reply to you: "It is not reasonable to give a good reward to one who has not merited it nor to punish someone who is not guilty of punishment. For we are of the opinion that the pleasantness of the good reward is His ultimate goodness and loving-kindness which He will bestow upon us. Besides all the good He has done for us in having brought us into existence out of nothing, He has taught us His ways, namely, to attain eternal blissfulness and the enjoyment after which there is no punishment, but only perpetual good."

If one will ask: "How can we attain this good?" we shall answer him: "By keeping the commandments and statutes of the Torah, and by abiding by the Will of the Creator."

If someone will object: "Since the Creator had known beforehand that the wicked one would provoke Him and that He will be obliged to punish him in the future world, why then did He create him? It would appear that He created him for his evil, and yet you contend that he created all creatures for their own good?" we shall reply: "The wicked one is not coerced to provoke the Creator, because the Creator knows beforehand that he would provoke Him. Were it not so the evil doer would be coerced at the time of his provoking, for this is the nature of coercion. The demonstration to demolish this theory is that if the Creator would coerce His creatures to do good or evil then it would not be right to reward one who does a good deed, for he was coerced at the time he did the good deed; nor to punish the evil doer, for he is coerced to do the evil act, and he does not commit a sin because of his coercion. A similar case would be if a master put his bond-servant in chains and then told him: 'If you do not appear before me tomorrow in such and such a city which is so many miles away from here, you will be sentenced to die'; notwithstanding that he [the master] knows that his servant could not go there, being unable to walk more than a few steps. Would not the one doing such a thing be a violent person?"

But the All-Wise, may He be praised, does not commit a violent action. His wisdom dictated Him because of the plenitude of His goodness and loving-kindness to create him [the evil doer] exactly like the pious one, with equal reason and

similar senses, and with all other equal equipment—even
though He knows beforehand that this one would be pious
and the other wicked. Moreover, out of His abundant mercy
for his servants, He admonished them and taught them the
ways of penitence so that the claim against them [if they
persist in their evil ways] will be stronger, as it is said: "And
they, whether they will hear, or whether they will forbear—
for they are a rebellious house—yet shall know that a
prophet hath been among them" (Ezekiel 2:5).

. . .

Thus it follows that wisdom is the cause for [moral] action.
For by means of wisdom and the action [resulting from it]
will the human soul be able to perfect herself. Moreover,
wisdom and action shatter the yoke of imprisonment which
nature has imposed upon man. In reference to this, the
philosopher said: "Not for you, ye who are doomed to die,
were the fetters broken with wisdom."

The great principle which we can derive from divine
service through wisdom is that man was created for her
sake and that primary accidents and primary substances
were imprinted in man in order that he may be instructed
and taught by them concerning secondary substances and
secondary accidents. To ascend from the primary to the
secondary ones is found to be difficult and deep because of
the abundant minuteness of the latter; but the existence of
the primary ones is evident if one proceeds from the secondary ones, because they are corporeal and well known.

The demonstration that man was created for the sake of
wisdom is that man was created only for the purpose of
attaining the blissfulness of the future world; but there is no
way to attain this except by practice, namely, divine service;
and there is no path to practice except wisdom. Therefore,
the reason and cause for the creation of man was only for the
sake of wisdom. By dint of wisdom man should know universal, eternal things, i.e., to know the existence of universals
and a fortiori the existence of God, may His name be sanctified. This is the ultimate purpose of knowledge.

*

Abraham ibn Ezra (1089-1164)

Ezra lived in Spain until 1140, after which he traveled throughout parts of Europe. He was a poet, grammarian, biblical commentator, philosopher, astronomer, physician, and scientist, and is known to have produced at least 108 works. The following brief excerpts are from Ezra's commentary on the Bible, translated by Nahum N. Glatzer, and *Yesod Mora*, translated by Leo Rosten.

COMMENTARY ON THE BIBLE

"And let us know, eagerly strive to know the Lord, his going forth is sure as the morning" (Hosea 6:3).

This [knowledge of the Lord] is the aim of all wisdom and solely to this end man was created. But man cannot know the Lord unless he has studied many branches of wisdom which are comparable to the steps of a ladder on which man ascends until he reaches the highest rung. The reason [why Hosea uses the image of] "the morning" is that like the morning commences [with but a little] light which grows bigger and bigger, so does the student [only gradually] recognize the Lord out of His works until he [finally] sees the truth.

YESOD MORA

Man was created to serve God and to cleave to Him, not to accumulate wealth and erect buildings which he must leave behind.

*

Abraham ibn Daud (1110–1180)

Daud lived and was martyred in Spain. One of the most rationalist of the Jewish philosophers, Daud was also an astronomer, physician, and historian. The following excerpt is from his work *Ha-Emunah ha-Ramah*, or *The Exalted Faith*, translated by Norbert M. Samuelson.

HA-EMUNAH HA-RAMAH

The Second Book

It [includes] an Introduction and six basic principles. The first basic principle is on the source of faith. The second basic principle is on oneness. The third basic principle is on [God's] attributes, may He be exalted, what is attributed to Him figuratively [in] species, what is attributed to Him figuratively [in] genus, and [the third basic principle includes] an explanation of the difficulty of attributing to [God], may He be exalted, [any] true essential attribute. The fourth basic principle is on [God's] actions, may He be exalted, and on the ordering of the [process of] drawing forth existent entities from Him. The fifth basic principle is on subsequent faith, which is faith in the prophets, peace be unto them, and in the tradition. [Also, the fifth basic principle is] on the conditions by which the word of the prophet is affirmed and established, and [by which] it is necessary to believe in it. [Also, the fifth basic principle is] on change in and the description of the [different] kinds of prophecy and the alternations of grades of people [who participate] in it. The sixth basic principle is on faith [in] and exhortation to [affirm] the truth [of the claim] that everything that is like them is said by way of metaphor and is distinct from Him.

Discussion of the Introduction

When it is seen that a certain thing [has] existence after nonexistence and perfection after defect in [its] order and grade, so that it reaches a certain end and it remains in it, [then] it is known that that end is the purpose [of the thing]. An example of this in the existence that is beneath the sphere of the Moon [is that] what is most deficient of what is in [the sublunar world] in grade is the existence of the matter that is associated with the four elements, because it has no existence in itself; rather, [it exists] in one of the forms of the elements. [In addition,] its existence is not for its own sake; rather, [it exists] in order to be combined with one of the elements. A better existence in this [sublunar world] is [that of] the elements themselves, because each one of them exists in itself. In that which we call "HYLE" there is already realized a form. However, we do not consider [the elements to exist] for their own sake; rather, [we consider them to exist] for [the sake of] the things that are composed from them, because they are matter in relation to the composite things. [What has] better existence than these [elements] is what is composed in earth from smoke and vapor. By saying "smoke" I do not mean the smoke of fire; rather, [I mean] dry vapors, because when smoke and vapor are mixed and remain in the belly of the Earth, they do not return to [be] earth afterward; rather, they remain [as they are] until at times boiling warmth acts on them or at [other] times cold freezes [them], so that from them minerals and gems come into existence. The minerals [come into existence] when the matter of the vapor is more dominant in them, so that [the mixtures] are more moist. Therefore, they are [capable of being] beaten out by a hammer. The gems [come into existence] when the matter of the smoke is more dominant. Therefore, [the mixtures] are dry, [so that] they are not [capable of being] beaten out by a hammer. All of these things approximate nature from the nature of the Earth. Therefore, none of them have any great active or

passive powers. Better than this in existence is the existence
of plants, because they have in them nutrition, growth, and
generation of what is of the [same] kind. The existence that
is better than this is the existence of nonrational animals,
because they have in them in addition to [the powers] that
are in plants animative and mental powers. [At] a better
level [than that of nonrational animals] in their species is
[the level of] the existence of man in that he has some rationality. Beyond man we do not find a species at a higher
level in grade. [Thus,] we know that he is the purpose of this
natural existence, and [we know] that everything that we
mentioned [exists for man's sake], since there is nothing in
[the sublunar world] more notable such that in [its] mix-
tures more notable forms and powers are caused to overflow. However, according to what a certain mixture becomes, a certain form suitable to [the mixture] is caused to
overflow upon it. [The reason for this is] that if the purpose
[of the sublunar world] was something higher in grade than
man, this thing would exist. But it does not exist. Therefore,
there is no purpose in this existence that is under the Sun
that has a higher grade than man. If the purpose was something lesser in grade than man from everything that we
mentioned, [then] existence would remain [at that level]
when [existence] reached [that level]. However, [existence]
does not remain at [that level]. Therefore, the final purpose
or the teleological cause is not something other than man.

These are true syllogisms [with] coherent conditions. We
learn that every [claim that is] an opposite of [our] conclusion is inferred [from] an opposite of [our] premise and
refutes [the syllogism's] postulate. Thus, we say that man
contains vegetative powers, above which in grade are animative powers, and above the animative ones in grade are
mental powers, above which is the rational power. We do not
find any other power above it. Therefore, [man] is the purpose of [the sublunar world]. It is impossible for the rational
power to be something other than those other things which
combine with and divide from one another, as has already
been explained.

This rational power has two aspects. By the higher aspect [man] receives from the angels [instances of] wisdom. By the lower aspect [man] judges the other powers of the body. [This aspect] does not leave alone [any]thing that can be used by [the body] more than is sufficient or without order. And wisdom is the superiority and the end of man. Some of the many [instances of] wisdom are [more] excellent than others. The purpose of all of them is knowledge of God, may He be exalted.

*

Moses ben Maimon—
Moses Maimonides (1135–1204)

Maimonides (known in rabbinic literature as the Rambam) was born in Spain and emigrated to Palestine in 1165. Later he became physician to the viceroy of Egypt. Maimonides was a philosopher, halakhist, medical writer, physician, scientist, and leader of Egyptian Jewry. Two of his greatest works are the *Mishneh Torah* and *Moreh Nevukhim* (*The Guide of the Perplexed*). He was the best known Jewish personality of the Middle Ages. The respect shown to Maimonides is expressed in the popular saying, "From Moses to Moses there was none like Moses." Following is M. Friedlander's translation of Part III, Chapter 13, from *The Guide of the Perplexed*.

THE GUIDE OF THE PERPLEXED

The Purpose of the Creation

Intelligent persons are much perplexed when they inquire into the purpose of the Creation. I will now show how absurd this question is, according to each one of the different theories [above-mentioned]. An agent that acts with intention must have a certain ulterior object in that which he performs. This is evident, and no philosophical proof is required. It is likewise evident that that which is produced with intention has passed over from non-existence to existence. It is further evident, and generally agreed upon, that the being which has absolute existence, which has never been and will never be without existence, is not in need of an agent. We have explained this before. The question, "What is the purpose thereof?" cannot be asked about anything which is not the product of an agent; therefore we cannot ask what is the purpose of the existence of God. He has not been created. According to these propositions it is clear that the purpose is sought for everything produced intentionally by an intelligent cause; that is to say, a final cause must exist for everything that owes its existence to an intelligent being: but for that which is without a beginning, a final cause need not be sought, as has been stated by us. After this explanation you will understand that there is no occasion to seek the final cause of the whole Universe, neither according to our theory of the Creation, nor according to the theory of Aristotle, who assumes the Eternity of the Universe. For according to Aristotle, who holds that the Universe has not had a beginning, an ultimate final cause cannot be sought even for the various parts of the Universe. Thus it cannot be asked, according to his opinion, What is the final cause of the existence of the heavens? Why are they limited by this measure or by that number? Why is matter of this description? What is the purpose of existence of this species of animals or plants? Aristotle considers all this as the result of a permanent order of things. Natural Philosophy investigates into the object of everything in Nature, but it does not treat of the ultimate final cause, of which we speak in this chapter. It is a recognized fact in Natural Philosophy that everything in Nature, has its object, or its final cause, which is the most important of the four causes, though it is not easily recognized in most species. Aristotle repeatedly says that Nature produces nothing in vain, for every natural action has a certain object. Thus, Aristotle says that plants exist for animals; and similarly he shows of other parts of the Universe for what purpose they exist. This is still more obvious in the case of the organs of animals. The existence of such a final cause in the various parts of Nature has compelled philosophers to assume the existence of a primal cause apart from Nature; it is called by Aristotle the intellectual or divine cause, and this cause creates one thing for the purpose of another. Those who acknowledge the truth will accept as the best proof for the Creation the fact that everything in Nature serves a certain purpose, so that one thing exists for the benefit of another; this fact is supported by numerous instances, and shows that there is design in Nature; but the existence of design in Nature cannot be imagined unless it be assumed that Nature has been produced.

I will now return to the subject of this chapter, viz., the final cause. Aristotle has already explained that in Nature the efficient cause of a thing, its form, and its final cause are identical; that is to say, they are one thing in relation to the whole species. E.g., the form of Zeid produces the form of his son Amr; its action consists in imparting the form of the whole species [of man] to the substance of Amr, and the final cause is Amr's possession of human form. The same argument is applied by Aristotle to every individual member of a class of natural objects which is brought to existence by another individual member. The three causes coincide in all such cases. All this refers only to the immediate purpose of a thing; but the existence of an ultimate purpose in every species, which is considered as absolutely necessary by every one who investigates into the nature of things, is very difficult to discover: and still more difficult is it to find the purpose of the whole Universe. I infer from the words of Aristotle that according to his opinion the ultimate purpose of the genera is the preservation of the course of genesis and destruction; and this course is absolutely necessary [in the first instance] for the successive formation of material objects, because individual beings formed of matter are not

permanent; [secondly], for the production of the best and the
most perfect beings that can be formed of matter, because
the ultimate purpose [in these productions] is to arrive at
perfection. Now it is clear that man is the most perfect being
formed of matter; he is the last and most perfect of earthly
beings, and in this respect it can truly be said that all
earthly things exist for man, i.e., that the changes which
things undergo serve to produce the most perfect being that
can be produced. Aristotle, who assumes the Eternity of the
Universe, need therefore not ask to what purpose does man
exist, for the immediate purpose of each individual being is,
according to his opinion, the perfection of its specific form.
Every individual thing arrives at its perfection fully and
completely when the actions that produce its form are complete. The ultimate purpose of the species is the perpetuation of this form by the repeated succession of genesis and
destruction, so that there might always be a being capable of
the greatest possible perfection. It seems therefore clear
that, according to Aristotle, who assumes the Eternity of the
Universe, there is no occasion for the question what is the
object of the existence of the Universe. But of those who
accept our theory that the whole Universe has been created
from nothing, some hold that the inquiry after the purpose
of the Creation is necessary, and assume that the Universe
was only created for the sake of man's existence, that he
might serve God. Everything that is done they believe is
done for man's sake; even the spheres move only for his
benefit, in order that his wants might be supplied. The
literal meaning of some passages in the books of the
prophets greatly support this idea. Compare: "He formed it
(viz., the earth) to be inhabited" (Isaiah 45:18); "If my covenant of day and night were not," etc. (Jeremiah 33:25); "And
spreadeth them out as a tent to dwell in" (Isaiah 40:22). If
the sphere existed for the sake of man, how much more must
this be the case with all other living beings and the plants.
On examining this opinion as intelligent persons ought to
examine all different opinions, we shall discover the errors
it includes. Those who hold this view, namely, that the exis-

tence of man is the object of the whole creation, may be asked whether God could have created man without those previous creations, or whether man could only have come into existence after the creation of all other things. If they answer in the affirmative, that man could have been created even if, e.g., the heavens did not exist, they will be asked what is the object of all these things, since they do not exist for their own sake but for the sake of something that could exist without them? Even if the Universe existed for man's sake and man existed for the purpose of serving God, as has been mentioned, the question remains, What is the end of serving God? He does not become more perfect if all His creatures serve Him and comprehend Him as far as possible; nor would He lose anything if nothing existed beside Him. It might perhaps be replied that the service of God is not intended for God's perfection; it is intended for our own perfection,—it is good for us, it makes us perfect. But then the question might be repeated, What is the object of our being perfect? We must in continuing the inquiry as to the purpose of the creation at last arrive at the answer. It was the Will of God, or His Wisdom decreed it; and this is the correct answer. The wise men in Israel have, therefore, introduced in our prayers (for Ne'ilah of the Day of Atonement) the following passage:—"Thou hast distinguished man from the beginning, and chosen him to stand before Thee; who can say unto Thee, What dost Thou? And if he be righteous, what does he give Thee?" They have thus clearly stated that it was not a final cause that determined the existence of all things, but only His will. This being the case, we who believe in the Creation must admit that God could have created the Universe in a different manner as regards the causes and effects contained in it, and this would lead to the absurd conclusion that everything except man existed without any purpose, as the principal object, man, could have been brought into existence without the rest of the creation. I consider therefore the following opinion as most correct according to the teaching of the Bible, and best in accordance with the results of philosophy; namely, that the Universe does not exist

for man's sake, but that each being exists for its own sake
and not because of some other thing. Thus we believe in the
Creation, and yet need not inquire what purpose is served by
each species of the existing things, because we assume that
God created all parts of the Universe by His will; some for
their own sake, and some for the sake of other beings, that
include their own purpose in themselves. In the same
manner as it was the will of God that man should exist, so it
was His will that the heavens with their stars should exist,
that there should be angels, and each of these beings is itself
the purpose of its own existence. When anything can only
exist provided some other thing has previously existed, God
has caused the latter to precede it; as, e.g., sensation precedes comprehension. We meet also with this view in Scripture; "The Lord hath made everything (*la-ma'anehu*) for its
purpose" (Proverbs 16:4). It is possible that the pronoun in
la-ma'anehu refers to the object; but it can also be considered as agreeing with the subject; in which case the meaning of the word is, for the sake of Himself, or His will which
is identical with His self [or essence], as has been shown in
this treatise. We have also pointed out that His essence is
also called His glory. The words, "The Lord hath made
everything for Himself," express therefore the same idea as
the following verse, "Everything that is called by my name:
I have created it for my glory, I have formed it; yea, I have
made it" (Isaiah 43:7); that is to say, everything that is
described as My work has been made by Me for the sake of
My will and for no other purpose. The words, "I have formed
it," "I have made it," express exactly what I pointed out to
you, that there are things whose existence is only possible
after certain other things have come into existence. To these
reference is made in the text, as if to say, I have formed the
first thing which must have preceded the other things, e.g.,
matter has been formed before the production of material
beings; I have then made out of that previous creation, or
after it, what I intended to produce, and there was nothing
but My will. Study the book which leads all who want to be
led to the truth, and is therefore called *Torah* (Law or In-

struction), from the beginning of the account of the Creation
to its end, and you will comprehend the opinion which we
attempt to expound. For no part of the creation is described
as being in existence for the sake of another part, but each
part is declared to be the product of God's will, and to satisfy
by its existence the intention [of the Creator]. This is expressed by the phrase, "And God saw that it was good"
(Genesis 1:4, etc.). You know our interpretation of the saying
of our Sages, "Scripture speaks the same language as is
spoken by man." But we call "good" that which is in accordance with the object we seek. When therefore Scripture
relates in reference to the whole creation (Genesis 1:31),
"And God saw all that He had made, and behold it was
exceedingly good," it declares thereby that everything
created was well fitted for its object, and would never cease
to act, and never be annihilated. This is especially pointed
out by the word "exceedingly"; for sometimes a thing is
temporarily good; it serves its purpose, and then it fails and
ceases to act. But as regards the Creation it is said that
everything was fit for its purpose, and able continually to
act accordingly. You must not be misled by what is stated of
the stars [that God put them in the firmament of the heav-
ens] to give light upon the earth, and to rule by day and by
night. You might perhaps think that here the purpose of
their creation is described. This is not the case; we are only
informed of the nature of the stars, which God desired to
create with such properties that they should be able to give
light and to rule. In a similar manner we must understand
the passage, "And have dominion over the fish of the sea"
(Genesis 1:28). Here it is not meant to say that man was
created for this purpose, but only that this was the nature
which God gave man. But as to the statement in Scripture
that God gave the plants to man and other living beings, it
agrees with the opinion of Aristotle and other philosophers.
It is also reasonable to assume that the plants exist only for
the benefit of the animals, since the latter cannot live without food. It is different with the stars, they do not exist only
for our sake, that we should enjoy their good influence; for

the expressions "to give light" and "to rule" merely describe, as we have stated above, the benefit which the creatures on earth derive from them. I have already explained to you the character of that influence that causes continually the good to descend from one being to another. To those who receive the good flowing down upon them, it may appear as if the being existed for them alone that sends forth its goodness and kindness unto them. Thus some citizen may imagine that it was for the purpose of protecting his house by night from thieves that the king was chosen. To some extent this is correct; for when his house is protected, and he has derived this benefit through the king whom the country had chosen, it appears as if it were the object of the king to protect the house of that man. In this manner we must explain every verse, the literal meaning of which would imply that something superior was created for the sake of something inferior, viz., that it is part of the nature of the superior thing [to influence the inferior in a certain manner]. We remain firm in our belief that the whole Universe was created in accordance with the will of God, and we do not inquire for any other cause or object. Just as we do not ask what is the purpose of God's existence, so we do not ask what was the object of His will, which is the cause of the existence of all things with their present properties, both those that have been created and those that will be created.

You must not be mistaken and think that the spheres and the angels were created for our sake. Our position has already been pointed out to us, "Behold, the nations are as a drop in a bucket" (Isaiah 40:15). Now compare your own essence with that of the spheres, the stars, and the Intelligences, and you will comprehend the truth, and understand that man is superior to everything formed of earthly matter, but not to other beings; he is found exceedingly inferior when his existence is compared with that of the spheres, and a fortiori when compared with that of the Intelligences. Compare: "Behold, he putteth no trust in his servants: and his messengers he charged with folly: how much less in them that dwell in houses of clay, whose foundation is in the dust, which are crushed before the moth?" (Job 4:18, 19). The expression "his servants," occurring in this passage, does not denote human beings; this may be inferred from the words, "How much less in them that dwell in houses of clay?" The "servants" referred to in this place are the angels; whilst by the term "his messengers" the spheres are undoubtedly meant. Eliphas himself, who uttered the above words, explains this [in the second speech] when he refers to it in one of his replies in other words, saying, "Behold, he putteth no trust in his holy ones; yea, the heavens are not clean in his sight, how much more abominable and filthy is man, who drinketh iniquity like water" (Job 15:15, 16). He thus shows that "his servants" and "his holy ones" are identical, and that they are not human beings; also that "his messengers," mentioned in the first passage, are the same as "the heavens." The term "folly" is explained by the phrase "they are not clean in his sight," i.e., they are material; although their substance is the purest and the most luminous, compared with the Intelligences it appears dark, turbid, and impure. The phrase, "Behold, he putteth no trust in his servants," is employed in reference to the angels, indicating that these do not possess perpetual existence, since, as we believe, they have had a beginning; and even according to those who assume the Eternity of the Universe, the existence of the angels is at all events dependent on and therefore inferior to, the absolute existence of God. The words, "How much more abominable and filthy is man," in the one passage, correspond to the phrase "How much less in those who dwell in houses of clay" in the other passage. Their meaning is this: How much less in man who is abominable and filthy, in whose person crookedness or corporeality is mixed up and spread through all his parts. "Iniquity" (*'avlah*) is identical with "crookedness," as may be inferred from the passage, "In the land of uprightness he will act with iniquity" (Isaiah 26:10), and *ish*, "man," is here used in the same sense as *adam*, "human being"; for "man" in a general sense is sometimes expressed in Scripture by *ish*. Comp. "He who smiteth a man (*ish*) and he die" (Exodus 21:12).

This must be our belief when we have a correct knowledge of our own self, and comprehend the true nature of everything; we must be content, and not trouble our mind with seeking a certain final cause for things that have none, or have no other final cause but their own existence, which depends on the Will of God, or, if you prefer, on the Divine Wisdom.

*

Berechiah ben Natroni ha-Nakdan (12th–13th century)

Little is known of Berechiah's life. He lived in Normandy and for a period in England. Berechiah was a fabulist, translator, thinker, copyist, and grammarian. The following selection is from his *Ethical Treatises*, translated by Hermann Gollancz.

ETHICAL TREATISES

XXI. The Gaon has said, that despite the fact of the multiplication of creatures and the great increase of created beings, we cannot possibly be amazed or perplexed, when our mind and reason make an endeavor to recognise which creature is the fittest and most select of the whole class of creatures; since nature herself and the elementary bodies afford us ample proof and evidence, as to which is the elect and special of all creatures, viz:—man alone. For it is well known and evident that it is the course and law of nature, and of the elementary bodies, to place that which is best and most precious in the centre, and to surround it with objects and substances of an inferior quality and of less importance.

This peculiarity is seen throughout all the fundamental principles of the world, their natural conditions and effects. First, we have to take the lightest and thinnest objects in the world, namely, plants and herbs, for it is known and evident that they are produced and receive their growth from the seed, which is consequently their origin and root. From it they blossom forth; and since it is the agent which brings forth the plant and raises the herb, it is always found in the very interior of these plants, and in the centre of the grasses and herbs, and in the innermost chamber; for this reason, because it is the best and most precious part of the growth. The same process holds good in the case of trees, in those instances in which they sprout forth and blossom with various species of food. The specific portion is (always) found in the centre which the bark surrounds, the like of which we may notice in almonds and nuts, etc. If again the trees receive their growth and their strength from grains, these grains will be found to lie in the central part of the trees, and enclosed in the innermost chamber of the tree. The food product is a secondary part of them and therefore encompasses them, since they do not form the root of the tree. But the seeds which are the root and origin exist in the centre, like the seeds of the pomegranate and the peach, etc. In the second degree are included dumb animals; we also find that the root and origin of their birth is derived from some internal substance lying within, like the yolk of an egg, from which the fowl takes life, since it is the basis of its formation. The third degree comprises the intellectual being, which is Man. Here we observe that the most precious and special thing within him, viz:—the seat of the soul, the residence of his spirit, the chamber of his life, the fountain of that peculiar blood with which his life is bound up, i. e., the heart of man, all this is placed and fixed in the centre of his body. And thus it is with the pupil of the eye of man, which sees and gives light; therein lies the source of all his perceptions, and therewith he can observe all his actions, and the actions of God. This again is placed in the middle between the

eyelids, and in the centre of the eye. Having adduced all
these proofs to show that the essence of everything is placed
in the centre, we now return and investigate, which is the
best and the most precious central portion in all the universe, and we find that the earth is the centre of all the
spheres, and that all the firmaments surrounding it encom-
pass it on every side; and since it is the centre of the whole
world, it is also the choicest and best of all created things
which exist. It is, however, impossible that it should be
peculiar on its own account, so as to be of itself the selected
one of all existing objects, considering that it is com-
pounded and mixed with another substance, viz:—water;
but the earth may, with propriety, be regarded as an object
of special favour and greatness, on account of the living
creatures dwelling thereon. It is, moreover, impossible for
every living creature to be included in that special cause,
for some of them, not being intellectual beings, minister to
the wants of those who are intelligent. Its selection and pre-
eminence result, therefore, properly speaking, from the
intellectual beings existing upon it. Hence we see that in all
the various groups in the world that contain within them
some integral central product, there is no product that is
really great, special, and selected but Man, that he it is who
is really the source and root of the life of the world, and for
whose sake the world was created. Nay further, at the
commencement of the Pentateuch we find, that God first set
in order all created things, and when He had completed
their plan, and finished creating them, He said: "Let us
make man in our image" (Genesis 1:26). This may be compared to one who, after building a palace, beautifies it,
adding sculpture work and adorning its walls with tapes-
try; and as soon as the house is swept down, and decked
with all manner of curious things, the owner of the palace is
introduced. Thus did God prepare the world for Man. As
soon as He had finished the work of Creation, and placed
every thing in order, He then, after due preparation, caused
Adam to enter the Garden of Eden.

*

Jonah ben Abraham Gerondi (c. 1200–1263)

Jonah lived in northern Spain and was head of a yeshivah in Toledo. He was known as "the pious." Perhaps his most popular work is *Shaarei Teshuvah*, or *The Gates of Repentance*. The following excerpt is from a translation of this work by Shraga Silverstein.

SHAAREI TESHUVAH

XXI. One who has been granted wisdom by the Blessed One will impress upon himself the fact that He sent him into this world to observe His charge, His Torah, His statutes, and His mitzvoth, and will open his eyes only to discharge His commission; and, in the end of days, if he has faithfully executed His trust, he will return in song, crowned with everlasting joy, as a servant whose master has sent him across the seas, whose eyes and heart are entirely intent upon his mission, until he returns to his master. As Solomon, may Peace be upon him, said, "That thy trust may be in the Lord . . . That I might make thee know the certainty of the words of truth, that thou mightest bring back words of truth to them that send thee" (Proverbs 22:19–21).

*

Moses ben Nahman (1194–1270)

Moses ben Nahman (also known as Nahmonides and the Ramban) was a Spanish Rabbi of Gerona. He was a commentator, kabbalist, and communal leader, and his knowledge was considered unrivaled in his day. Nahmonides had to leave Spain because of his victorious participation in the forced Barcelona Disputation. His most celebrated works were his glosses on the Talmud and Bible commentaries. Following are two excerpts, the first from *Commentary on the Torah* translated by Charles B. Chavel, and the second from *Has the Messiah Come?*, translated by Nahum N. Glatzer.

COMMENTARY ON THE TORAH

Deuteronomy 32, Ha'Azinu

This plea is not meant to demonstrate His power among His enemies, for *All the nations are as nothing before Him; they are accounted by Him as things of nought, and vanity* (Isaiah 40:17). Rather, [the explanation thereof is as follows:] God created man among the lower creatures in order that he acknowledge his Creator and be thankful to His Name, and He placed in his hand the choice to do evil or good. But when people sinned willingly and they all denied Him, only this people [Israel] remained devoted to His Name, and so He made known through them by means of signs and wonders that *He is God of gods, and Lord of lords* (Isaiah 10:17), and this became known to all nations. Now, if He were to reconsider and their memory [i.e., of Israel] be lost, the nations will forget His wonders and His deeds and they will no longer recount them. And if a person should mention them, they will think that it was [done by] one of the powers of the constellations which is *overflowing as he passeth through* (Isaiah 8:8), and thus the purpose of the creation of man will be annulled completely, for no one will be left among them who knows his Creator—only those who provoke Him. Therefore, it is appropriate as a consequence of the [Divine] Will which existed at the creation of the world to establish for Himself a people for all time, who are nearer to Him and who know Him more than all the [other] peoples. And the meaning of the verse *For the Eternal will judge His people, and for His servants He will reconsider* is, that God will remember in mercy that they are His people of old, and He will remember that they are His servants, for they stood by Him in their exile like servants to suffer the troubles and the bondage, similar to what is stated, *For He said: 'Surely, they are My people, children that will not deal falsely'* (Isaiah 63:8). I have already suggested that in the creation of man there is a sublime and recondite secret which requires that we be His people and He be our God, similar to what is stated, *Every one that is called by My Name, and whom I have created for My glory, I have formed him, yea, I have made him* (Isaiah 43:7).

HAS THE MESSIAH COME?

"And God said, Let us make man" (Genesis 1:26). The reason for this signal honor is that there was nothing comparable in the preceding creations to his being. The true interpretation of the word *na'aseh* ("Let us make") is that God created *ex nihilo* [out of nothing] only on the first day. From then on He used the elements [which He had created on the first day]. In the same way as He gave the waters the power to swarm with living creatures and brought forth beasts from the earth, He now said, "Let us . . . ," that is, I and the earth, make man. Out of the earth shall come forth the material elements to make up the body of man, just as is the case with animal and the wild beast, and I, the Lord will give him spirit from above . . . Thus man is like the lower creatures [in his physical structure], and like the higher beings in appearance and beauty, which is evidenced by his urge for wisdom, knowledge, and the doing of good deeds.

The eminence of the human soul, its distinction and superiority, lie in the fact, as the Torah informs us, that it was God who "blew the soul of life into the nostrils" of man (Genesis 2:7). This teaches us that man's soul does not originate in the material elements of his body, as is the case with all lower living creatures, nor is it even a substance evolved from the Separate Intelligences; instead, it is of the essence of the Holy One, since he who blows into the nostrils of another bestows upon him the breath of his own soul. Man's powers of learning and understanding come thus directly from Him.

Prior to his sin man performed his duties by inherent disposition; he was like the heavens and their hosts who [in the words of the sages] "are creatures of truth, whose achievement is truth, and who do not deviate from the path set for them." Love and hatred do not enter into the performance of their functions. It was the eating of the fruit of the Tree of Knowledge that brought desire and will into the heart of man. From then on he began choosing between one mode of action and another in accordance with his disposition for good or bad. [. . .] For this reason prior to the sin all parts of the human body were to Adam and Eve as the face and hands; they entertained no thoughts of shame concerning any part of the body. But after they ate of the tree they acquired the power to choose between good and evil. The power is indeed divine; but as far as man is concerned it also contains a potential of evil, since his deeds became dependent upon his desires and passions.

Consider it in your heart that the Holy One, blessed be He, has created all lower creatures for the benefit and use of man, since we know of no purpose for the creation of all objects who have no recognition of the Creator, except this— that they serve man. Now man has been created for the prime purpose that he recognize his Creator. Should he fail to know his Creator altogether, and what is even worse, should he fail to gain a realization of the fact that certain deeds are pleasing to God and others are displeasing, then man becomes as the unknowing beast. If man shows no desire to acquire a knowledge of God, and the realization that there is a difference between good and bad, the whole purpose of the world is lost.

The intent of all the commandments is that we acquire a firm belief in God, and proclaim Him as the One who has created us all. This is, in fact, the very purpose of Creation. The Supreme Being desires of man only that he know Him and acknowledge that He is the Creator. The prayers we recite, the synagogues we build, the holy convocations we hold, are all designed to give us an opportunity to gather and give outward expression to our inner conviction that He is our Creator and that we are His creatures.

*

The Zohar (13th century)

The Zohar, or Book of Splendor, is considered the fundamental work of the kabbalah or mystic teachings of Judaism. The book was written in the Aramaic language. There are divergent opinions regarding the authorship of the work. According to tradition, it was written by Rabbi Simeon ben Yohai, who lived in the second century. Some contend that the work is the result of a number of contributors over a period of time. However, Gershom Scholem, perhaps the greatest scholar of Kabbalah, is of the opinion that the book's sole author is Rabbi Moses de Leon, and that it was written in Spain about the year 1290. To date, only half of its content is available in English. The following excerpts are from the Soncino publication, translated by Harry Sperling and Maurice Simon.

THE ZOHAR

Terumah (Exodus) 155a

R. Eleazar then discoursed on the verse, LET THY GARMENTS BE ALWAYS WHITE, AND LET THY HEAD LACK NO OINTMENT (Ecclesiastes 9:8). 'This verse', said he, 'has been variously interpreted, but it may also be expounded thus. God created man

in the mystery of Wisdom, and fashioned him with great
art, and breathed into him the breath of life, so that he
might know and comprehend the mysteries of wisdom, to
apprehend the glory of his Lord; as it is written: "Everyone
that is called by my name: for I have created (*beratiw*) him
for my glory, I have formed (*yezartiw*) him, yea, I have
made (*asitiw*) him" (Isaiah 43:7). "I have created him for
my glory", literally, the inner meaning being that, as we
have learnt, the glory of the holy Throne is fixed firmly and
compactly in its place through the co-operation of the children of this world; that is, through the co-operation of righteous and saintly men, and those who know how to effect
adjustments. So the words really mean: "I have created the
world in order that, by means of their work, the righteous
on earth may cause my glory to be established on mighty
pillars to provide it with adornments and completion from
below, that it may be exalted, through their merit." *Beriah*
(creation, i.e. creative ideas) appertains to the left side;
Yezirah (creative formation) appertains to the right side, as
it is written, "Who formeth (*yozer*) light and createth (*bore*)
darkness" (Isaiah 45:7); while '*Asiyah* (making, finishing)
lies between them, as it is written, "I make ('*ose*) peace and
create evil: I the Lord do ('*ose*) all these things" (Isaiah 45:7)
and again, "He maketh ('*ose*) peace in his high places" (Job
25:2). Hence, because man is on the earth, and it is incum-
bent on him to establish firmly My glory, I have provided
him with the same supports as the supernal Glory: as in it
there are "creation", "formation", and "making", so of man
it is written, "I have created him, I have formed him yea, I
have made him." Thus man is after the pattern of that
supernal Glory that he may confirm it and make it complete on all sides. Blessed is the man whose works entitle
him to be regarded thus. Concerning this it is written: "Let
thy garments be always white", etc. And, as the Supernal
Glory has no lack of "holy ointment", from the mystery of
the world to come, the man whose works are "white" will
not lack this "holy ointment". Through what does a man

merit participation in that supernal joy? Through his table: yea, when at his table he has satisfied the wants of the poor: as it is written: "If thou draw out thy soul to the hungry and satisfy the afflicted soul. . . . then shalt thou delight thyself in the Lord. . . ." (Isaiah 58:10-14). Such a man will the Holy One satisfy; he will anoint him with holy supernal "ointment", which ever streams upon that Supernal Glory.' . . .

Terumah (Exodus) 161a

R. Hiya then followed with an exposition of the verse: *Thou hast been shown (har'eta) to know that the Lord he is God; there is none else beside him* (Deuteronomy 4:35). 'What does this peculiar expression, "thou hast been shown to know", denote? When the Israelites came out of Egypt, at first they knew nothing of the true meaning of faith in the Holy One, blessed be He, because, while they were in captivity in Egypt, they had worshipped foreign gods and had forgotten the essentials of the Faith, that legacy which the Twelve Tribes had received from Father Jacob. So, when Moses came, he had to teach them that in the universe there is a supreme God. Then they were witnesses of all the signs and wonders connected with the crossing of the Red Sea, and more than that, of all the wonders that took place in Egypt itself before it; then, later, they experienced the mighty acts of God in connection with the manna and the water in the wilderness. And by and by the Torah was given to them, and, gradually, they learned the ways of the Holy One, blessed be He, until eventually they reached that point when the words quoted were said unto them. Moses said, in effect: "Till now I had to teach you as little children are taught"; thou "hast been shown to know", and thou hast learnt by now to know and penetrate into the mystery of the Faith, namely, this, that "the Lord (*YHVH*) He is God (*Elohim*)", which is no small matter, since concerning this it says: "know therefore this day and consider it in thine heart that the Lord he

is God in heaven above and upon the earth beneath, there is
none else" (Deuteronomy 5:39). The whole mystery of the
Faith depends upon this; from this comes the knowledge
of the mystery of mysteries, the secret of secrets. *YHVH
ELOHIM* is a full Name, and the whole is one. Herein is a
mystery of mysteries to the masters of the esoteric knowledge. And, indeed, blessed are they who endeavour to comprehend the Torah. When the Holy One resolved to create
the world, He guided Himself by the Torah as by a plan, as
has been pointed out in connection with the words "Then I
was by him as *amon*" (Proverbs 8:30), where the word *amon*
(nursling) may also be read *uman* (architect). Was the
Torah, then, an architect? Yes; for if a King resolves to build
him a palace, without an architect and a plan how can he
proceed? Nevertheless, when the palace has been built, it is
attributed to the King: "here is the palace which the King
has built", because his was the thought that thus has been
realized. Similarly, when the Holy One, blessed be He, resolved to create the world, He looked into His plan, and,
although, in a sense, it was the plan which brought the
palace into being, it is not called by its name, but by that of
the King. The Torah proclaims: "I was by Him an architect,
through me He created the world!" —for the Torah preceded
the creation of the world by two thousand years; and so,
when He resolved to create the world He looked into the
Torah, into its every creative word, and fashioned the world
correspondingly; for all the words and all the actions of all
the worlds are contained in the Torah. Therefore did the
Holy One, blessed be He, look into it and create the world.
That is why it says not merely "I was an architect", but "I
was, alongside of Him, an architect". It may be asked, How
can one be an architect with Him? God looked at His plan in
this way. It is written in the Torah: "In the beginning God
created the heavens and the earth"; He looked at this expression and created heaven and earth. In the Torah it is written:
"Let there be light"; He looked at these words and created
light; and in this manner was the whole world created.

When the world was all thus created, nothing was yet established properly, until He had resolved to create man, in order that he might study the Torah, and, for his sake, the world should be firmly and properly established. Thus it is that he who concentrates his mind on, and deeply penetrates into, the Torah, sustains the world; for, as the Holy One looked into the Torah and created the world, so man looks into the Torah and keeps the world alive. Hence the Torah is the cause of the world's creation, and also the power that maintains its existence. Therefore blessed is he who is devoted to the Torah, for he is the preserver of the world.

Vayehi (Exodus) 235a

R. Eleazar put the following question to R. Simeon. 'Since it is known to God that men will die, why does He send souls down into the world?' He answered: 'This question has been discussed many times by the teachers, and they have answered it thus. God sends souls down to this world to declare His glory and takes them back afterwards. This mystery can be explained from the verse: "Drink water from thy cistern and flowing streams from the midst of thy well" (Proverbs 5:15). As we have laid down, the term "cistern" designates the place from which the waters do not naturally flow. But they do flow when the soul is perfected in this world and ascends to the place to which it is attached, for then it is complete on all sides, above and below. When the soul ascends, the desire of the female is stirred towards the male, and then water flows from below upwards, and the cistern becomes a well of flowing waters, and then there is union and foundation and desire and friendship and harmony, since through the soul of the righteous that place has been completed, and the supernal love and affection has been stirred to form a union.'

*

Sefer Hayashar (The Book of the Righteous) (13th century)

This anonymous work was one of the most popular ethical books during the Middle Ages. It was first printed in 1544, and has since been reprinted many times. Following is the opening section of the work, translated by Seymour J. Cohen.

SEFER HAYASHAR

Chapter I
The Mystery of the Creation of the World

It is obvious that anything that is desired testifies to the nature of him who desires it and that every deed testifies to the nature of him who performs it. It is, therefore, fitting for every intelligent person to engage in the choicest of occupations so that this will be a sign of his intelligence. From this we know that there is no occupation more choice and no deed more honored than the service of God, may He be exalted. For this testifies to the degree of intelligence that a man possesses and to his perfection. All the wise men of the world believe and understand that the intellect is able to grasp only two concepts: first, the Creator and second, that which was created. There is nothing else besides these. They thus believe that the Creator is first, and that that which was fashioned is created ex nihilo, that the Creator is without a beginning and an end, and that every living thing has a beginning and an end. They thus believe that the Creator has no need of anything. For one who is in need lacks the thing of which he is in need, and by securing the thing which he needs, he becomes complete. But since the Creator is perfect, He has no need of anything at all. Since He has no need of anything, it follows that He did not create the world to fill any need of His. Since He did not create the world for any need of His, we can deduce that He created it as a loving act to reward the good who merit such reward. Even as it is said (Isaiah 43:7), "Everyone that is called by My name, [And whom I have created for] My glory, I have formed him." Proof of this is in the way Scripture describes the Creation of the world. In the act of the Creation concerning the lights, it says (Genesis 1:17), "And God set them in the firmament of the heaven to give light upon the earth", and it does not say, "to give light to the heavens" or "toward the heavens," but "upon the earth." If this is so, we know that the luminaries were not created for any use of the Creator and not to give light to the heavens, but to give light to the earth and its inhabitants.

We can also recognize logically that if that which was created was for the benefit of the Creator, then it would be just as eternal as He, for His benefit would not be separated from Him, but would be found with Him always. But since we know that the world is created and not eternal, we know that before there was a world the Creator did not have any need of it. Just as He had no need of it before it came into being, so did He have no need of it after it came into being; but all of His intent in His creation of the world was for our benefit. Furthermore, we know and understand that the Creator did not create the world for the sake of the wicked or those who anger Him, for reason cannot lead us to such a conclusion, but He created it for the sake of the pious, who acknowledge His divinity and serve Him properly. His intent was only to create the pious, but the wicked were created by virtue of the nature of creation. Just as a piece of fruit has a peel and that which is choice is what is within the peel, so the pious are the fruit of the creation of the world and the wicked are the peel. Just as we see that the intent of the sower of the seed is to cause wheat alone to grow, but that the strength of the sprout brings forth evil weeds with the wheat and that with the rose come all sorts of thorns, thus it is the intent of the Creator to create the pious, but by the virtue of the nature of creation, the wicked are brought forth with the pious.

There is nothing that is created that cannot be divided into three parts: the choice or the purest part, which is like the finest flour; the inferior part, which consists of offal and worthless parts, such as straw or rubbish, and there is the part in between. Thus you find among human beings one part which is choice and pure, and these are the pious ones; they are like the fine flour or the choicest fruit. And then there is the less worthy and the rejected, and they are the wicked that are like the rubbish or straw. Therefore, we can say that the world was not created for the sake of the wicked, but for the sake of the pious. Just as in the case of a tree, its master did not plant it and labor for the sake of the peel, but for the sake of the choicest fruit that it will yield.

Furthermore, we see that the heavens are in motion, and every moving thing has a beginning to its motion. Since there was a beginning to its motion, we know that it has a beginning and that it is created, for the beginning of its motion is in fact its genesis. Since we know that it has a beginning, we know that before its creation the Creator had no need of it. Just as He had no need of it before its creation, so did He have no need of it after its creation. For the same power which the Creator had before its creation remained with Him after its creation; there was nothing lacking in it, there was nothing added to it, nor did it change it. Inasmuch as this is so, we know that just as He did not need it before its creation, so did He not need it after its creation. But if you should say that the motivation which obligated the Creator to create the world was His need for the world, we will say that the power of an obligation bends the one obligated to do the thing. With regard to the Creator, however, there is no power that can bend Him to do any act, but it was His own power that compelled the created objects to go forth from nothingness into existence. If you should ask why he obligated the created things thus, it was in order to make His divinity known and to show the glory of His greatness and to rejoice in His acts. For when the Creator creates a pious man, He rejoices in him, just as a father rejoices when he begets an intelligent and wise son, who recognizes the glory of his father and honors his father properly. [In such a case] the father rejoices and glories in him, and thus it is said (Psalms 104:31), "Let the Lord rejoice in His works!"

Now that it has been made clear that the world was not created for any need of God, we can say that the world was created for a great reason and that that reason is the service of the Creator, blessed be He. For just as a king is not called king until he has a people, as it is said (Proverbs 14:18), "In the multitude of people is the king's glory", so similarly the name "Creator" cannot be applied to one unless there is something that He has created. He is not called "God" until He has a people, as it is said (Leviticus 26:12), "And I will be your God and ye shall be My people." Even though the Divine name does not lack anything because of the lack of men nor does It gain by them, nevertheless, in the creation of the world, it was fitting that the name of the Creator should be "God." For example, the smiter can smite, but he is not called "the smiter" until he has smitten something. Even if there is no smitten object, there may be nothing lacking in the strength of the smiter, yet only when there is a smitten object is it proper to call the smiter by that name. Thus with the Creator, nothing was lacking in His power before the world was created, but in the creation of the world His perfection increased. This is the cause for which the world was created. Thus we know and understand that the Creation of the world was the perfection of God's name.

Just as we know that when an artisan does a task he has only one intention, to do it to the very best of his ability, and that according to the greatness of his skill will be the accuracy of his work, and since we see that the world is created with the utmost accuracy, we know that God created it with the utmost wisdom. Just as the good artisan has but one intent, to do lovely and good work, and just as a good and wise potter whose whole intention is to fashion very beautiful vessels; if one of them should come forth unattractive, crooked or imperfect, he will reject it and he will not include it with the beautiful vessels, but he will cast it aside or will break it—so, too, the Creator, blessed be He, had only one intent, to create in His world the good and the pious. And if there exists sinners, God rejects them, for they do not perfect the work of creation. Just as the wise artisan when he produces a beautiful piece of work boasts of it to all who see him, so does the Creator, blessed be He, glory in His pious ones, as it is said (Isaiah 44:23), "And he doth glorify Himself in Israel." And it says further (ibid., 49:3), "Israel, in whom I will be glorified." He vaunts Himself in His pious ones, for they testify to the perfection of His work and offer clear evidence to the righteousness of His deeds. As for the wicked, they are the opposite of which we have spoken. They place a blemish on His creation. They are a cause of the profanation of His glorious name. So that those who see them say that the work of the Creator, blessed be He, is not good, as it is said (Ezekiel 36:20), "And when they came unto the nations, whither they came, they profaned My holy name; in that men said of them: These are the people of the Lord, and are gone forth out of His land."

*

Bahya ben Asher ben Hlava
(?–1340)

Bahya was a Spanish Bible exegete, homilist, and kabbalist. He was known for his fourfold method of interpretation: literal, philosophical, homiletical, and mystical. One of Bahya's most popular works is *Kad Hakemach*. The following excerpt is from Charles B. Chavel's translation of this work entitled *Encyclopedia of Torah Thoughts*.

KAD HAKEMACH

Man was created primarily to study Torah. Therefore, one should be disconcerted by the sinful neglect of the study of the Torah by the majority of people. Most people concentrate all their efforts upon vanity and totally forget their duty to set aside regular hours for study on the Sabbaths and festivals and to study occasionally on weekdays and even nights. One should consider that if he received a written communication from a mortal king and he was unsure about its meaning, he would certainly endeavor with all his might to understand it. If this is true with respect to the writing of a mortal king, who is alive today and dead tomorrow, it is so much more true of the Torah, the writing of the King of kings, for the Torah is man's life and deliverance, as it is written, *For that is thy life and the length of thy days!* (Deuteronomy 30:20). Our Sages commented: "Every day, a Heavenly Voice bursts forth from Mount Horeb [Sinai] and proclaims, 'Woe to men for their contempt of the Torah.'" Thus you learn that man was primarily created to engage in the study of Torah.

The world exists only for the sake of Torah, as it is said, *Were it not for My covenant* [i.e., the Torah], *I would not have appointed day and night, the ordinances of heaven and earth* (Jeremiah 33:25). We also find that Malachi, the last of the prophets, warned us concerning [the neglect of the study of] Torah and concluded his prophecy with that subject. He said, *Remember ye the law of Moses My servant,* etc. (Malachi 3:22). *Lest I come and smite the land with utter destruction* (Malachi 3:24). It is thus as if he said, "*Remember the law of Moses My servant* (*Berachoth* 8a), and I will bless the entire world; if not, I will destroy the entire world." From here you derive that the entire world depends upon Torah. The Sages commented, "The Holy One, blessed be He, has only the four cubits of law in His world." That is to say, He has no desire or craving in His world except for the kind of human being who engages in the study of the law and who occupies but four square cubits. How sinful then is the person who has the time for studying Torah and fails to use it, for the Sages expounded: "*Because he hath despised the word of the Eternal* (Numbers 15:31). This refers to one who could have engaged in the study of Torah but failed to do so."

*

Joseph Albo (1380–1435/1444?)

Albo was a Spanish philosopher and pupil of Hasdai Crescas. His major work, *Sepher ha-Ikkarim*, or *Book of Dogmas*, is a treatise on Jewish articles of faith. The following excerpt is from Isaac Husik's translation of this work.

SEPHER HA-IKKARIM

'Ikkarim
Chapter 2

Every natural existent has in its specific form a certain property and purpose which distinguish it from other species. This purpose which exists in every species is the cause which determines its existence in that specific form. Man is also a natural existent, being the noblest and most perfect of them, as we have explained. He must therefore also have a proper purpose which is related to his specific form. It can not reside in the faculties of nutrition and sensation, for in that case the perfection and purpose of the ass and the pig would be the same as that of man. It is clear therefore that the perfection of man must consist in something which he has over and above the other animals.

Now we see that man has a potentiality and capacity of apprehending concepts, discovering sciences and bringing them from potentiality to actuality, more than all the other animals. Therefore human perfection must depend upon this intellectual power. And this power being divided into theoretical and practical, human perfection must depend upon the theoretical part rather than upon the practical, for the former bears closer relation to man's nature.

We can not say that the purpose of the human intellect is exclusively practical, to enable man to invent arts and trades. For it is made clear in the *Treatise on Animals*, composed by the Brethren of Purity, that as a general rule the lower animals are more adept in practical skill than man. Moreover if this were the case, then since the purpose is more important than that which comes before the purpose, the practical arts would be more noble than the speculative, and those speculative arts which lead to no practical result at all would be vain and of no value whatever. But this is contradicted by our nature and universal opinion. For all agree that the theoretical arts are superior to the practical. Again, the joy we feel in a thing relates to the purpose, and to that which is near to the purpose more so than to that which is far from it. But we find that the satisfaction and joy derived from a little theoretical knowledge are infinitely greater than all the satisfaction derived from practice. This proves that the real purpose of man depends upon the theoretical part of the intellectual power.

This is why we find that man has a stronger desire for the sensibilia of sight and hearing than for those of smell and taste. Nature has put in us a stronger desire for the former because we are more apt through them to acquire theoretical knowledge, upon which human perfection depends. The other sensibilia, on the other hand, bear a closer relation to the corporeal sensations and desires, which are far away from the specific perfection of man. Man has them only for the maintenance of his body, like the other animals. Now as every existent has a greater desire for that which has a bearing on his specific form and proper purpose, he has also a strong desire for the powers and instruments which lead to that purpose. Therefore man has a greater desire for these two sensibilia than for the others, because they play a greater part in leading man to his purpose than the others.

And this is the reason why the Bible ascribes to God the formation of these two senses, rather than the others. Solomon says, "The hearing ear, and the seeing eye, The Lord hath made even both of them" (Proverbs 20:12). And since instruction which is imparted by a teacher is more permanent than that which is not so acquired, the author of Proverbs explains in another verse that hearing is superior to sight, "The ear that hearkeneth to the reproof of life abideth among the wise" (Proverbs 15:31). In allusion to the superiority of these two senses over the others because they are instrumental in man's acquisition of perfection, Solomon says in the Song of Songs, "O my dove, that art in the clefts of the rock, in the covert of the cliff, let me see thy countenance, let me hear thy voice; For sweet is thy voice, and thy countenance is comely" (Proverbs 2:14). In poetic figure he speaks to his own soul, which he pictures as a dove, and speaks of her as being in the clefts of the rock, in the coverts of the cliff, alluding to the fact that the soul is hidden in the body, its seat not being known. The word countenance in the above passage is expressed in the Hebrew by the plural to indicate two things, letters in a book, and the sensibilia, both of which are necessary means of acquiring knowledge, and both of them are comely. Then he says, "Let me hear thy voice," meaning to say that though the voice of the dove is not sweet, the voice of this one is sweet, meaning the voice through which the soul learns concepts from the teacher; that voice, he says, is very sweet. Therefore he says, Let me hear thy voice, that which thou hast received from thy teacher, for thy voice is sweet, and thy countenance is comely. For through these two senses man's capacities are realized *in actu*, and he attains his perfection if he uses them properly.

But if he directs them to the world's vanities, he is as though he were deaf and blind. Thus, the prophet calls those who occupy themselves with the vanities of the world, deaf and blind, "Hear, ye deaf, and look, ye blind, that ye may see" (Isaiah 42:18). The reason is, because they do not employ their senses properly, i.e., to actualize their potential perfections, which is the only way by which man can realize his purpose.

In explanation of this we must say that there are two kinds of perfection, a first and a last. The first is that perfection which a thing has as soon as it comes into existence, the *perfection of existence*. The other is the perfection which a thing has not solely by existing. It is only potential in the existing thing, which attains that perfection when its potentialities are actualized. This is called the *perfection of purpose*. This is the perfection that is intended for man. Take a chair, for example. Its first perfection is attained as soon as it comes into existence, as soon as its manufacture is completed. The last perfection of the chair, the perfection of purpose, is not attained until it is sat on. In the lower animals the only perfection that is expected of them is the perfection of existence. Hence in speaking of their formation, the Bible says, "And God saw that it was good," to indicate that as soon as they come into existence, the good of which they are capable is attained and completed, and no other good is expected of them. But in the account of the formation of man there is no statement "that it is good," which seems strange. For it would seem that the formation of man should be characterized as good just like the formation of animals. The reason for the omission is in order to indicate that the good that is intended in the creation of man is not the perfection of existence merely, as in the other animals, but another nobler perfection, which can be attained only when he has actualized his potentialities. But as long as his intellect does not actualize its potentialities, the perfection intended, namely the perfection of purpose, is not attained.

This is the meaning of Solomon's statement, "A good name is better than precious oil; and the day of death than the day of one's birth" (Ecclesiastes 7:1). The meaning is, a good name acquired by good qualities is better than good oil, for a good name is heard much farther away than extends the odor of good oil. But a good name is not an essential and ultimate good of the soul. Therefore the day of death, when a man has attained his complete knowledge, is better than the day of his birth; for on the day of death he has already actualized the potentialities of his intellect, which is not the case on the day of his birth, for then the perfection of the soul has only potential existence, though the perfection of the body is actual.

The difference between man and animals in the purpose of their creation is alluded to also in variation of expression. Thus in the account of the formation of animals, we find the expressions, "after its kind," "after their kind," "And God made the beast of the earth after its kind, and the cattle after their kind, and every thing that creepeth upon the ground after its kind" (Genesis 1:25), to indicate that in animals there is no difference between the purpose of one species and that of another. Nor is there a difference between the creation of the male and that of the female. There is one general purpose including them all, and that is the perpetuation of the species, which is the perfection of existence. This is the same for all species and for male and female, for the male has no superiority in this matter over the female. But in the case of man, since the purpose of his creation is not merely the perpetuation of the species, but also the perpetuation of the individual, the expression "after his kind" is not mentioned, and the female was not created at the same time as the male, to indicate the great difference between the two kinds of creation (man and animal). The purpose in the latter is perpetuation of the species, wherein male and female are equal. The purpose of the former is perpetuation of the individual, in which the female is not equal to the male, but was created to help him that he might attain the intended perfection, which was there potentially, at the time of creation, and must be brought into actuality.

As this perfection is in man potentially, and potential existence stands midway, as it were, between existence and non-existence, the Bible calls it nothing. Thus Solomon says, "The pre-eminence of man above the beast is *nothing*; for all is vanity" (Ecclesiastes 3:19). The meaning is, the pre-eminence of man above the beast is something whose existence is weak. If the passage read: "There is no pre-eminence of man over the beast," it would have the meaning of a purely negative proposition. But since he says: "The pre-eminence of man above the beast is *nothing*," the judgment is affirmative, equivalent to the statement that man has pre-eminence over the beast, but this pre-eminence is nothing, i.e., something whose existence is weak, because it is mere potentiality. The student of logic will understand that this judgment has the value of an affirmative proposition rather than a negative. In reference to this power Job said, "But wisdom shall arise from nothing" (Job 28:12). The meaning is that wisdom comes from a potentiality residing in man, which is called "nothing" (*ayin*). Man's final perfection is attained when it becomes actual, not before. And the manner in which this power can attain wisdom is by answering the question, "What is it?" in defining things. Hence he says in the sequel, "And 'what' is the place of understanding."

*

Judah Loew ben Bezalel
(1512–1609)

Rabbi Loew spent most of his life in Moravia and Prague, where he was a talmudist, moralist, and mathematician. Numerous legends are associated with him, including the making of the most famous golem. Following, are two excerpts from *Netivot Olam* and *Derekh ha-Hayyim* translated by Ben Zion Bokser.

NETIVOT OLAM, TORAH, 15

Man is in a state of potentiality, and he was created for self-realization through the study of Torah and the performance of the commandments. It is for this reason that he is called

adam, alluding to the name *adamah*, which means *land* . . .
He is like the land which has been seeded with grain, a clean
seed, and the land will bring the seed to fruition, until it will
be an actual fruit. Similarly, the human body, which was
created from the earth, has been seeded with the soul, which
is pure and clean and free of base ingredients. Man is under
a commitment to bring to fruition that with which he has
been seeded: for this reason he bears the name *adam*. The
Torah acquired and the good deeds performed are the fruit,
as the verse suggests (Isaiah 3:10): "Say of the righteous that
it shall be well with them; they will eat the fruit of their
labors." But one who does not activate his soul is called in
Hebrew *bur*, a barren one, like a barren field. . . .

DEREKH HAHAYYIM ON AVOT 1:2

All creatures were created because of the good inherent in
them, and if the beings in existence did not have some good
inherent in them they would not have been created. For
whatever is not good in essence is unworthy of existence.
And as has already been made clear, you must realize that
all creatures depend on man, for they were created for
man's sake. If man does not live up to *his purpose*, then all
becomes void . . . Therefore man must achieve the good,
which is his end, thereby justifying his existence, and when
his existence has been justified, the whole universe has been
justified, since all hinges on man . . . Therefore must a person cultivate good qualities. And what makes a person good
so that one may say of him, "What a fine creature he is!" One
requirement is that he must be good in relation to himself
. . . The second category is that he must be good toward the
Lord who created man, to serve Him and to do His will. The
third category is that he must be good to others. For a person
does not exist by himself, he exists in fellowship with other
people . . . And when a person acts with kindness toward
other people there is a bond between him and his fellowman
and thus is the person as God intended him to be.

*

Isaac ben Solomon Luria (1534–1572)

Luria was the principal personality in the religious center of Safed and creator of a new kabbalistic trend expounding the ideas of exile and redemption. As he did not commit his teachings to writing, the dissemination of his doctrine was largely due to the rich literary activity of his disciple Hayyim Vital.

*

Hayyim Vital (1542–1620)

Vital was one of the greatest kabbalists. He was a pupil of Moses Cordovero and closely associated with Isaac Luria. Vital published the teachings of Luria in *Etz Hayyim* (*Tree of Life*) and many other works. The following excerpt is from Louis Jacobs' translation of Treatise 1, part 2 of *Etz Hayyim*.

ETZ HAYYIM

God's Withdrawal
The Mystery of God's Creation
of the Universe

Know that before there was any emanation and before any creatures were created a simple higher light filled everything. There was no empty space in the form of a vacuum but all was filled with that simple infinite light. This infinite light had

nothing in it of beginning or end but was all one
simple, equally distributed light. This is known as
"the light of *Ēn Sof*."

These extremely difficult meditations are those of R. Isaac
Luria but were written down by his disciple R. Hayyim
Vital. Vital wrote a number of books expounding his master's theories and they are the major source books of the
Lurianic *Kabbalah*. The Zohar, we have seen in an earlier
passage, holds that the world was created by means of ten
emanations, the Ten *Sefirot*. The Lurianic *Kabbalah* considers what happened even before these were caused to be
emanated. This is more than an effort to explain the ancient
puzzle of how creation came to be. By this teaching Luria
wants to explain the continuing relation between the Infinite and the finite, and to lay the groundwork for explaining
how evil came into the good God's creation. *Ēn Sof* (without
limit) is, as we have seen, the *Kabbalistic* name for God as
He is in Himself, i.e., apart from His self-revelation to His
creatures.

Two things have to be said before studying this passage.
First, although the *Kabbalists* use terms like "before" and
"after" in describing *Ēn Sof*'s creative activity, they really
think of these processes as occurring outside time altogether. (It is, of course, impossible for us to grasp this idea of
existence outside of time, but for the *Kabbalists*, as for some
of the philosophers, time itself is a creation.)

Secondly, all the illustrations of a vacuum, an empty
space, a line and the like are seen by the *Kabbalists* as
inadequate pointers to spiritual realities. They never tire of
warning their readers not to take them literally as if there
really is, for instance, a space in God. God is outside time
and space. Similarly, terms like *above* and *below* are only
figurative. Unless this is appreciated the whole subject becomes incredibly crude.

There arose in His simple will the will to create
worlds and produce emanations in order to realize

His perfect acts, His names and His attributes. This was the purpose for which the worlds were created.

In the "simple light of *Én Sof*" there emerged a will to create. (Note the way in which it is avoided saying that *Én Sof willed* directly, because this is considered as touching on a mystery too deep for human understanding.)

Én Sof then concentrated His being in the middle point, which was at the very center, and He withdrew that light, removing it in every direction away from that center point.

In the Lurianic *Kabbalah* creation is only possible by God withdrawing Himself. The logic is simple. Where there is God there cannot be any creatures since these would be overpowered by His majesty and swallowed up, as it were, into His being. This idea of Luria's is known as *Tzimtzum* (withdrawal).

*

Benedict (Baruch) Spinoza (1632–1677)

Spinoza was a Dutch philosopher descended from a family of Portuguese marranos. He was excommunicated from the Jewish community in 1656 at the age of 24, and died of tuberculosis at the age of 45. Most of his works were published posthumously. Spinoza was one of the foremost exponents of rationalism. His work *Ethics* is cited as among the greatest single works in the literature of philosophy. Following is R. H. M. Elwes's translation of the Appendix from Spinoza's *Ethics*.

ETHICS

Appendix

In the foregoing I have explained the nature and properties of God. I have shown that he necessarily exists, that he is one: that he is, and acts solely by the necessity of his own nature; that he is the free cause of all things, and how he is so; that all things are in God, and so depend on him, that without him they could neither exist nor be conceived; lastly, that all things are pre-determined by God, not through his free will or absolute fiat, but from the very nature of God or infinite power. I have further, where occasion offered, taken care to remove the prejudices, which might impede the comprehension of my demonstrations. Yet there still remain misconceptions not a few, which might and may prove very grave hindrances to the understanding of the concatenation of things, as I have explained it above. I have therefore thought it worth while to bring these misconceptions before the bar of reason.

All such opinions spring from the notion commonly entertained, that all things in nature act as men themselves act, namely, with an end in view. It is accepted as certain, that God himself directs all things to a definite goal (for it is said that God made all things for man, and man that he might worship him). I will, therefore, consider this opinion, asking first, why it obtains general credence, and why all men are naturally so prone to adopt it? secondly, I will point out its falsity; and, lastly, I will show how it has given rise to prejudices about good and bad, right and wrong, praise and blame, order and confusion, beauty and ugliness, and the like. However, this is not the place to deduce these misconceptions from the nature of the human mind: it will be sufficient here, if I assume as a starting point, what ought to be universally admitted, namely, that all men are born ignorant of the causes of things, that all have the desire to seek for what is useful to them, and that they are conscious of such desire. Herefrom it follows first, that men think them-

selves free, inasmuch as they are conscious of their volitions
and desires, and never even dream, in their ignorance, of the
causes which have disposed them to wish and desire. Secondly, that men do all things for an end, namely, for that
which is useful to them, and which they seek. Thus it comes
to pass that they only look for a knowledge of the final causes
of events, and when those are learned, they are content, as
having no cause for further doubt. If they cannot learn such
causes from external sources, they are compelled to turn to
considering themselves, and reflecting what end would have
induced them personally to bring about the given event, and
thus they necessarily judge other natures by their own. Further, as they find in themselves and outside themselves
many means which assist them not a little in their search for
what is useful, for instance, eyes for seeing, teeth for chew-
ing, herbs and animals for yielding food, the sun for giving
light, the sea for breeding fish, etc., they come to look on the
whole of nature as a means for obtaining such conveniences.
Now as they are aware, that they found these conveniences
and did not make them they think they have cause for
believing, that some other being has made them for their
use. As they look upon things as means, they cannot believe
them to be self-created; but, judging from the means which
they are accustomed to prepare for themselves, they are
bound to believe in some ruler or rulers of the universe
endowed with human freedom, who have arranged and
adapted everything for human use. They are bound to estimate the nature of such rulers (having no information on the
subject) in accordance with their own nature, and therefore
they assert that the gods ordained everything for the use of
man, in order to bind man to themselves and obtain from
him the highest honors. Hence also it follows, that everyone
thought out for himself, according to his abilities, a different
way of worshipping God, so that God might love him more
than his fellows, and direct the whole course of nature for
the satisfaction of his blind cupidity and insatiable avarice.
Thus the prejudice developed into superstition, and took
deep root in the human mind; and for this reason everyone

strove most zealously to understand and explain the final causes of things; but in their endeavor to show that nature does nothing in vain, i. e., nothing which is useless to man, they only seem to have demonstrated that nature, the gods, and men are all mad together. Consider, I pray you, the result: among the many helps of nature they were bound to find some hindrances, such as storms, earthquakes, diseases, etc.: so they declared that such things happen, because the gods are angry at some wrong done them by men, or at some fault committed·in their worship. Experience day by day protested and showed by infinite examples, that good and evil fortunes fall to the lot of pious and impious alike; still they would not abandon their inveterate prejudice, for it was more easy for them to class such contradictions among other unknown things of whose use they were ignorant, and thus to retain their actual and innate condition of ignorance, than to destroy the whole fabric of their reasoning and start afresh. They therefore laid down as an axiom, that God's judgments far transcend human understanding. Such a doctrine might well have sufficed to conceal the truth from the human race for all eternity, if mathematics had not furnished another standard of verity in considering solely the essence and properties of figures without regard to their final causes. There are other reasons (which I need not mention here) besides mathematics, which might have caused men's minds to be directed to these general prejudices, and have led them to the knowledge of the truth.

I have now sufficiently explained my first point. There is no need to show at length, that nature has no particular goal in view, and that final causes are mere human figments. This, I think, is already evident enough, both from the causes and foundations on which I have shown such prejudice to be based, and also from Proposition xvi., and the Corollary of Proposition xxxii., and, in fact, all those propositions in which I have shown, that everything in nature proceeds from a sort of necessity, and with the utmost perfection. However, I will add a few remarks, in order to overthrow this doctrine of a final cause utterly. That which is really a cause it considers as an effect, and *vice versâ*: it makes that which is by nature first to be last, and that which is highest and most perfect to be most imperfect. Passing over the questions of cause and priority as self-evident, it is plain from Propositions xxi., xxii., xxiii. that that effect, is most perfect which is produced immediately by God; the effect which requires for its production several intermediate causes is, in that respect, more imperfect. But if those things which were made immediately by God were made to enable him to attain his end, then the things which come after, for the sake of which the first were made, are necessarily the most excellent of all.

Further, this doctrine does away with the perfection of God: for, if God acts for an object, he necessarily desires something which he lacks. Certainly, theologians and metaphysicians draw a distinction between the object of want and the object of assimilation; still they confess that God made all things for the sake of himself, not for the sake of creation. They are unable to point to anything prior to creation, except God himself, as an object for which God should act, and are therefore driven to admit (as they clearly must), that God lacked those things for whose attainment he created means, and further that he desired them.

We must not omit to notice that the followers of this doctrine, anxious to display their talent in assigning final causes, have imported a new method of argument in proof of their theory—namely, a reduction, not to the impossible, but to ignorance; thus showing that they have no other method of exhibiting their doctrine. For example, if a stone falls from a roof on to some one's head and kills him, they will demonstrate by their new method, that the stone fell in order to kill the man; for, if it had not by God's will fallen with that object, how could so many circumstances (and there are often many concurrent circumstances) have all happened together by chance? Perhaps you will answer that the event is due to the facts that the wind was blowing, and the man was walking that way. "But why," they will insist, "was the wind blowing, and why was the man at that very time walking that way?" If you again answer, that the wind had then sprung up because the sea had begun to be agitated the day before, the weather being previously calm, and that the man had been invited by a friend, they will again insist: "But why was the sea agitated, and why was the man invited at that time?" So they will pursue their questions from cause to cause, till at last you take refuge in the will of God—in other words, the sanctuary of ignorance. So, again, when they survey the frame of the human body, they are amazed; and being ignorant of the causes of so great a work of art conclude that it has been fashioned, not mechanically, but by divine and supernatural skill, and has been so put together that one part shall not hurt another.

Hence any one who seeks for the true causes of miracles, and strives to understand natural phenomena as an intelligent being, and not to gaze at them like a fool, is set down and denounced as an impious heretic by those, whom the masses adore as the interpreters of nature and the gods. Such persons know that, with the removal of ignorance, the wonder which forms their only available means for proving and preserving their authority would vanish also. But I now quit this subject, and pass on to my third point.

After men persuaded themselves, that everything which is created is created for their sake, they were bound to consider as the chief quality in everything that which is most useful to themselves, and to account those things the best of all which have the most beneficial effect on mankind. Further, they were bound to form abstract notions for the explanation of the nature of things, such as GOODNESS, BADNESS, ORDER, CONFUSION, WARMTH, COLD, BEAUTY, DEFORMITY, and so on; and from the belief that they are free agents arose the further notions PRAISE and BLAME, SIN and MERIT.

I will speak of these latter hereafter, when I treat of human nature; the former I will briefly explain here.

Everything which conduces to health and the worship of God they have called GOOD, everything which hinders these objects they have styled BAD; and inasmuch as those who do not understand the nature of things do not verify phenomena in any way, but merely imagine them after a fashion, and mistake their imagination for understanding, such persons firmly believe that there is an ORDER in things, being really ignorant both of things and their own nature. When phenomena are of such a kind, that the impression they make on our senses requires little effort of imagination, and can consequently be easily remembered, we say that they are WELL-ORDERED; if the contrary, that they are ILL-ORDERED or CONFUSED. Further, as things which are easily imagined are more pleasing to us, men prefer order to confusion—as though there were any order in nature, except in relation to our imagination—and say that God has created all things in order; thus, without knowing it, attributing imagination to God, unless, indeed, they would have it that God foresaw human imagination, and arranged everything, so that it should be most easily imagined. If this be their theory they would not, perhaps, be daunted by the fact that we find an infinite number of phenomena, far surpassing our imagination, and very many others which confound its weakness. But enough has been said on this subject. The other abstract notions are nothing but modes of imagining, in which the imagination is differently affected, though they are considered by the ignorant as the chief attributes of things, inasmuch as they believe that everything was created for the sake of themselves; and, according as they are affected by it, style it good or bad, healthy or rotten and corrupt. For instance, if the motion whose objects we see communicate to our nerves be conducive to health, the objects causing it are styled BEAUTIFUL; if a contrary motion be excited, they are styled UGLY.

Things which are perceived through our sense of smell are styled fragrant or fetid; if through our taste, sweet or bitter, full-flavored or insipid, if through our touch, hard or soft, rough or smooth, etc.

Whatsoever affects our ears is said to give rise to noise, sound, or harmony. In this last case, there are men lunatic

enough to believe that even God himself takes pleasure in
harmony; and philosophers are not lacking who have persuaded themselves, that the motion of the heavenly bodies
gives rise to harmony—all of which instances sufficiently
show that everyone judges of things according to the state of
his brain, or rather mistakes for things the forms of his
imagination. We need no longer wonder that there have
arisen all the controversies we have witnessed and finally
scepticism: for, although human bodies in many respects
agree, yet in very many others they differ; so that what
seems good to one seems bad to another; what seems well
ordered to one seems confused to another; what is pleasing to
one displeases another, and so on. I need not further enumer-
ate, because this is not the place to treat the subject at
length, and also because the fact is sufficiently well known.
It is commonly said: "So many men, so many minds; everyone is wise in his own way; brains differ as completely as
palates." All of which proverbs show, that men judge of
things according to their mental disposition, and rather
imagine than understand: for, if they understood phenomena, they would, as mathematics attest, be convinced, if not
attracted, by what I have urged.

We have now perceived, that all the explanations commonly given of nature are mere modes of imagining, and do
not indicate the true nature of anything, but only the constitution of the imagination; and, although they have names, as
though they were entities, existing externally to the imagination, I call them entities imaginary rather than real; and,
therefore, all arguments against us drawn from such abstractions are easily rebutted.

Many argue in this way. If all things follow from a necessity of the absolutely perfect nature of God, why are there so
many imperfections in nature? such, for instance, as things
corrupt to the point of putridity, loathsome deformity, confusion, evil, sin, etc. But these reasoners are, as I have said,
easily confuted, for the perfection of things is to be reckoned
only from their own nature and power; things are not more

or less perfect, according as they delight or offend human senses, or according as they are serviceable or repugnant to mankind. To those who ask why God did not so create all men, that they should be governed only by reason, I give no answer but this: because matter was not lacking to him for the creation of every degree of perfection from highest to lowest; or, more strictly, because the laws of his nature are so vast, as to suffice for the production of everything conceivable by an infinite intelligence, as I have shown in Proposition xvi.

Such are the misconceptions I have undertaken to note; if there be any more of the same sort, everyone may easily dissipate them for himself with the aid of a little reflection.

*

Israel ben Eliezer Baal Shem Tov (c. 1700–1760)

The Baal Shem Tov was the charismatic founder and leader of Hasidism in Eastern Europe. Though he did not put his teachings in writing, after his death, his disciples published hundreds of sermons and homilies learned from their master. The basic core of his teachings is devekut—man's adhesion or cleavage to God. Following is a brief excerpt from Louis I. Newman's *The Hasidic Anthology*.

THE PURPOSE OF CREATION

In the hour of his death the Baal Shem said: "Now I know the purpose for which I was created."

*

Moses Hayyim Luzzatto (1707–1747)

Luzzatto, a kabbalist and poet, was born and educated in Padua, Italy. Due to conflicts with the local Jewish leaders he migrated to various parts of Europe and finally settled in Palestine, where he died of the plague. Luzzatto's *Mesillat Yesharim* (*The Path of the Upright*) is an ethical work considered a classic. The following excerpt is from Mordecai Kaplan's translation of the first chapter.

MESILLAT YESHARIM

Concerning Man's Duty in the World

The foundation of saintliness and the root of perfection in the service of God lies in a man's coming to see clearly and to recognize as a truth the nature of his duty in the world and the end towards which he should direct his vision and his aspiration in all of his labors all the days of his life.

Our Sages of blessed memory have taught us that man was created for the sole purpose of rejoicing in God and deriving pleasure from the splendor of His Presence; for this is true joy and the greatest pleasure that can be found. The place where this joy may truly be derived is the World to Come, which was expressly created to provide for it; but the path to the object of our desires is this world, as our Sages of blessed memory have said (*Avoth* 4:21), "This world is like a corridor to the World to Come."

The means which lead a man to this goal are the mitzvoth, in relation to which we were commanded by the Lord, may His Name be blessed. The place of the performance of the mitzvoth is this world alone.

Therefore, man was placed in this world first—so that by these means, which were provided for him here, he would be able to reach the place which had been prepared for him, the World to Come, there to be sated with the goodness which he acquired through them. As our Sages of blessed memory have said (*Eruvin* 22*a*), "Today for their [the mitzvoth's] performance and tomorrow for receiving their reward."

When you look further into the matter, you will see that only union with God constitutes true perfection, as King David said (Psalm 73:28), "But as for me, the nearness of God is my good," and (Psalm 27:4), "I asked one thing from God; that will I seek—to dwell in God's house all the days of my life . . ." For this alone is the true good, and anything besides this which people deem good is nothing but emptiness and deceptive worthlessness. For a man to attain this good, it is certainly fitting that he first labor and persevere in his exertions to acquire it. That is, he should persevere so as to unite himself with the Blessed One by means of actions which result in this end. These actions are the mitzvoth.

The Holy One Blessed be He has put man in a place where the factors which draw him further from the Blessed One are many. These are the earthy desires which, if he is pulled after them, cause him to be drawn further from and to depart from the true good. It is seen, then, that man is veritably placed in the midst of a raging battle. For all the affairs of the world, whether for the good or for the bad, are trials to a man: Poverty on the one hand and wealth on the other, as Solomon said (Proverbs 30:9), "Lest I become satiated and deny, saying, 'Who is God?' or lest I become impoverished and steal . . ." Serenity on the one hand and suffering on the other; so that the battle rages against him to the fore and to the rear. If he is valorous, and victorious on all sides, he will be the "Whole Man," who will succeed in uniting himself with his Creator, and he will leave the corridor to enter into the Palace, to glow in the light of life. To the extent that he has subdued his evil inclination and his desires, and withdrawn from those factors which draw him further from the good, and exerted himself to become united with it, to that extent will he attain it and rejoice in it.

If you look more deeply into the matter, you will see that the world was created for man's use. In truth, man is the center of a great balance. For if he is pulled after the world and is drawn further from his Creator, he is damaged, and he damages the world with him. And if he rules over himself and unites himself with his Creator, and uses the world only to aid him in the service of his Creator, he is uplifted and the world itself is uplifted with him. For all creatures are greatly uplifted when they serve the "Whole Man," who is sanctified with the holiness of the Blessed One. It is as our Sages of blessed memory have said in relation to the light that the Holy One Blessed be He stored away for the righteous (*Chagiga* 12*a*): "When the Holy One Blessed be He saw the light that He had stored away for the righteous, He rejoiced, as it is said (Proverbs 13:9), 'The light of the righteous rejoices.'" And in relation to the "stones of the place" that Jacob took and put around his head they said (*Chulin* 91*b*), "R. Yitzchak said, 'This teaches us that they [the stones] gathered themselves into one spot, each one saying, "Let the righteous one lay his head upon me." Our Sages of blessed memory drew our attention to this principle in Midrash Koheleth, where they said (*Koheleth Rabbah* 7:28) "'See the work of God . . .' (Ecclesiastes 7:13). When the Holy One Blessed be He created Adam, He took him and caused him to pass before all the trees of the Garden of Eden. He said to him, 'See how beautiful and praiseworthy are my works; and all that I have created, I have created for your sake. Take heed that you do not damage and destroy my world.'"

To summarize, a man was created not for his station in this world, but for his station in the World to Come. It is only that his station in this world is a means towards his station in the World to Come, which is the ultimate goal. This accounts for numerous statements of our Sages of blessed memory, all in a similar vein, likening this world to the place and time of preparation, and the next world to the place which has been set aside for rest and for the eating of what has already been prepared. This is their intent in saying (*Avoth* 4:21), "This world is similar to a corridor . . . ," as our Sages of blessed memory have said (*Eruvin* 22a), "Today for their performance and tomorrow to receive their reward," "He who exerted himself on Friday will eat on the Sabbath" (*Avodah Zarah* 3a), "This world is like the shore and the World to Come like the sea . . ." (*Koheleth Rabbah* 1:36), and many other statements along the same lines.

And in truth, no reasoning being can believe that the purpose of man's creation relates to his station in this world. For what is a man's life in this world! Who is truly happy and content in this world? "The days of our life are seventy years, and, if exceedingly vigorous, eighty years, and their persistence is but labor and foolishness" (Psalm 90:10). How many different kinds of suffering, and sicknesses, and pains and burdens! And after all this—death! Not one in a thousand is to be found to whom the world has yielded a superabundance of gratifications and true contentment. And even such a one, though he attain to the age of one hundred years, passes and vanishes from the world.

Furthermore, if man had been created solely for the sake of this world, he would have had no need of being inspired with a soul so precious and exalted as to be greater than the angels themselves; especially so in that it derives no satisfaction whatsoever from all of the pleasures of this world. This is what our Sages of blessed memory teach us in Midrash (*Koheleth Rabbah*), "'And also the soul will not be filled' (Ecclesiastes 6:7) What is this analogous to? To the case of a city dweller who married a princess. If he brought her all that the world possessed, it would mean nothing to her, by virtue of her being a king's daughter. So is it with the soul. If it were to be brought all the delights of the world, they would be as nothing to it, in view of its pertaining to the higher elements." And so do our Sages of blessed memory say (*Avoth* 4:29), "Against your will were you created, and against your will were you born." For the soul has no love at all for this world. To the contrary, it despises it. The Creator, Blessed be His Name, certainly would never have created

something for an end which ran contrary to its nature and
which it despised.

Man was created, then, for the sake of his station in the
World to Come. Therefore, this soul was placed in him. For
it befits the soul to serve God; and through it a man may be
rewarded in his place and in his time. And rather than the
world's being despicable to the soul, it is, to the contrary, to
be loved and desired by it. This is self-evident.

After recognizing this we will immediately appreciate
the greatness of the obligation that the mitzvoth place upon
us and the preciousness of the Divine service which lies in
our hands. For these are the means which bring us to true
perfection, a state which, without them, is unattainable. It is
understood, however, that the attainment of a goal results
only from a consolidation of all the available means employ-
able towards its attainment, that the nature of a result is
determined by the effectiveness and manner of employment
of the means utilized towards its achievement, and that the
slightest differentiation in the means will very noticeably
affect the result to which they give rise upon the fruition of
the aforementioned consolidation. This is self-evident.

It is obvious, then, that we must be extremely exacting in
relation to the mitzvoth and the service of God, just as the
weighers of gold and pearls are exacting because of the
preciousness of these commodities. For their fruits result in
true perfection and eternal wealth, than which nothing is
more precious.

We thus derive that the essence of a man's existence in this
world is solely the fulfilling of mitzvoth, the serving of God
and the withstanding of trials, and that the world's pleasures should serve only the purpose of aiding and assisting
him, by way of providing him with the contentment and
peace of mind requisite for the freeing of his heart for the
service which devolves upon him. It is indeed fitting that his
every inclination be towards the Creator, may His Name be
blessed, and that his every action, great or small, be moti-
vated by no purpose other than that of drawing near to the
Blessed One and breaking all the barriers (all the earthy

elements and their concomitants) that stand between him and his Possessor, until he is pulled towards the Blessed One just as iron to a magnet. Anything that might possibly be a means to acquiring this closeness, he should pursue and clutch, and not let go of; and anything which might be considered a deterrent to it, he should flee as from a fire. As it is stated (*Psalm* 63:9), "My soul clings to You; Your right hand sustains me." For a man enters the world only for this purpose—to achieve this closeness by rescuing his soul from all the deterrents to it and from all that detracts from it.

After we have recognized the truth of this principle, and it has become clear to us, we must investigate its details according to its stages, from beginning to end, as they were arranged by R. Pinchas ben Yair in the statement which has already been referred to in our introduction. These stages are: Watchfulness, Zeal, Cleanliness, Separation, Purity, Saintliness, Humility, Fear of Sin, and Holiness. And now, with the aid of Heaven, we will explain them one by one.

*

Elimelech of Lizensk (1717–1787)

Elimelech was one of the founders of Hasidism in Galicia. He helped to build the theoretical foundations for the establishment of "dynasties" of tzaddikim. His book *Noam Elimelech*, or *Elimelech's Delight*, was published by his son after his death. The two excerpts that follow were translated by Aryeh Kaplan.

NOAM ELIMELECH

HaAzinu (97b)

Our sages teach us, "At first there was a thought to create the world with the Attribute of Justice. God saw that the world could not endure, so He combined it with the Attribute of Love."

Earlier commentators have already questioned this teaching. How is it possible to say that the Creator, who is absolutely simple [and unchanging], could first have one thought, and then later realize that the world could not endure with it. Heaven forbid that we should imagine any change with regard to the Creator!

In order to understand this we must first ask another question. How can we say that God's first thought was to create the world with the Attribute of Justice? We know that the main purpose of creation was to bestow good to His creation. [How was this meant to be accomplished through unmitigated justice?]

In order to understand this, we must realize that creation was brought into existence primarily for the sake of the righteous.

We find this in the Midrash: "It is written, 'And God saw . . .' (Genesis 1:4). What did He see? He saw the souls of the righteous."

The righteous, however, are actually worthy of receiving good because of their good deeds. They can therefore receive it as their reward, even according to Justice.

[The righteous do not need the Attribute of Love] since Love implies that which goes beyond the requirements of justice. [Through the Attribute of Love] God gives good to people as a free gift, even though they do not deserve it. [Since it is not earned, however,] it is called the "bread of shame."

The righteous, however, receive their reward according to Justice. The world was created in order to benefit creation, and the main benefit is good which is bestowed through Justice, since this is not "bread of shame." [It is for this reason that we are taught that the world was created for the sake of the righteous.]

The nature of creation is like any other natural growth [containing both the essential and the secondary].

Thus, for example, when a person plants wheat, his main

intent is to grow grain. The nature [of wheat, however,] is that it grows with extraneous chaff as well. The same is true of all creation, as we find in the *Sefer Ha Yashar*.

We are taught that, "At first there was a thought to create the world with the Attribute of Justice." This is called the "first thought" because it is the main [purpose of creation] and its beginning. This was for the sake of the righteous who would exist in the future, who would receive their reward with justice and fairness. This remained in effect forever, and this thought actually never changed. At all times it is true that the righteous receive their reward through Justice.

Creation contained a balance [of good and evil], however, and therefore, extraneous things would automatically come into existence. These [extraneous things] include the wicked.

It was because of the wicked that there had to be a combination with the Attribute of Love so that the world could endure. They cannot be worthy through Justice, and must therefore depend upon God's Love.

All this was a single thought, and it took place in a single instant of time. The only reason why God's thought with regard to the righteous is called "first" is because it was His main purpose and desire in creation.

Likutey Shoshanim (103d)

It is written, "God desires for the sake of His righteousness. He made the Torah great and mighty" (Isaiah 42:21).

It is known that God's main purpose in creation was so that He should grant good to His handiwork.

[It is written that] God is, "great in love" (Exodus 34:6). Since nothing existed with whom He could do good, He had to bring the world into existence, so that He could maintain the attribute of love.

This takes place through the righteous, since it is they who transmit all influences through an "awakening from below." Through their actions, the righteous can transmit whatever they desire, whether it be Love or Strength.

This is accomplished through the Torah. Through God's great mercy, He placed the Attributes of Love and Strength in the Torah. When a person studies Torah for God's sake, he can transmit the Attributes of both Love and Justice—Love for Israel, and Justice toward the wicked . . .

This is the meaning of the above verse. God wanted to act righteously to all worlds, and it is thus written, "God desires for the sake of His righteousness." He therefore, "made the Torah great and mighty." He placed both the greatness [of His Love] and the might [of His Justice] in the Torah, in order that the righteous should be able to use the Torah to transmit [these attributes].

*

Moses Mendelssohn (1729–1786)

Mendelssohn was born in Dessau, Germany, a philosopher, translator, and leader of German Jewry. He was an advocate of Jewish emancipation and enlightenment. The following excerpts are from Eva Jospe's *Moses Mendelssohn: Selections from His Writings.*

WHAT IS MAN'S DESTINY?
[EXCERPTS FROM LETTERS
TO THOMAS ABBT]

Our all-wise Benefactor has sent us here so that we might steadily exercise and thereby improve our faculties. That this represents His will is evidenced not merely by the very nature of our drives, desires, and passions but also by the character of our pleasures, displeasures, and tastes and even by our wilfulness and sense of self-importance. The uneducated man senses the force of all these impulses, though he may not be able to articulate his emotions. The educated

man tries to control his inclinations rationally, and is happi-
est when he can make his own will correspond closely to the
real purpose of his natural drives, the purpose intended by
God.

But does our Benefactor's plan for us extend beyond our
destiny here on earth? Since no substance is ever destroyed,
it continues throughout its existence to serve its [divinely]
intended purpose.

Is there, then, some inner connection linking our future to
our present state? There is indeed, and it is as perfect as the
order of all God's designs, or as the syllogism of a logical
demonstration in which the conclusion follows from all
preceding premises.

The blossom torn off by the north wind, the seed that will
not take root and sprout—they are blown away and disinte-
grate. Yet their components, reorganized, assume another
form, fulfilling, in their new shape, the divine intent. Would
they be able to do so had they not first been either blossom or
seed? Just as in a logical demonstration one argument must
proceed from the other to arrive at a correct conclusion, so
God, too, proceeds in the most direct manner toward the
realization of the goals He has set for man.

There [in the beyond] too, O man, there too you will serve
mankind. But you could never do so had you not first exercised your faculties here on earth, just as you could never
become a man had your basic constitution not already rudi-
mentarily existed in your father's blood.

The divine order of things is characterized by unity of
purpose. All intermediate ends are at once means, all means
ends. Do not think of our life here as merely preparatory, or
of our future life as an end in itself. Both are means, and
both are ends. God's plan extends into all eternity, and the
transformation of all substances continues indefinitely.

Questions and Answers

1) What is man's destiny?—To serve, in congruence with
   his rational insights, his divinely intended purpose;

perpetually to become more perfect, and to attain eternal bliss through that state of perfection. . . .

GOD'S CREATURES: WHAT IS THEIR PURPOSE? [TO THOMAS ABBT]

Berlin, March 26, 1765

. . . The well-known dictum that in God's creation all means are ends and all (intermediary) ends merely means may yield more insights than we have thus far assumed. If Maupertuis, for instance, asks: "Is the fly so wonderfully built for the sole purpose of being devoured by the rapacious spider in a single instant?" I should like to reply: "The works of God do not provide us with ready answers or definite statements of purpose." The primary purpose of this flying machine's artful construction is evidently the mere existence of this small insect. But why? For the simple reason that those things that look like flies may be alive and have sensations. And if you continue with your nearsighted "but why?" you might as well turn all creation into a desert. That proud yet poverty-stricken thing, man, asks of anything that seems of no use to him personally: "What is it for?"

The fly's existence may well serve some secondary purpose. In fact, this is the way it must be, unless my conception of the interrelatedness of ends and means in nature is totally wrong. Flies probably clean the air; or they may possibly announce an impending change of weather by stinging us; in addition, they also provide nourishment for spiders. Moreover, God probably has definite intentions with regard to every single fly. But who can fathom those?

Similarly, natural science asks: "Why is there such an infinite number of tiny organisms and cells in the seeds of animals and plants, if only a single one will come to fruition while all the others perish?" My reply is: "The small animals and plants are proportionately as important in nature as the

large ones, and one cannot say that the former exist merely
to give rise to the latter. True, semen and seed have an
inherent disposition to become grown animals and plants.
But who says they must undergo this transformation in
every instance? And why does one deny any purpose to their
existence merely because they have not developed fully or
grown to their full size? Though the majority of them do lose
their ability to grow, they grace creation even in their infinitesimal smallness. Still, even those reduced to infinitesim-
ally small organisms stop neither living nor fulfilling God's
intent. And if their inner organization had not been exactly
the way it is, they would in all likelihood have been unable to
fulfill this intent.

But what exactly is this intent? Here, I believe it is time to
touch one's finger to one's lips and seal them. Despite all our
searching inquiries, this wise "I do not know" remains our
last resort. This, however, does not at all mean a negation of
those things we do know.

With this, I am coming closer, I think, to the meaning of
your question. For it may be similar with man and his life on
earth, if, that is, one can clearly define those specific characteristics that make us rational beings. Since we exist, we
may deduce with some certainty that the world would have
been less complete without human beings. And what is our
purpose, what are we to do down here? All of us must do not
only what we have to do but in fact what we can never fail to
do—namely, develop our mental faculties, though some will
necessarily do so to a higher degree than others.

In what way does man's destiny differ from that of other
beings? Only in the way in which we make use of our specific
gifts on earth to achieve that degree of perfection given us
[as our potential goal].

Why are only so few men aware of the purpose of their
existence? Because man can fulfill his purpose even when he
is unaware of it. Few men ever realize the purpose of their
hunger, and those who do may have the poorest appetite.
Man, you say, does not know why he is here. Oh, but he does
know it rather well, if only because he sees, feels, compares,

incessantly exercises his ability to think. And he does all this
with great gusto. The only thing is that he lacks such abstract notions as "purpose," "existence," "means," et cetera,
so that he is unable to sum up logically his incessant emotions and acts. I for one do not even see why you insist that
this is particularly necessary.

Some people die before reaching that level of development
possible here on earth. This is true enough when you consider mankind's total potential. But if we look upon it [a
prematurely ended life] as a partial potential, seeing the
single individual as determined and circumscribed by certain conditions, we may well arrive at a different judgment.
For then we should see that each person reaches the level of
development he could and should have reached in the given
circumstances and context.

This would also hold true for the seminal cell that was
never conceived and therefore neither could nor should have
developed at this time. But this does not mean that its innate
disposition, even its rudimentary development or potential,
is completely lost. For, as I said before, except for their
general main purpose, God's works do not demonstrate His
intent so unequivocally, so obviously, that one would be justified in saying that every means is lost merely because we do
not see the end to which it might be leading.

MAN: THE ULTIMATE END
IN THE COSMIC PLAN
[TO THOMAS ABBT]

... You ask me what I think concerning my destiny as a
man: first of all, I must worship [God] and perform good
deeds. Then, I must strive for happiness. I realize that by the
same token by which God Himself cannot be happy without
acts of kindness and goodness, His lowliest creature cannot
be entirely unhappy as long as he can do some good. True, I

cannot determine with any degree of certainty the part I was assigned in all of creation, nor can I know how far I and my kind have progressed within the cosmic plan.

But this much I do know: I am a member of a group of beings who must and can worship God and perform good deeds, beings who represent not merely means to higher ends within the cosmic plan but ends in themselves—and ultimate ends at that. Thus, my heart and mind can be filled with the sweet consolation that I shall one day exist in a different state, one of enhanced ability to worship and do good. I shall then see in a clearer light the great truth that goodness toward others constitutes happiness, and that the more happiness I can create the happier I shall become. And I can create happiness in this world by trying to promote order and harmony, gladness and enjoyment, wisdom and virtue.

This expectation of mine (surely neither deception nor delusion!) is fully commensurate with the nature of things— my own nature as well as that of the most exalted Wisdom's kind rule. To be sure, I cannot flatter myself that I shall ever be able to divest myself entirely of whatever foolishness occasionally troubles me or makes me unhappy down here. In fact, I have the feeling that even in the beyond I shall occasionally have to suffer so that others may become happier, and shall frequently do something unwise simply because it seems wise to me.

Moreover, I realize that I shall never become entirely one with the source of all perfection; shall never be able to enjoy completely untroubled the pure pleasure of comprehending the whole truth. But I shall come ever closer to my goal. I shall become increasingly more aware that I cannot ever suffer for others without becoming a better and, in an inward sense, a more perfect person. Mine will be an ever deeper realization that all my wisdom is but foolishness if it desires anything other than what an all-wise Providence has arranged for me. And I shall become increasingly aware that like all others of my kind I have been singled out and destined by our Creator to be righteous and happy in that righteousness; to search for truth; to love beauty and do the best I can—which means to worship Him and to do good.

*

Israel ben Shabbetai Hapstein— the Magid of Kozience (1733–1814)

Israel was a fourth-generation hasidic leader. His eloquent preachings gained him the title of Magid of Kozience. Israel's principal work on Hasidism is *Avodath Yisroel* (*Israel's Worship*). This selection was translated by Aryeh Kaplan.

AVODATH YISROEL

TeTzaveh (34b)

It is known that the purpose of creation was that we should serve the "God of Israel." This was the goal and reason for creation.

We cannot delve or philosophize into God's will, trying to find out how and why He desired this. It is thus written, "Does one exist who can search out God?" (Job 11:7). Maimonides speaks of this, and it is a fundamental basic of our faith.

The wicked . . . however, foolishly said that it would be a defect in the Infinite Being if He desired the worship of those below [in the physical world]. Since they could not understand it with philosophical reasoning, they therefore denied the concept of the "God of Israel," that is, the fact that He deals with us according to our observance of the Torah and its commandments.

Instead, they called Him the "God of gods," claiming that He does not pay any attention to the lower world. [According to their philosophy] God gave all power to the stars and other astrological forces, and it is these forces that control the world. For this reason, [they felt that] it was necessary to worship [the stars] rather than the Highest of the High.

They continued [philosophizing in this manner] until they ultimately denied the Will of Wills. They said that creation was not a willful act [on the part of God] since it is impossible to conceive how will can relate to the Infinite Being. They thus concluded that there was a "potential" that had to create the world, and that there was a formless matrix that had always existed [without beginning].

But from the miracles and wonders, with which God punished [these wicked individuals] through . . . the righteous, it became apparent that He does desire that we serve Him, and that He acts with love according to our ways. It is in this respect that He is called "the God of Israel."

[At the Red Sea, the Jews thus said], "This is my God and I will glorify Him" (Exodus 15:2)—and each one pointed with his finger. Even though God is utterly incomprehensible, and "no thought can grasp Him at all," we still have some grasp of His will through the Torah and commandments.

*

Levi Yitzchok ben Meir of Berdichev (1740–1810)

Levi Yitzchok was a founder of Hasidism in central Poland. Although he founded no dynasty, he had many disciples. He is most remembered for his *Kedushath Levi* (*Holiness of Levi*). This abbreviated excerpt was translated by Aryeh Kaplan.

KEDUSHATH LEVI

It is written, "These are the histories of the heaven and the earth when they were created (*be-HiBaRAM*, בְּהִבָּרְאָם)" (Genesis 2:4). Our sages comment, "Do not read 'when they were created' (*be-HiBaRAM*), but 'for Abraham' (*be-ABRa-HaM*, בְּאַבְרָהָם)." [The world was thus created for the sake of Abraham.]

The universe was only created because God knew that a righteous man would arise, who would publicize God's existence to the world, declaring that He is the Authority in His universe, the one absolute Unity, doing great wonders by Himself; that He is the Creator of all, and that besides Him there is no good. Out of this individual would come Isaac, Jacob, the twelve tribes, and the Children of Israel.

God would bring about great miracles for the sake of Israel, and as a result, His existence would become known in the world. He would then give them the Torah, and His being would be revealed to all Israel at Mount Sinai. It is thus written, "Face to face, God spoke to you" (Deuteronomy 5:4). All creation trembled before God at that time.

Israel would then build the Tabernacle [in the desert] and the Sanctuary (*Beth HaMikdash*, בֵּית הַמִּקְדָּשׁ) [in Jerusalem]. This would cause God to rejoice in His universe. It is thus written, "the day of His wedding, the day His heart rejoiced" (Song of Songs 3:11). Our sages interpret this saying: "the day of His wedding" is the giving of the Torah, and "the day His heart rejoiced" is the building of the Holy Temple.

The Creator thus has pleasure when He speaks and His will is done.

*

Moses Leib of Sasov (1745–1807)

Leib was a hasidic rabbi and writer. He taught many of the future hasidic leaders. The following selection is from Martin Buber's *Tales of the Hasidim: The Later Masters*, translated by Olga Marx.

WHEN IT IS GOOD TO DENY THE EXISTENCE OF GOD

Rabbi Moshe Leib said:

"There is no quality and there is no power of man that was created to no purpose. And even base and corrupt qualities can be uplifted to serve God. When, for example, haughty self-assurance is uplifted it changes into a high assurance in the ways of God. But to what end can the denial of God have been created? This too can be uplifted through deeds of charity. For if someone comes to you and asks your help, you shall not turn him off with pious words, saying: 'Have faith and take your troubles to God!' You shall act as if there were no God, as if there were only one person in all the world who could help this man—only yourself."

*

Schneur Zalman of Lyady— the Alter Rebbe (1745–1813)

Schneur Zalman was born in central Russia. He was the founder of Habad (Chabad) Hasidism and is considered one of the greatest hasidic leaders. Schneur Zalman

wrote a number of works, the most famous of which is
Tanya. This work is unique in that it is not just a collection of discourses but a complete, systematic exposition
of the originator himself. The first selection from *Tanya*
was translated by Aryeh Kaplan and the second, *Likkutei
Torah*, by Ben Zion Bokser.

TANYA 36 (45b)

Our sages teach us that the reason why the physical world
was created was because "God longed to have a dwelling in
the lower world."

This [is very difficult to understand] since God fills all
worlds equally, and therefore such distinctions as "above"
and "below" do not apply to Him.

The explanation is as follows. Before the world was
created, God was alone, being one and unique. He filled the
entire place in which He would create the universe.

With respect to God, this is still exactly the same [even
after creation]. The only change is with regard to those who
receive His Light and Life Force.

Those who receive God's Light must receive it through the
many Garments that hide and conceal it. It is thus written,
"No man can see Me and live" (Exodus 33:20). Our sages
comment on this and explain that even the highest angels
cannot see . . .

This is the concept of the [downward] gradation of the
universes, and their descent, step by step. This takes place
through a multitude of Garments, concealing the Light and
Life Force that emanate from God. It continues in this fashion until the lowest possible level, which is the physical,
material world.

The physical world is at the lowest possible spiritual level,
and is hence in a state of [spiritual] darkness, where God's
Light is concealed. It is filled with the [evil] Husks and
[forces of] the Other Side, which are literally opposite to

God. The essence of these forces is, "I exist, and there is nothing besides me" (Isaiah 47:8).

The purpose of the downward gradation of the [spiritual] universes, and their descent, step by step, is clearly not for the sake of the higher worlds. With respect to [these higher worlds], the Light of God's presence must descend [to a lower level]. This must therefore be for the sake of this physical world.

God willed that He would have pleasure when the Other Side is subdued, and when Darkness is transformed into Light. The places of Darkness and the Other Side in this physical world are then illuminated with the Infinite Light of God, with even more intensity and strength.

This is the Light that emerges from darkness. It is even greater than the Light of the higher [spiritual] universes. [In the higher worlds] this Light only shines through Garments and through a concealment of their presence. This screens the Light of the Infinite Being, hiding it so that the existence [of these upper worlds] should not be nullified.

It is for this reason that God gave us the Torah. The Torah is called "strength and power." [This "strength" is alluded to in the teaching of] our Sages, which states that God gives the righteous the power to accept their reward in the Ultimate Future.

This is necessary in order that their existence not be utterly nullified in the Light of God that will ultimately be revealed without any [coverings or] Garments whatsoever. It is thus written, "Your Teacher will no longer hide Himself . . . but your eyes shall behold your Teacher" (Isaiah 30:20). It is also written, "For eye to eye will they see [God returning to Zion]" (Isaiah 52:8). It is furthermore written, "God shall be to you for an everlasting Light . . ." (Isaiah 60:19).

It is known that the culmination and fulfillment of creation will take place in the days of the Messiah, and particularly, after the resurrection of the dead. It was for this reason that the world was initially created.

LIKKUTEI TORAH

The goal in the creation of man is that he might make himself submissive to God. This is to be explained thus: the descent of the divine potency through many stages of self-limitation was to serve as a prelude to its return upward, so as to transform darkness to light; and it is for this role that God created man on earth. Since this world is the lowly realm, covered with darkness, and there is need for many lights to illumine the darkness, God created man whose vocation is to serve as a light, and as a candle, as it is suggested in the verse (Proverbs 20:27): "For the soul of man is a candle of the Lord." Man illumines the world with the light of the divine Name, revealing it from its concealment, thus transforming darkness to light. In this sense we are to understand the call to Abraham (Genesis 12:2) to "be a blessing." He was to spread blessing throughout the earth; and it is similarly written of the children of Israel (Isaiah 61:9): "They are a seed blessed by the Lord." The terms for blessing and blessed, *berakhah* and *berakh*, suggest the words *mavrikh* and *markhiv*, which mean "to graft" or "to merge," and this defines their role as a source of blessing. They were to spread the influences from one world to another, from the world of concealment to the world of disclosure. Thus would the divine realm be disclosed. Those who effect this disclosure are the Jewish people. They are the seed that discloses the Lord; and as the soul of man is a candle of the Lord, the multitude of souls are a multitude of candles. The extent of the darkness determines the number of candles burning in souls that are needed to overcome it . . .

The disclosure of the divine must be "with all your heart," with the two hearts, the inner and the outer . . . The inner heart reveals the divine impact through excitation felt over the awareness of His being, that He is beyond comprehension . . . This is the hidden love in man's nature, but its effect is visible always. The "outer heart" means that the love spread, curbing the evil impulse and in the end redirecting that impulse to serve a positive end. At first we are to curb it, as is suggested in the verse which defines the man worthy of being in God's presence as "he who shuts his eyes from seeing evil" (Isaiah 33:16), and we have a similar admonition (Numbers 15:39): "not to stray after your heart and after your eyes." This expresses a desire that the outer world reveal its divine dimension, for the term *olam* which means world suggests the word *elem*, which means concealed, it hides the divine light, and one must curb the evil impulse to make the light manifest. The next step is to convert the darkness to light. This means that the passion of one's bodily nature which is bent on lusting after all kinds of lusts shall be redirected from its worldly disposition, to yearn for God, praised be He . . . Thus will he fulfill the call to love God with his whole heart.

*

Hayyim ben Isaac Volozhiner (1749–1821)

Volozhiner was a rabbi, educator, and student of the Gaon of Vilna. He was also the acknowledged spiritual leader of non-hasidic Russian Jewry of his day. In 1802, he founded a successful yeshivah at Volozhiner. Although Volozhiner was a moderate opponent of the hasidim, he did not sign a ban against them. Among his works are a number of responsa, a commentary on the Mishna Avot, and *Nefesh ha-Hayyim* (his major work, published posthumously). The following selection is from Rabbi Zechariah Fendel's *The Torah Ethic*.

THE PRIMARY PURPOSE OF CREATION

Rav Aharon Kotler, citing Rabbeinu Chaim Volozhin, regards this as a means of fulfillment of man's primary purpose in creation. The great significance of rendering rebuke is that, *The world is built by loving-kindness*. [Psalm 89:3] The *gaon*, Rabbeinu Chaim of Volozhin, writes that the primary purpose of man's creation is [the Creator's desire] to render benefit to others. And just as the Creator, be He blessed, created all of creation because of His desire to perform kindness, so, too, must we follow in His footsteps. The most significant kindness one can perform for others, is to cause them to have the merit of Torah study and mitzvah-fulfillment, and to dissuade them from the wiles of the evil inclination. This is the greatest kindness in the world which one can possibly perform for his fellow man.

*

Nachman of Braslav (1772–1811)

Nachman is another of the great hasidic leaders. He lived in the central Ukraine. Nachman's most famous work is the *Likutey Moharan* (*Anthology of Our Master*). The two excerpts from this work were translated by Aryeh Kaplan.

LIKUTEY MOHARAN 18:1,2

One must realize that everything has a purpose. Each purpose has yet another purpose, one above the other.

For example, the purpose of building a house is so that a person should have a place to rest. But the purpose of his resting is so that he should have enough strength to serve God. And the purpose of serving God . . .

The purpose of each thing is attached to some thought and intellect more than the actual thing that results from this purpose.

"The end of a thing is its first thought." Therefore, the purpose is closer to the thought than the thing itself. The thing's end and purpose begins in thought and is close to it. It is then from this purpose that action is derived.

For example, when a person decides to build a house, it is certainly not built all at once. He must first obtain wood. Then he must smooth and shape each piece of wood, depending on how it will be used. Only then can the house be built and completed.

The completion of the house, however, is the end of and purpose of its being built, and this is the first thought. This goal is closer to the original thought than is the first actual work.

One must realize that the goal of creation is the delight that will exist in the World to Come.

It is impossible to bring this goal close to people's thoughts. Regarding [the World to Come] it is written, "No eye has seen it . . ." (Isaiah 64:3). Those who are truly righteous, however, can grasp the goal, which is the Future World, in their thoughts.

LIKUTEY MOHARAN B39

The manner in which God created the universe is really very wonderful and marvelous. It contains many wondrous, awesome things—"How great are Your deeds O God" (Psalms 92:6, 104:24). He created lifeless things, growing things, [as well as living animals and man]. Who can even estimate God's greatness in creating the universe?

[If this is true of our physical universe,] how much more must it be true of the [higher spiritual] universes!

All this was created only for the sake of Israel. And Israel itself was created for the sake of the Sabbath.

The Sabbath was the completion of the act of creation. The Sabbath is therefore the concept of purpose.

The Sabbath is the concept of the World of Souls, which is a world where "all is Sabbath."

In the World of Souls, people will comprehend God as they should, without any restrictions, and without any barriers separating them. Everything will then be complete unity. Each one will be able to point with his finger and say, "This is God, in whom we hoped" (Isaiah 25:9), as our sages teach us.

This is the purpose for which God brought all creation into existence.

Each thing that was created in the universe therefore certainly has an aspect of this purpose.

Each thing that exists has a beginning and an end.

It has a beginning in the place from which it originated [and existed] until it finally entered the realm of the physical, with shape and form. It also has an end and a purpose, for which it was created.

Israel can delve into this very deeply. Through each detail in creation, they can know and comprehend God's greatness. They can make use [of such knowledge as] the structure, shape and form of man's body, and use it to serve God.

This continues higher and higher, until the end point where each thing itself partakes of Purpose. Each and every thing thus has a grasp on the purpose for which it was created.

Through each thing, a person can grasp that end point, where that particular thing ends and approaches Purpose. He can thus perceive God and serve Him.

Each individual must concentrate deeply on this, in order that he should be able to know and recognize God's greatness in each and every thing . . . so that he should make use of it in serving God.

[One must do so] until he comes to the ultimate purpose of that particular thing, which is an aspect of the Sabbath, the World of Souls. . . .

Our sages teach us, "It is better that man not have been created . . ." (*Eruvin* 13b). It is also written, "Better than both [the living and the dead] are those who have not yet been born" (Ecclesiastes 4:3).

This is really very surprising, for if it is actually true, why was man created?

Actually, this refers only to the physical world. People have so much suffering and pain in this world, it would certainly be better if they were not created into it. But with regard to the World to Come, it is certainly better that they were created. It is precisely through this that they attain the Purpose.

Furthermore, even with respect to this world, our sages say, "Better one hour of repentance and good deeds in this [physical] world, than all of the World to Come" (*Avoth* 4:17).

*

Isaac Leeser (1806–1868)

Leeser was born in Westphalia, Germany and, in 1824, emigrated to the United States to work for his uncle. He was a rabbi, writer, and educator. Leeser founded the first successful Jewish newspaper (*The Occident*), the first Jewish Publication Society of America, and the first Hebrew high school. In addition, he published the first Hebrew primer for children, the first English translation of the Sephardi Prayer Book, and the first American translation of the Bible. The following excerpt is from the *Discourses on the Jewish Religion*.

DISCOURSES ON THE JEWISH RELIGION

Discourse XXI

The Object of the Creation

O God of our fathers! how exalted is thy glory in all the earth! From the first moment that thy creative word went forth to build and to establish, every thing spoke of thy

goodness and greatness, and with the increase of years, with
the progress of all things to their ultimate consummation
nothing is diminished of thy power and mercy, and Thou art
the same as at the time Thou didst sit on the throne, when
the waters of the flood passed over the sinful generation that
had incurred thy displeasure. All the earth proclaims
thy kingdom, and from the rising of the sun to the setting
thereof is thy name great among the nations. But above all
have we received thy light and thy guidance, that we might
proclaim thy name and the august majesty of thy kingdom;
and thus are thy people Israel blessed above all tongues and
nations; since theirs is the blessed privilege of calling on thy
name alone, and to worship no other God besides Thee. Do
Thou therefore, O Father! establish firmly the work which
thy hands have founded, and prosper our endeavours to
spread thy kingdom, and show unto the gentiles that it is
indeed thy wisdom and thy word which dwell imperishably
among us. So that we may be strengthened and comforted,
and live to receive the blessings which Thou hast treasured
up for thy servants; and that through us thy glory may be
diffused and thy memorial hallowed on earth as it is in
heaven, amidst the assemblies of thy spotless messengers
who surround thy throne in purity and love, even now and
forever. Amen.

Brethren!

Among the maxims which our wise men have handed down
to us as the fruits of their research in the law of God, we find
the following at the conclusion of the sixth and last chapter
of the Proverbs of the Fathers:

כל מה שברא הקדוש ברוך הוא בעולמו לא בראו אלא לכבודו שנאמר כל הנקרא
בשמי ולכבודי בראתיו יצרתיו אף עשיתיו: אבות ו' ט':

Whatever the holy One, blessed be He, has created
in his world, He has created only for his glory; for

it is written [Isaiah 43:7], Whoever is called by my
name and whom I have created for my glory, I
have formed, also made him.

Whatever exists is not in this world by chance: this is the
doctrine of the teachers of Israel; it is not here merely to be
beautiful, great or intelligent for no ulterior object uncon-
nected with itself; but since it stands in a necessary connex-
ion with the Creator as its producer, it of necessity has a
relation to Him by which the object of its existence will be
fulfilled. A workman may make an instrument and part
with it forever; since he cannot be beyond the spot where he
happens to be at any one period of time, because the finite-
ness of his nature limits his presence to one place for the
time being. Not so the Fashioner of our frame; He has
created and called forth innumerable creatures of a thousand varying forms, of a thousand varying natures; they fill
the spaces both in the immeasurable heavens, and on the
earth on which we live, and in the waters that are cast
around our globe. And still they are not beyond the reach of
God, they are near Him, at all times, in every place; for walls
shut not out his presence, oceans and deserts do not divide
Him; hence none of his works have passed out of his reach,
although each one moves and lives, and works in its own
peculiar sphere.

Whatever exists was made for the glory of God. It is,
however, not selfishness which dictates this limited object of
all creation. Were it, that a man should say, that all he did
had but one object, and this his own personal aggrandize-
ment, we could with truth call him selfish and contracted;
because for the most part the sole advantage of one is to the
manifest injury of the many. If a man becomes distinguished for power, there are many who must submit to his
will, whether this submission be founded in reason and con-
sent or not. If a man becomes wealthy, many around him
may stand in need of the necessaries of life, whilst he riots in
superfluous plenty. If a man attains to renown by his wisdom and learning, he is but too apt to make use of this

mental power to impose his views upon those less favoured than himself. It is not well in man therefore to regard himself only as of the first importance in the scale of beings; for thus he will become an injury to his fellow-creatures instead of the blessing which his particular position could easily render him. Far different however is the case with the Creator. His glory can never interfere with our well-being. His power is that which sustains all existence; if therefore we submit ourselves yieldingly to his rule, we only do what prudence would counsel us; for thus we best secure our own happiness, seeing that at all moments of our presence on earth we are within his dominion, where his eye always beholds our deeds, where his power is ever ready to seize us.—God's riches consist of the abundance which decks all nature with splendour and beauty; the smallest insect is supported by his bounty, and the highest angel is there only by his bidding; from his munificence then all is fed, from his wide-spread table all is sustained; none therefore are hungry while in his abode there ruleth plenty, none are sighing because his granaries are filled to overflowing.—And his wisdom is not a means of injury to the weak and foolish. For whatever knowledge there is springs immediately from his spirit, and the light that illuminates the souls of the sons of man springs from his own essence, which is the brightest and purest that thought can conceive and the imagination reach, in their farthest and most painful search for truth and instruction.

To be therefore created for the glory of God, means nothing else than to be destined to the highest perfection. The Lord is the most perfect, the holiest of all beings; there is no imperfection, no defect in his nature, no obscurity in his ken, no hesitation in his judgment. Whatever glorifies Him must thus partake, no matter in how minute a degree, of his perfection and greatness, and the nearer any one thing approaches to the nature of the Author of all, the more can it administer to his glory: the more will it be capable of obtaining and enjoying the happiness for which its nature has fitted it.

If you therefore turn your view on high, and behold the mighty sun that dazzles the eyes, so that you cannot contemplate his radiant beauty; if you in ecstasy admire the silvery moon as she majestically ascends the pinnacle of the firmament in the silent, eloquent nights of the warm season of the year; if you look up to the blue vault of heaven in a frosty night when the satellite of our earth is hid from view, and behold the thousands of brilliant suns that gleam and sparkle, as though they were the jewels set in the diadem which encircles the throne of our Father and King: what can you feel, if you have a heart alive to the glories of God's worlds that roll around you on all sides, what can you say but that these all tell of a Creator, a Preserver, a Ruler who is wise, good, great and glorious? And how do all these things harmonize! Constellation after constellation rises; and planet after planet pursues its course, and comets speed along athwart the boundless waste in the brilliancy of their array, and the beauty of their apparel: and yet there is a place assigned to each, to all; there is no crowding, no interfering with each other's orbit; but every one of all these travels the path which is peculiarly its own, and all obey the law which the Energy that called them forth prescribed unto them from the beginning.

But if you descend from the contemplation of all these mighty glories as we may aptly call them, and cast your searching eye over the earth on which we are placed, the nether world, as our Rabbis style it, what do you not find to admire? what, to be thankful for?—Here before you is the ocean; for thousands of years it has rolled, and it has heaved; its bosom has been tranquil, and been placid as the face of innocence in its moments of joy; and it has risen in mountain waves, and been covered with foam, and been upturned to its centre when the spirit of the storm rushed along over it in his swift-flying chariot. It has borne the commerce of nations, and the warships of contending empires have ploughed its plains, and vented there their rage in their deadly conflicts against each other. And many are the treasures it has swallowed up when its waves roared, and many are the gallant hearts that sleep in its coral caves till the day of the resurrection; and many a country have its surges overflowed in their inroad upon the land; and thus in many cases it has been a messenger of weal, the agent of woe, as its Creator commanded it to bless or to punish.—And think well, how mysterious is this power: you know not the causes which agitate it; the reasons why its roarings cease; and together with its equally mysterious companions the winds of heaven, which become cognizable only when they are called into action, and then die away to return no more, it speaks of the glory of Him who cast it around our globe as the belt for the union of distant nations, as the girdle that is to bind all mankind into one bond of brotherhood.

And there are the rivers that flow onward from their source till they meet with ocean's floods to be swallowed up in that common receptacle of the waters beneath the firmament. How small their origin! how insignificant their rise! still as onward they move, how they deepen! how they expand! and the humble rill, that on the mountain height sparkled at your feet like a silver thread, pours a mighty volume in deep ocean's lap, and is at its termination great and wonderful, and offers a refuge to the despairing mariner whose bark has long been tossed upon the sea, and dispenses blessings to many a town, to many a hamlet, that are scattered along its banks. What would the earth be without these rivers! a desert waste, a howling wilderness! But now these are the means to fructify the soil, to enliven the landscape, to facilitate travel, to perform labour for man; and they tell that the great Being who created them is indeed glorious, wise and good, and they admonish you to be thankful that in his mercy He has appointed them to be servants unto you, the ministers of his bounty.

Now turn to the dry land; and here too you will constantly and universally find cause to glorify your God. If you have examined with the eye of science the objects that are everywhere around you, the animal that bears you gaily along, the flower that blooms in your garden, even the dust on which you tread: you will have discovered in each, in all, evidence of matchless skill, of surpassing wisdom. Few are the elements which enter in the combinations of which every material thing is constituted; but with all there is something too ethereal for human search to define, why and how these few elements should form such a variety, such an infinite succession of substances, all differing, all admirable in their construction. Who but a God that is all-powerful could have contrived these creatures, who but the Lord can be their Creator! Look at the various animals that move on the earth; the birds that flit beneath the sky; the fishes that sport in lakes, rivers, and seas; the insects that dance in the light of the sun, or buzz on the face of the waters; the reptiles that glide along in the brilliancy of colour; the worms that crawl in the dust: and who does not find each adapted to the sphere for which it is destined? The humble silk-worm that weaves its own sepulchre is admirable, wonderful, surprisingly gifted with its peculiar instinct; and humble as is its lot, short as is its life, it is built with the same matchless skill which gives strength to the eagle's wings, and points out his way beyond the region of the clouds.—Nothing which you survey, nothing which you contemplate, but must preach to you of the greatness and glory of God, and call on you to fall down and worship the great Mercy that has subjected all these things to your service, and made you the lord of all that is placed on the earth.

And your body, the house in which your soul lives, proclaims the glory of God! They who have carefully studied our structure, and have as it were looked into man himself to teach them how to adore their Maker, have proved that for variety, for strength, for use, for beauty, nothing could have been contrived by human ingenuity, granting even that man could have formed a creature like himself, half so admirable as the outward frame of the human race. The hand that performs so many acts, that opens and shuts, expands and closes at the merest wish, how well is it calculated to perform the infinity of labours which it momentarily executes! What animal has a hand like man?—what being is skilled in the use of instruments as is man, the favourite of God's creation? And there is the tongue, the organ of speech, by which soul is opened to soul! how well does it execute the object for which it was made. The heart desires, the soul frames the thought, and incontinently the tongue becomes the messenger of what dwells within the recesses of the spirit, and other heart's desire, other souls frame thoughts, all urged by the power of speech of the first who conceived and thought. Within our soul burns the law of God with a brightness, a living power, which fill up her whole being. And she arrays her emotions in the outward garment of intelligible sounds, and steps abroad with what she is imbued, and enkindles in other souls the life and light that are within herself, and revives and refreshes many that otherwise would have languished and died. O truly is our frame a tabernacle of the Lord, a fit temple for his glory; and in thinking on yourselves therefore, in pondering over your own being you must acknowledge that you were, as outward men, created for the glorification of your Maker, as a part of the creation that constantly and silently hymns his praise.

But glorious as is outward creation in its manifold varieties, more glorious far is the creation of the word of God which has been bestowed on us for our happiness. For, just as the earth would be a desert without the rivers and streams that render it fruitful, so would human life be a waste, a starless sky, a raging ocean, without the revelation of the Lord, which teaches us how to act, how to live, how to hope, how to die. If man teaches, there may be doubts on our mind whether he has fully comprehended the subject, whether there may not be falsehood, whether there may not be some selfish and unworthy motive which lies at the foundation of his instruction. When, however, the Lord comes to teach, we cannot fear of being deceived, we can only listen, and say as the prophet did of old "Speak, Lord, for thy servant heareth." His guidance is a sure protection amidst dangers, his faithfulness a safe refuge amidst the storms of existence; and whatever therefore He tells us, is that which must be the best for us in every position in which we may be

placed. And if we examine with such faith the book which
He has written, we will always find the glory of God combined with the benefit of mankind; and the punishment of
the sinner, the death of the wicked even, an admirable commentary upon the text "for in the image of God, hath He
made man;" since, because man has received so high a destiny, his conduct requires to be more fenced in, to use a
Jewish expression, to be more circumscribed, than it would
need to be were he to die the death of the beast that perishes
away, when its appointed time is over. No, man must be
guarded, in order to fit him for immortality; and this guarding he discovers in the wisdom of God which we have in our
possession, and in following its directions he will surely and
safely arrive at the portals of bliss, which his Father in
heaven has appointed for all those who seek his mercy. If we
wish to know how we are to love God, we are shown a series
of duties by which we can display to our own satisfaction,
whether we have sufficient control over our evil inclinations
to sacrifice them to the command we have received. If we
seek to be informed how to love our fellow-man, we will be
told to be directed by that unsurpassed system of ethics, or
of moral duties, which is contained in the Bible. It is not a
system of mawkish sensibility, which only sees the evil-doer,
which only regards with affection and indulgence the violent aggressor on his neighbour's property, and on his brother's life; but it surveys all mankind, and can see peace to the
entire mass only in guarding the rights, life, and property of
every member of the human family; it therefore punishes
the wicked that the others "may hear thereof and be afraid,
and do no more like these deeds of wickedness" for which the
punishment is awarded. If then a man violently assails the
life of another so that he dies, his own life pays the forfeit. If
a man steals his fellow-being and sells him for a slave, his
own life pays the forfeit. If a man enters the home of his
brother and robs him of his dearest treasure, the wife of
his bosom, the malefactor's life pays the forfeit. If a man,
rebelling against the authority of the Lord, openly forswears
his duty by worshipping idols, thus sapping the foundation,

as far as he can do it, of God's own state, his life must pay the
forfeit.—And so for minor crimes, minor punishments are
ordained; but no offence can pass with impunity. And where
the sin is only against Heaven, where the soul only trans-
gresses, as in matters of faith, whilst the body lends not its
aid to display the sentiments by outward action, no matter
how great the infidelity, how great the inward rebellion, the
soul alone becomes answerable to her Maker; no human
tribunal can judge of such guilt, no human judgment can be
executed upon such a criminal. The sin is a moral one, and
moral must be the visitation; it is the Lord, who is the
Master of all spirits, and He can and will send due visitation
as soon as, and whenever He may deem it requisite to have
his name glorified by the prostration of the rebellious worm,
the less than a fragment of a potter's vessel, who dares to
doubt of his Maker's power, of his Saviour's mercy, of his
God's providence.—Well may we say: "The commandment of
the Lord is pure, it enlighteneth the eyes;" it is indeed a
study for the simple, but also a wonder to the wise; and
search through it when young, search through it when old,
and it reviveth the spirit, it makes the simple wise; and truly
may we therefore say that, great as is the creation, greater
far is the revealed word; and it too glorifies the Lord, and
speaks of his perfection, and it proves that He has made it
for the sake of the holiness of his name, that he might be
sanctified among the sons of man. —We could add much
more, we could descant for hours on the beauty and sublimity of the theme; but what need is there to prove what you all
know? what all mankind acknowledge if they have but received the proper instruction?—And then I speak to Israelites who, with me, believe in the same law, worship the
same God; and they will surely ascribe glory to his name,
and love the wisdom of his ordaining, and bless his holy
name for having the law of truth and the life everlasting to
his people Israel.

This consideration brings us at once to the subject to
which I wished to direct your attention, by applying our text
to ourselves as members of the house of Jacob. We too are a

creation, a special work of the Lord, that He may be glorified. If by the formation of man as the image of God, by the bestowal of the Bible which is the word of God, the world was greatly benefitted, and the name of the Lord magnified and extolled: He is not the less apparent in his glory by the selection of Israel as his own peculiar treasure. Look on the image of God! how often has he deteriorated from his noble calling; how did he fall in Adam when he ate of the tree of knowledge, though everything was allowed him, save the fruit of the one tree which was in the midst of the garden; how had he swerved from the path pointed out when the waters of the flood came over the earth, "because she had been filled with violence;" and how woefully was he derelict when, at the building of the tower and city in the land of Shinear, he sought to frustrate the councils of his Maker, to spread the human family over the face of the earth.—And the word of God! how has it been contemned at all times and under all circumstances! In all ages, man has striven against its decrees, as though some dire evil were hidden in its pages, as though destruction would follow in the path pointed out to us as the one in which we should walk. If then man had been made in the image of God only, and the word had been merely cast abroad without a human guardian to watch over it in its struggles for supremacy over sin and death: mankind would never have become perfected, and the rank offspring of superstition and folly would have overshadowed the purest and best gift of God to his children. You may ask: "Why does sin exist?" This is a question not for us to solve; perhaps God wished to form a creature that should struggle for salvation, that should, not like the angels, who are nothing but purity, and whose beatitude is inherent in their very being, labour with diligence to become exalted and accepted on High. This we do know that, if we have received feelings which excite to sin, we have inherent in us stronger powers than sin, which enable us to struggle successfully, and to overcome the evil, and be obedient in all things. But above all, free choice was imparted to our nature; and hence we are at liberty to refuse the kingdom of

Heaven if in our perversity we may choose to do so.—We
therefore say, that without a custodian of the Bible, the
glorious work of the Lord would have sunk under and beneath the dominion of sin, unless the Lord himself had come
to rescue this blissful gift from amidst the destruction.—
Now this precisely came to pass.—First, the age of the flood
proved by their iniquity that they would not live under the
law. Next the age of the Babylonian Tower testified likewise, that they did not value the kingdom of the Lord. In the
days of Abraham also, though he preached and taught the
truth, crime had again become prevalent, and Sodom and its
sister towns were overwhelmed, because there were not ten
righteous men to obtain pardon for their city. And when we
look unto Egypt at the time when sixty myriads of Israel's
sons were slaves and bondmen in its boundaries, a tyranni-
cal Pharaoh exclaimed, "Who is the Lord!" It was therefore
that the Lord willed to "form to himself a people that they
might tell his praise," as the prophet Isaiah expresses himself in chapter 43:22. False to their God were Noah's generation; false to their God the generation of Babel; false the men
of Abraham's age; false the wise rulers of Egypt. But the
truth was not to perish, because it was not loved; God's glory
was not to be hidden to everlasting, because man loved idols
and vanity. The Lord for this reason educated our fathers in
the midst of tribulation, that they might know Him as their
sole Redeemer, as their only God and Father; as says the
same prophet whom we just quoted (Isaiah 48:10): "Behold, I
have refined thee, though not unto silver, I have approved
thee in the crucible of affliction." And in good truth, they
were tried in the iron furnace, even in Egypt, to make them
fit to be the recipients of the precious word, and to look
forever unto the Lord as their sole Refuge, as their only
Saviour in the midst of tribulations. And thus did you arise,
O men of Israel! spring up as does the noble plant from the
midst of the corruptions of the earth, to blossom in the
presence of the nations as the blissful tree which is to ripen
the fruit of salvation. And when after your establishment
you endeavoured to throw off your allegiance to your King,

the law claimed you back as its own, as its servants, who can only live in God. When many fell off and would have no portion in David, nor inheritance in the son of Jessé, again the sword was unsheathed, and you were rendered few instead of having been as numerous as the stars of heaven. But yet a remnant remained, a remnant glorious as your ancestry, noble as your progenitors. And they stood unflinchingly on the day of battle, and they defied the foe whilst the warm life-blood flowed freely from their deadly wounds; and dying, these blessed men handed the standard to the almost unconscious youth, who had grown up in the midst of these struggles, that they might bear it onward till that time, when it should float triumphant over the walls and ramparts of the newly risen Jerusalem. And you, brethren! are here this day, as the descendants of these undaunted heroes and martyrs, who glorified the Name which angels mention in dread and adoration, and the legacy which they carried away as the only treasure which they saved from the wreck of their empire, is still yours,—yours, if you will bear it in your hearts, if you will treasure it in the inmost recesses of your spirit.—O how the heart of the patriot Hebrew warms, when he looks back upon the long line of nobles in the kingdom of the Lord from whom he has sprung! ay! untitled they were on earth, poverty and affliction were their estate; but they are registered in the book of the righteous before the Lord, and their riches are those which perish not, their treasures are those over which death has no dominion, and their chaplets are those which never fade, the flowers of which are ever fragrant, the green of which is always bright. And these were your fathers! and such as these were your mothers! What does this all say to you, brothers and sisters of the house of Israel? Does it tell you to live a life of indolence? of self-indulgence? of vanity? of worldly pursuits? Would this be for the glory of the Lord? would this be combining in yourselves the perfection of the divine image, the nature of man, with the perfection of divine wisdom, the word which God has revealed?—No; Israel can only be Israel when they are active in all that is asked of them; active in their earthly calling, for our body too must not be neglected, it is the dwelling of the soul, the image of God; labour therefore cheerfully in the sphere pointed out as the field of your labours, depend on the blessing of God for success, and seek neither gifts nor loans from man, unless dire necessity compels you; but above all, fly to your religion as the chief means of your welfare; labour in it without ceasing, it is the glory of God, it is your own happiness. Know, that all earthly greatness has received an appointed time when it must vanish, pass away, and leave a woful void behind. But our faith—our hopes—our trust—cannot remain unfruitful, they will blossom amidst decay, bear fruit amidst corruption. Seek not therefore to lead a life of pleasure, but submit yourselves, your wishes, your aspirations, your desires, to the faith, the law which you have received from your fathers, for thus only can you be justified, thus only can you be said to labour for the glory of God.—You perhaps feel yourselves drawn away by worldly desires; you see the gentiles around you enjoy what your religion prohibits unto you; you see them labour on the Sabbath day, and gaining wealth and distinction which you cannot attain. You may therefore feel indifferent to your birthright, and be anxious to throw off the hated name, the hated faith, the contemned hopes of salvation which are yours. But beware! you may do all these things, and still you cannot escape the responsibility which your fathers assumed when at Sinai, they said   נעשה ונשמע "We will do and obey." The promise was made amidst the gratitude of overflowing hearts for innumerable benefits received, in the midst of admiration at the greatness of the Lord, displayed to the understanding and knowledge of all. This promise was ratified when your fathers entered the holy land, when Joshua, before he died, again asked them "whom they would serve;" they then again chose the Lord. Again, when Solomon built the temple, the people came in the covenant and rejoiced before the Lord "seven and seven days, even fourteen days."—And when Ezra and Nehemiah restored the state, the covenant was renewed, and from that moment idolatry was banished from among us. And in each

generation since then, there have been those who bore testimony to the sacredness of the oath, and to the permanence of
the obligations, and though they suffered martyrdom and
persecution on earth, they no doubt have been accepted on
High as well-tried servants and faithful children. And can
we escape the obligation? will there be no retribution, if we
fall off? Let him believe this who does not confide in Providence; "but ye who cleave to the Lord your God, who are here
alive this day," ye who have ever known that there is no
virtue without reward, no sin without retribution: you
surely will fly for protection and safety to the law, and
endeavour to avoid sinning against its precepts, if you wish
to escape that punishment which ever pursued your fathers
when they attempted to follow the ways of the gentiles, and
to walk in the ordinances which are not from God.

You, brethren, have been formed for the glory of the Lord;
He has, in forming you, combined the image of himself with
his word, so that both should exist in the same persons.
Israel without the law is an impossibility; without it we
should be like the other nations of the earth, with it we are
separate and distinct amidst the families of man, though we
are but few in each town, "men of number" in all lands.
Without us the evidence of the truth of God's law and the
certainty of his ultimate sole reign on earth would be entirely obliterated; and still they are facts which are of the
utmost importance both to us and other portions of mankind, although these now may not recognize the truth,
amidst the din and confusion which the bad passions and the
inventions of designing men have raised on earth.—But
believing is not all that is required; a nominal Jew is but a
useless specimen of the testimony which we are to bear. If
you wish to be Jews, bearers of God's standard, be so in full
earnestness and sincerity. Make yourselves acquainted with
your duties by a careful education and the study of God's
word; and when you are instructed, omit no opportunity to
prove that the faith which dwells within you is active and
full of life and immortality. When the hour of the Sabbath
arrives, welcome ye the heavenly bride with joy and holi-

ness, because she has come again to bid the labourer cease
his toil, and to bring rest to the weary spirit. Welcome, yea
welcome the day! it is a sign between God and you; on it He
will be glorified; it is a part of his creation, it is a rest which
springs from Him, and on the resting day of the Lord the
sons of Jacob should sanctify the holy Name.—Honour the
festivals; they are seasons which remind you of the wonders
which were wrought in your behalf, that you might be re-
deemed from bondage, and your soul be enlightened by the
wisdom and will of God.—Live in your own houses in absti-
nence of all, which the God of your fathers has set aside as
unclean, and let all the world see that you have dominion
over your animal appetites, and that you can sacrifice them
to the blessed principles of your ancestral religion.—But in
faith, too, be erect! Hope for the welfare of Jerusalem; pray
for the coming of the redeemer under whose shadow we
shall live in peace among the gentiles.—Honour the Lord
alone in your hearts; associate with Him no being in any
manner whatever; since He alone is God, since He alone is
our Saviour.—Confess this faith aloud, and let not shame of
the world withhold you from publicly appearing as profess-
ing Jews; and rest assured that even in a worldly point of
view you will not lose by a profession and practice under
which the pious ones, whose name we have inherited, flour-
ished like the cedars on Lebanon. Even assume that you
should lose much in standing and wealth by being Jews:
then rise above the perishable world, and seek for true
happiness where alone it can be found, in the presence of the
Lord who dwells in heaven, and whose reign is unto all
eternity.

Israelites! you are God's servants, the heralds of his glory;
you are the perfection of men, your destiny is the perfection
of all the hopes which the pious of every age have ever
prayed for, of which all the prophets speak. Live so that you
may glorify the Lord in the eyes of man, and educate your
offspring so that none of your latest descendants may be
wanting in the family of Jacob, when the Lord returns to
Zion in mercy.—In brief, live in the law and for the law, and

cast on God all your wishes, and be sure He will bring to pass whatever tends for your happiness, that is, at last, whatever tends to his glory.—And may our eyes behold the consummation of all things, when all mankind like ourselves will belong to the same flock, to the same household, when the idols shall be no more, and God be glorified alone on earth as He is one alone in heaven; on that day when the earth shall be full of knowledge of the Lord, and He shall be the God one and his name be One. Amen.

*

Samson Raphael Hirsch
(1808–1888)

Hirsch was born in Hamburg, Germany. He attended the University of Bonn and, in 1846, became the Chief Rabbi of Moravia. Hirsch was a rabbi, writer, community leader, and foremost exponent of Jewish Orthodoxy in Germany during the nineteenth century. He was an opponent of religious reform, arguing that reform would lead to the degeneration of Judaism and empty it of its content. In addition, Hirsch was active in the struggle to obtain emancipation for Austrian and Moravian Jewry. His chief work is *The Nineteen Letters of Ben Uziel.* Following is the fourth letter from this work, translated by Bernard Drachman.

THE NINETEEN LETTERS OF BEN UZIEL

Fourth Letter

Man—what is he in this God-filled world? What is his place in this throng of creatures of God, this choir of servants of the Lord? Though the Torah were silent, would not the

contemplation of creation, would not your own breast tell
you? Man, is he not also a creature of God? Should he not also
be a servant of God? Every fiber of your body is a creation
from the hand of God, formed by Him, arranged by Him,
endowed by Him with power. Your spirit, that world of
powers, is the creation of God from beginning to end. The
divine spark, your personality, which, invisible as Deity,
weaves and works in this microcosm, and under whose control stand intellect and body and the power to use the entire
realm of nature for its purpose, this mysterious spiritual
force in you is itself emanation of Deity. Learn to deem
yourself holy as creature of God and, while contemplating
heaven and earth and the great chorus of servants of the
Lord, consecrate yourself to your mission, and proclaim
yourself with mingled solemnity and joy, "servant of God!"
Since all things, the smallest and the greatest, are God's
chosen messengers, to work, each in its place, and with its
measure of power, according to the law of the Most High,
taking only that it may give again, should man alone be
excluded from this circle of blessed activity? Can he be born
only to take?—to revel in lavish plenty or to starve in misery,
but not to work?—not to fill any place, nor fulfill any purpose, but to let all end in himself? The world and all which is
therein serves God; is it conceivable that man alone should
only serve himself? No! Your consciousness pronounces you
as does the Torah, צלם אלהים "an image of God." That is what
man should be. Only when working out some end canst thou
know God in love and righteousness; to work out ends of
righteousness and love art thou called; not merely to enjoy or
suffer. All which thou possessest, spirit, body, human beings, wealth, every ability and every power, they are means
of activity; לעבדה ולשמרה to promote and preserve the world
were they given—love and righteousness. Not thine is the
earth, but thou belongest to the earth, to respect it as Divine
soil and to deem every one of its creatures a creature of God,
thy fellow-being; to respect and love it as such, and as such
to endeavor to bring it nearer to its goal, according to the
will of God. For this reason every being impresses upon thy

spirit an image of itself; for this reason thy heart-strings
pulsate sympathetically with every cry of distress heard
anywhere in creation, or with every tone of joy which issues
anywhere from a gladsome being; therefore thou rejoicest
when the flower blooms and sorrowest when it fades. *The
law to which all powers submit unconsciously and involuntarily, to it shall thou also subordinate thyself, but consciously and of thy own free will.* "*Knowledge and freedom,*"
these words indicate at once the sublime mission and the
lofty privilege of man. All forces stand as servitors around
the throne of God, their capacity is hidden from themselves
and covered are their countenances, so that they can not see
the reason of their mission, but they feel within them
winged power to act, and act in accordance with their purpose. Thou, O man, thy countenance is half uncovered, thy
capacity is half revealed, thou canst comprehend thyself as
creature of God—canst at least faintly appreciate the notion
of the mission which He breathed into thy ear; canst thou see
thyself encompassed round about by God's active servants,
canst thou feel in thyself power to act and wilt thou not
joyously join in the cry of the great chorus of servants,
נעשה ונשמע "we will do and therefore hearken? We will obey,
and fulfilling strive to comprehend the import of the command!" Consciously and freely! Therefore thou shalt be first
and highest servitor in the company of servants!

Not by that which we gain, my dear Benjamin, can our
vocation be determined, not according to the extent of external or internal possessions which we gather in external or
internal storehouses, should we estimate the value of our
lives; what we accomplish, what results proceed from us,
these should fix our vocation, and in proportion as we use
our external and internal possessions to fulfill the will of
God and utilize every capacity, small or great, for a truly
human, God-serving deed, will be the measure of our value.
The attainment of internal or external possessions has only a
value as the means of securing ability for such activity.
From the slightest mental power and the nerve ganglia
which minister to it, to the executive force of your hand with

which you alter creation, and to which the entire realm of
nature is subject, and every being which ever came within
your reach—all of these are means lent to you—which one
day will appear as witnesses for or against you, before the
throne of God, and will testify whether you neglected or used
them well, whether you wrought with them blessing or
curse. There exists, therefore, an external measure for the
deeds of men, correspondence to the will of God—and an
internal measure for the greatness of men—not the extent of
powers conferred, not the amount of results achieved, but
the fulfillment of the Divine will in proportion to the power
possessed. Life, therefore, may be an utter failure in spite of
the purest sentiments, if the deeds done be not right; or may,
on the other hand, be most sublime despite infinitesimal
results, if the means did not suffice for more. Happiness and
perfection are, therefore, nothing but the greatest plenti-
tude of external and internal possessions which, only when
employed in accordance with the will of God, constitute the
greatness of man. The angel whose province it is to super-
vise the coming into existence of man, says one of the sages,
takes the germ which is to be a human being, brings it
before the Holy One, blessed be He, and asks, "This germ,
what shall become of it in life? Shall he that proceeds from it
be strong or weak, wise or simple, rich or poor?" He does not
ask whether he will be good or bad, pious or sinful, for all
things depend upon the decree of God, except virtue and the
fear of the Lord, the pious reverence of heaven, these the
Almighty leaves to the free will of men. Let us not, therefore, judge man according to that which is hardly half in his
hands, but rather according to that which God put entirely
into his control, and which, therefore, can alone constitute
his greatness. The mission of mankind, thus comprehended,
is attainable by all men, in every time, with any equipment
of powers and means, in every condition. Whoever in his
time, with his equipment of powers and means, in his condition, fulfills the will of God toward the creatures who enter
into his circle, who injures none and assists every one ac-

cording to his power, to reach the goal marked out for it by God—he is a man! He practises righteousness and love in his existence here below. His whole life, his whole being, his thoughts and feelings, his speech and action, even his business transactions and enjoyments—all of these are service of God. Such a life is exalted above all mutation.

Whether enjoyment or privation, whether abundance or need be one's lot, whether tears of resigned sorrow or joy exultant be shed—the truly human personality, unchangeable almost as Deity, sees in every gain or loss only another summons to solve afresh the same problem. Thus man in his earthly frame belongs to earth, and his terrestrial existence is full of significance. As no passing breath, and no ephemeral grass-blade or butterfly exists for nought, but furnishes its contribution, slight though it be, which God's wisdom uses for the upbuilding of the All; thus also no pleasure, no thought, no deed, trifling though it be, is empty and purposeless; those which are right are finished work delivered into the hand of God that He may employ them for the completion of His universe-plan. Fulfillment of the Divine will with our property and our pleasures, with our thoughts, words, and deeds, that should be the contents of our lives. And we should strive to ascertain this will. For that is the special and peculiar greatness of man, that whereas the voice of God speaks *in* or *through* all other creatures, to him it speaks directly that he accept voluntarily its precepts as propelling force of his life-activity. Go to, my Benjamin, and examine yourself; examine yourself in comparison with a grass-blade or a rolling thunder-peal, and if you do not, despite all your wealth of property and enjoyment of inner and outer possessions, blush with shame and veil your face in the presence of the angelic grandeur of such creatures, because of your selfish pettiness; and if you do not then rouse yourself with all your strength, with every spark of your being, to acquire for yourself such angelic power, then go and lament the degradation which the age has brought upon you.

Bless, O my soul, the Lord,
And all my inner parts recognize His holiness!
Bless, O my soul, the Lord,
And forget not all which He lets ripen for thee.
That He forgiveth all thy perversities,
That He healeth all thy ailings,
That He redeemeth from the grave thy life,
That He crowneth thee with loving kindness and
    mercy,
That He satisfieth thee with good things, which
    adorn thee,
That thou mayest renew as the eagle thy youth.

.   .   .   .

Sunken man—as grass are his days,
As the flower of the field he bloometh;
The wind bloweth over him, he is no more,
No more doth his place know him.
But the loving kindness of the Lord is from eternity
    to eternity
Unto those who revere Him, and His mercy endu-
    reth unto the children's children,
Of those who regard His covenant,
And remember His commandments, to do them.
For He—who hath founded His throne in Heaven,
Ruleth in majesty throughout the All.
Bless Him, therefore, ye His messengers!
Ye who, girded with strength, fulfill His word
Obeying the voice of His word;
Bless Him, all ye His hosts!
His servants, fulfillers of His will!
Bless Him, all ye His creatures, in every place of
    His kingdom,
Bless also thou, O my soul, the Lord. [Psalm 103]

*

Moritz Lazarus (1824–1903)

Lazarus was born in Filehne (now Wielen), Germany. He was a German philosopher and psychologist. As a child, Lazarus received an intense Jewish education. He was a professor at the University of Berne and later at the University of Berlin (1873–1896). Lazarus served almost twenty-five years as a member of the Berlin Jewish Community Council. In addition, he wrote many works on the psychology of nations. According to Lazarus, the central concept underlying his Jewish view of life is holiness—which is the "ultimate goal of morality." Below are several excerpts from his major work *Ethics of Judaism*, a two-volume work translated from the German by Henrietta Szold and published in 1900–1901 by the Jewish Publication Society.

ETHICS OF JUDAISM

Principle of Jewish Ethics

81. The same thought runs through the whole of Rabbinic literature. The Divine Being and therefore the knowledge of His moral attributes, combined with the endeavor to emulate them in man's finite way, constitute at once the rule and the reason of morality: "Because I am merciful, thou shalt be merciful; as I am gracious, thou shalt be gracious, etc." (מה אני רחום וכו׳).

In a word, the fundamental doctrine of Judaism reads: Because the moral is divine, therefore you shall be moral, and because the divine is moral, you shall become like unto God. It may be said that the highest form and ultimate purpose of human life is likeness to God, and the ethical ideals are conceived as attributes of God, in whose image man was created, and whose copy and image it is man's task to strive to become.

82. The Bible does not expound, and the Rabbis do not inculcate, metaphysical notions or dogmatic teachings concerning the divine nature, for the purpose of deducing the legislative authority of God. Man's duty of obedience is based neither upon God's omnipresence, nor his omnipotence, nor even his supreme wisdom. The ethical ideals are presented as attributes of God, and for the sake of their realization man is called upon to strive to become like unto God. When the "glory of God" is made manifest to Moses, only moral attributes are enumerated (Exodus 34:6), and in the well-known verse from Jeremiah, we have a clear statement of what man can and should know concerning God: "Let not the wise man glory in his wisdom, neither let the mighty man glory in his might, let not the rich man glory in his riches; but let him that glorieth glory in this, that he understandeth and knoweth me, that I am the Lord which exercise loving-kindness, judgment, and righteousness in the earth" (Jeremiah 9:22, 23).

Sanctification Is Moralization

189. As was pointed out above, this aim is ethical holiness, that is, the sanctification of human life, and it is the task of ethics to define its character and content.

The ethical notion of sanctification is neither extravagant nor mystical. Still it implies an ideal infinitely beyond the highest yet attained by human conduct. But though this ideal is so remote as to seem quite unattainable, it is, after all, the impelling force that determines every step in its direction, and, therefore, for finite man each step in itself constitutes an aim.

190. Ethical holiness means the perfection of morality.

The perfection of morality demands above and beyond all else that morality shall be absolutely unconditioned. Its meaning, worth, and dignity inhere in itself. It is to be practised for its own sake, for no other reason, for no ulterior purpose. Life develops an abundance of purposes which man strives to realize, and an abundance of values which he seeks to acquire, both increasing with the advance of civilization: and their number is exceeded by the sum of progressive means contrived to avoid evils, and to attain enjoyments and secure their permanence. The moral life is crossed and interlaced with all these purposes and the means, negative and positive, for their realization. But morality may not serve them; it should dominate them, make them subservient to itself, in fact. It may never be considered the means to attain some other purpose; it is its own and sole purpose and at the same time the purpose of all purposes.

For, to be perfect, morality may not even be regarded as co-ordinate with other purposes, distinct from them but resembling them in kind; in the same way, for instance, as science and art, industry and trade, economic organization and administration stand next to each other in the reciprocal relation of means and end. Morality to be perfect, to be the expression and incarnation of holiness, must occupy a solitary position opposite to the aggregate of all other human purposes. It is holy when it is independent and absolute: when it asserts itself as the final and the highest motive of all action, as the force that makes for nobility of character, as energy rejoicing to create and produce.

Many in the Rabbinical world, and among them superior minds, went to such length in the development of this idea as to maintain, not only the independence and predominance of the ethical motive, but also its absolute exclusiveness. When we come to treat of the relation of morality to the natural impulses, the purposes of nature, we shall see that the fundamental idea of Judaism requires a modification of this extreme view.

Natural Law and Moral Law

230. Thence arises the fundamental view, that the whole machinery of the natural world is but the material and the occasion for the display of the moral order of things—an

idea that is maintained with full consciousness of the fact
that only an infinitesimal fraction of natural objects, forces,
and substances serves moral ends directly. Comparatively
few molecules of the enormous quantity of oxygen that permeates the terrestrial atmosphere are dignified with the
mission of invigorating human blood, and so entering as
efficient agents within the confines of the spiritual realm.
Yet the service rendered by them would surely be desig-
nated the most distinguished virtue of oxygen. In the form of
an allegory, Rab, as reported by R. Jehudah, expressed the
same idea. "Daily," he says, "a voice calls out aloud proclaiming: The whole world is fed (supported) for the sake of
my son Chanina, yet my son Chanina contents himself from
Sabbath eve to Sabbath eve with a basket of St. John's
Bread (*Charubim*)" (*Berakhoth* 17b). In various turns of expression, the fundamental thought is urged, that the moral
ideal is a phenomenon transcending the universe of natural
objects and seeking to realize its own, the very highest purpose. This, for instance, is the meaning of the saying: "Every
human being is obliged to believe that the world was created
for his sake" (*Sanhedrin* 37a). For the individual, conceiving
himself to be an ethical person in the true sense, is called
upon to supplement the creation of the world by the creation
of his character. In every individual as creator and as agent
of morality, and only in such a one, the world-purpose is
achieved.

231. In view of the fundamental importance of the relation of the ethical to natural existence and to the natural
course of events, it is proper to cite some of the Rabbinical
sayings that convey the above thought in manifold forms,
though with but slight variations of content. The frequent
repetition of this primary principle in the Rabbinical writings proves that the authors were acutely aware of the tell-
ing difference between the moral doctrine that is based
upon a purely ethical reason on the one hand, and on the
other all utilitarian, naturalistic, and eudæmonistic systems. A sentence by Kant may serve as the focus of all these
Rabbinical sayings—Kant, the original, genial thinker, never

perhaps more original and genial than in the sphere of ethics. His sentence expresses in simple, crisp words the same idea as the Rabbis doubtless meant to convey by their poetical and allegorical dicta.

"If justice is perverted," says Kant, "man's existence on earth is of no value."

R. Simon ben Lakish expresses almost the same thought: "God made a compact with the universe he created: If the children of Israel—and through them all the nations—accept the Torah, the moral code, well and good! Otherwise I shall resolve you into chaos again" (*Abodah Zarah* 3a). In Kantian phrase, the existence of a world were "of no value" then. R. Dimi bar Choma puts it more fantastically and less universally: "God inverted Mount Sinai over the congregation of Israel, and said: If you accept the Torah, well and good! If not, this shall be your grave" (*Abodah Zarah* 2b). Again, as Kant would have said, the existence of the people of Israel were "of no value," if they did not accept the Law, if they did not lay hold on the ideas of morality, whose development, dissemination, and realization alone form the nucleus and the reason of their peculiar existence.

232. R. Eliezer ben Hyrcanos expresses the same thought in directer language: "Great is the Torah! If it were not for the Torah, for the moral law, heaven and earth would not continue to exist" (*Nedarim* 32a). R. Meïr said of him who occupies himself with the Law for its own sake, not for selfish, or ambitious, or other by-purposes, "the whole world, as it were, exists for him alone" (*Aboth* 6:1). Raba's saying presents another phase of the same shade of the thought: "If a man does moral deeds, but not from moral motives, it were better for him had he never been born" (*Berakhoth* 17a), for, as man is destined (was born) for the moral world, for the second world transcending nature, he does not fulfill his destiny whose motives are not moral. His acts count as nothing more than an element in the natural conflict of interests, a peg in the mechanism of the natural order of things. Finally, mention must be made of R. Nehemiah's version: "A solitary man is equal in value to the whole

of creation." That not an individual is meant, but man, the
human being, humanity, the human kind represented by
one specimen, appears from the reference to Genesis 5:1.
Ben Azai's interpretation of which has been mentioned as of
fundamental importance. . . .

*

Israel Meir Ha-Kohen (Kagen)— the Hafetz Hayyim (1838–1933)

Kagen was a rabbi, talmudist, and prolific writer who
lived in Eastern Europe. Hundreds of sayings of practical
wisdom are attributed to him. He became universally
known as the Hafetz Hayyim, after the title of his first
work. Following is an excerpt from *The Hafetz Hayyim on
the Siddur*, translated by Y. A. Dvorkas.

THE HAFETZ HAYYIM ON THE SIDDUR

91
The Purpose of Life

ומשטן המשחית

May it be thy will . . . to save me today . . . from the destructive Satan. A man once complained to the *Hafetz Hayyim*
that evil impulse (Satan) was giving him no peace. The sage
answered him: This is your good fortune, and the good fortune of the whole world. For if not for him (Satan), the
purpose of Creation would not be perceived. A clock runs
because the spring within it is wound up, and the spring
activates the wheels, that each should revolve in an opposite

direction; and by the opposing revolutions of the wheels, the operation of the clock is made exact.

So also the affairs of a man in this world revolve. The good inclination draws him in its direction, and the evil inclination, in the opposite way. By mustering his strength and overcoming the evil inclination, remembering his Creator, he acquires a share in the world-to-come. And this, you see, is the goal and purpose of his life.

*

Hermann Cohen (1842–1918)

Hermann Cohen was a German philosopher. Soon after earning his doctorate he became professor of philosophy at the University of Marburg (1873–1912). Here, he founded the so-called Marburg School of Neo-Kantianism. Cohen also wrote defenses of the "Jewish Question." The sections that follow are from his *Religion of Reason*, translated by Simon Kaplan.

RELIGION OF REASON

Chapter VI
The Attributes of Action

1. The Talmud contains the following report: "In the presence of Rabbi Chanina somebody once prayed the words: O God, great, powerful, fearful, sublime, and so on. Then Rabbi Chanina said to him: have you now exhausted the praise of your Lord?" And he limits the right to invoke the characteristics of God in prayer to the invocation expressed in the scripture (*Berachoth* 33b). The scripture, however, names in the theophany, which we considered above . . . , the "thirteen characteristics" the Talmud recounts: "merciful

and gracious, long-suffering, and abundant in love and truth (*Treue*); keeping love unto the thousandth generation, forgiving iniquity and transgression and sin; and that will by no means clear the guilty" (Exodus 34:6–7). These thirteen characteristics are actually only two: love and justice.

Unity is not even contained in them, not to mention that there is no reference to omnipotence and omniscience. The characteristics of *being* are therefore entirely omitted, and what is there left in the modifications of love and justice? The characteristics are thought through and ordered in an entirely new relation, namely, as "attributes of action" (תוארי המעשה), as Maimonides designates them. The place of being is taken by action. And the place of causality, therefore, is taken by purpose.

2. What does action mean in the case of God? Is it not fulfilled with the creation? However, creation and revelation both come under the realm of causality; their cause is not purpose, but simply being. From these causalities of God one must distinguish action, which is determined by love and justice. Action therefore does not ensue according to causality, but according to the new kind of causality that is formed by purpose. What, accordingly, does action mean in the case of God?

This question finds its answer through another question: what does purpose mean in the case of God? This question already implies the problem of correlation. For, properly speaking, with regard to being there can be no question of its purpose. The question of the purpose of being transcends being proper and relates itself to correlation. The same is the case with the problem of action, which as love and justice is distinguished from the causality of creation.

Action in the case of God is related to the possibility of action in becoming, namely, in man. And this possibility is related not to causality but comes under the viewpoint of purpose. Hence the attributes of action are not so much characteristics of God, but rather conceptually determined models for the action of man. The unity of the concepts of love and justice in the concept of action, and consequently in purpose, elevates characteristics to norms (י"ג מדות).

And already this term "norm," which is otherwise only logically valid, and which in the Talmud is established for these thirteen characteristics, shows their designation as precepts and models, which are clearly distinguished from the determination of being. These norms are contained in the essence of God, but it is impossible to imagine that they could exhaust this essence: they could have been conceived for man only, could be valid for the actions of man only.

3. We here come again to the same thought to which we were led while considering the biblical passages concerning Moses' entreaty for God's appearance. . . . God wants to reveal only the effects of his essence to Moses, not his essence itself. These effects, which there we recognized as aftereffects of God's essence, were the only knowable characteristics of God. Now these effects become more precisely known as actions. They are now therefore no longer merely aftereffects, which would still be connected with causality, but as norms of action, as love and justice, they originate not in causality but in the purpose of the action, which is determined by love and justice. At this point, again, being steps out of its confines and enters into correlation with becoming in man.

If we now turn from the philosophical designation of these legitimate thirteen characteristics, for which we are particularly indebted to Maimonides, and consider other biblical sources, we find above all two concepts in which these moral characteristics of God are comprised: *holiness* and *goodness*.

There is a question as to which one of these concepts precedes the other in the development of the biblical thinking; or, rather, the question is answered by the relation Deuteronomy has to the so-called laws of holiness, whereas it is only later that the concept of God's goodness, as the unique good one, becomes the leading thought, as it does in the psalms. The thought may have been instrumental in bringing about the lyrical style of the psalms.

4. *Holiness* originally means separation. As the myth generally separates from common usage particular places, houses, vessels, animals and finally also persons, so the sacrificial worship in the sanctuary and with the priest intensi-

fied and made distinct this meaning of holiness as separation. Polytheism does not go beyond the holiness of things. If God is also called holy in polytheism, the reference is to his statue in the separated place of his temple.

A great center of gravitation comes into the world with the words: "Ye shall be holy; for I the Eternal your God am holy" (Leviticus 19:2). This word "holy" has a twofold meaning: it relates holiness to God and to man. And one is to assume that only through this unified relation to God, as well as to man, can holiness be thought of as possible with regard to God himself; as on the other hand one might say that only through the coming to be of holiness in God does its relation to man simultaneously become possible. The correlation becomes effectual and with it mythology and polytheism cease to be. Holiness becomes *morality*.

5. What is the difference between that which we scientifically call morality and the religious expression of holiness? The difference is to be derived from the difference of the tense of the verb in the sentence in which holiness is used with regard to God and man. With God it is being: "For I am holy." With regard to man, however, it says: "Ye shall be holy." Hence one may translate: "Ye shall become holy." Holiness thus means for man a task, whereas for God it designates being.

This designation of being with regard to God is not concerned with his metaphysical causality but with his purposive acting, which is the model for the purposive action of man. In holiness God becomes for man the *lawgiver* who sets tasks for him. Only as a holy one can he set these tasks; for holiness, already according to its original meaning, separates God from all sensibility. And this elevation above sensibility is the thing that is set as a task for man.

If one were not to shun the paradox, one could think that holiness exists not so much for God as for man. Out of God's being, out of his uniqueness, holiness separates itself and does so only out of consideration for man. It is, however, not a particular characteristic, but rather is the unity of all characteristics of action.

The contrary question, therefore, whether holiness is possible for man, cannot be asked. This is a question of causality, which at this point entirely recedes before the new interest in and the new problem of purpose. Without the purpose of holiness the being of man becomes void. Holiness is his purpose, which sets for him his task, God's task.

6. Modern biblical research damages its own understanding of the ethical meaning of holiness and its connection with the fundamental concepts of monotheism because it cannot refrain from blindly mixing a historical interest in the literary and cultic development of these concepts with the inner connection that permeates them. Therefore its objective understanding is constantly hampered by historical elucidation. Philological research has not yet been enlightened by the understanding that all spiritual progress is accompanied by secondary material factors. These factors, much as they might hinder and limit, work not only as forces of opposition, but very often they give wings to the flight of ideas.

Biblical research, in any case, influenced by dogmatic tendencies, has a predilection for clinging to secondary material, to the state of affairs of the time and to political circumstances; but it neglects to investigate and to illuminate the inner, relentless chain of the motivation of ideas. Holiness, to be sure, originated with sacrifice, and developed with the sacrifice, but as sacrifice is surpassed by morality, so is holiness removed from sacrifice and together with morality brought to a new separation.

7. We shall better understand this development of the concept of holiness if we do not start from the laws of holiness but with the innovation in the name of the unique God that Isaiah brings about by designating him as the "Holy one," the "Holy one of Israel." Isaiah's style makes it evident that he is conscious of the fact that he is introducing a new concept of God, a new knowledge of God. He does not abrogate the four-letter name, which was so solemnly introduced to Moses at the first revelation. But he feels the vocation not

only to deepen the knowledge and reverence of the Unique One, of the only unique being, but also to further this knowledge practically through the new knowledge of holiness.

Therefore he begins his career with this vision of holiness, in which, characteristically enough, he imitates Moses' humility. For as the latter shies away from his vocation because of a bodily impediment, so this humility in Isaiah becomes even more moralistic: the uncircumsized lips become the unclean lips. And yet the call comes to him: holy is the Eternal.

Why does Isaiah repeat this call three times? Did he intend to write the text for the musical treatment of the Sanctus? It is obvious that the three times holy, which the angels called one to another, has the meaning of a proclamation of a new content of the divine teaching. The final clause itself, which is also attributed to the angels, confirms this idea: "the whole earth is full of His glory." The separation of heaven and earth ceases; God does not live only in heaven, but the whole earth is full of his glory. This seeming extension of God's location also is rather an intensification of the spirituality that does away with the primitive meaning of holiness. And finally the moral meaning of the new holiness is confirmed by the threat of punishment which Isaiah has to announce to his people.

8. The "Holy One of Israel" is therefore the prevailing name of God in Isaiah and is also preserved in the Deutero-Isaiah. "His name is the Holy One of Israel" (Isaiah 47:4). "And the neediest among men shall exult in the Holy One of Israel" (Isaiah 29:19). "The High and Lofty One that inhabiteth eternity, whose name is Holy" (Isaiah 57:15). Holiness is substituted for the place on high as God's abode: "I dwell in the high and holy" (Isaiah 57:15). Also it is identified with God's unity: "There is none holy as the Eternal; for there is none beside Thee" (1 Samuel 2:2). The spiritualization, which the psalm produces by putting the praises of Israel in the place of Zion and Jerusalem, is also joined to holiness: "Thou art holy, that are enthroned upon the praises of

Israel" (Psalm 22:4). Thus holiness is connected with spirituality but develops out of the latter into morality.

And what is the essence of morality? It consists of the correlation of God and man. Correlation is therefore based on holiness and therefore is entirely different from separation. Morality branches off into the reciprocal relations of men and therefore also into the correlation with God. Holiness develops into an embodiment of all these branchings out of the correlation. Thus God, the holy one, *is* for the sake of the holiness of man. And holiness also becomes the embodiment of the thirteen characteristics of God: it comprises justice and love; it makes love akin to justice.

9. Isaiah still uses the expression the "mighty One of Israel." It nearly corresponds to the name "Almighty God" (אל שדי), which name was replaced by that of the One that is. But the expression occurs in Isaiah only once, which shows how much might recedes before holiness. And the connection of holiness with human things and institutions, which Deuteronomy maintains, becomes decisive for the prophets. Thus everywhere the idea of Deuteronomy was effective, that the truth of the Torah is to be proven by the "statutes and ordinances."

It would, however, be mechanical, and in truth unhistorical, if one were to demand a strict realization of this connection between God and man in all human endeavors, and if one were to consider each exception as a proof that this connection was not grasped in all its clarity. Who is going to expect clarity in the development of these basic eternal concepts, a clarity which in the naive stage of the development is bound to be lacking? Clarity is a sign of reflection; in its primitive steps the naive course of history falters everywhere. This proves all the more the naiveté of historical development, but it cannot be counted as an argument against the general tendency of the development. Thus holiness, to be sure, also progresses side by side with its primitive meaning, which, however, it outgrows. This connection should not mar the new formation, which is a new flowering on the old stem, a new fruit from the old root. For sacrifice is the root of worship, just as polytheism is undisputably the root of monotheism. But a new sun rises above the old root and brings to light a new growth.

What then is morality? This question has a different meaning when the sociologist rather than the moralist asks it. Therefore, one should not ask of religion in its naive stage of development a definite treatment and realization of this concept. Morality is indeed called holiness there, and with this is expressed the connection of the old with the new. The only symptom of development that can be required is the preponderance of human morality.

*

Kaufmann Kohler (1845–1926)

Kohler was born in Germany and studied there before emigrating to the United States in 1869. He was a rabbi, a leader of Reform Judaism, President of Hebrew Union College, and a prolific writer in the fields of philosophy and theology. The best known of his many works is *Jewish Theology Systematically and Historically Considered*, from which an excerpt is presented below.

JEWISH THEOLOGY SYSTEMATICALLY AND HISTORICALLY CONSIDERED

Chapter XXXV
The Origin and Destiny of Man

1. Of all created beings man alone possesses the power of self-determination; he assigns his destiny to himself. While

he endeavors to find the object of all other things and even of his own existence in the world, he finds his own purpose within himself. Star and stone, plant and beast fulfill their purpose in the whole plan of creation by their existence and varied natures, and are accordingly called "good" as they are. Man, however, realizes that he must accomplish his purpose by his manner of life and the voluntary exertion of his own powers. He is "good" only as far as he fulfills his destiny on earth. He is not good by mere existence, but by his conduct. Not what he is, but what he ought to be gives value to his being. He is good or bad according to the direction of his will and acts by the imperative: "I ought" or "I ought not," which comes to him in his conscience, the voice of God calling to his soul.

2. The problem of human destiny is answered by Judaism with the idea that God is the ideal and pattern of all morality. The answer given, then, is "To walk in the ways of God, to be righteous and just" (Genesis 18:19, Deuteronomy 8:6, 10:12, 32:4), as He is. The prophet Micah expressed it in the familiar words: "It has been told thee, O man, what is good, and what the Lord doth require of thee: Only to do justly, and to love mercy, and to walk humbly with thy God" (Micah 6:8). Accordingly the Bible considers men of the older generations the prototypes of moral conduct, "righteous men who walked with God." Such men were Enoch, Noah, and above all Abraham, to whom God said: "I am God Almighty; walk before Me, and be thou whole-hearted. And I will make My covenant between thee and Me" (Genesis 5:22, 6:9, 17:1-2). The rabbis singled out Abraham as the type of a perfect man on account of his love of righteousness and peace; contrasting him with Adam who sinned, they beheld him as "the great man among the heroes of the ancient times." They even considered him the type of true humanity, in whom the object of creation was attained (Genesis *Rabbah* 12:8, 14:6, 14:15).

3. This moral consciousness, however, which tells man to walk in the ways of God and be perfect, is also the source of

shame and remorse. With such an ideal man must feel constantly that he falls short, that he is not what he ought to be. Only the little child, who knows nothing as yet of good and evil, can preserve the joy of life unmarred. Similarly, primitive man, being ignorant of guilt, could pass his days without care or fear. But as soon as he becomes conscious of guilt, discord enters his soul, and he feels as if he had been driven from the presence of God.

This feeling is allegorized in the Paradise legend. The garden of bliss, half earthly, half heavenly, which is elsewhere called the "mountain of God" (Ezekiel 12:14), a place of wondrous trees, beasts, and precious stones, whence the four great rivers flow, is the abode of divine beings. The first man and woman could dwell in it only so long as they lived in harmony with God and His commandments. As soon as the tempter in the shape of the serpent called forth a discord between the divine will and human desire, man could no longer enjoy celestial bliss, but must begin the dreary earthly life, with its burdens and trials.

*

Felix Adler (1851–1933)

Adler was born in Germany and moved to the United States with his family in 1857. He graduated from Columbia University and for a brief period of time, was rabbi at Temple Emanu-El in New York. Adler was the founder and leader of the Ethical Cultural Movement, an educator, and an author. His last major work was An Ethical Philosophy of Life (1918) from which a portion is presented below.

AN ETHICAL PHILOSOPHY OF LIFE

Chapter X
The Last Outlook on Life

The view of life that man has on leaving it is the final test of
his philosophy of life. These are my thoughts: It is time to
detach thyself from this earth. The shadows are lengthen-
ing. Look around you and note the strange changes that have
taken place in the men and women of your acquaintance.
Those that you once knew in their prime are now old and
wrinkled,—and how many already dead! As you survey the
procession of life, how many vacant places are there in it!
How many true and loyal comrades have been swept away!
Or go into the busy streets of the city, and look at the
multitude passing through them. You are still one of this
multitude. Presently you will drop out. There will perhaps
be a little ripple on the surface, and then the stream will
flow on as before. How curious is it to think that this frame
of life which sustains such high faculties should crumble
into a little heap of dust at the touch of the wand of death!
Detach thyself, therefore, relax thy hold by anticipation as
thou shalt soon relax it actually. But detachment does not
mean cold inattention or unnatural shrinking from the
earthly scene, like that of the monk in his cell. Relax thy
hold on what is earthly in the earthly scene, and fix thy
loving attention all the more on what is *spiritually significant* in it. Regard with a friendly eye the beauty of the
natural landscape around thee—yonder lake and yonder
noble mountain summit. They are earthly, yet are they also
hieroglyphs and symbols.

Still more is this true of thy social relations. Detach thyself means relax thy hold on what is transient in those
relations. Cling all the more firmly to what is spiritual in
them. The earth is thy foundation, thou art Antæus as long
as thou remainest in contact with the earth. Until the very

last thou must lean for strength upon the earthly bases and
substrata.

Consider the drive of the human race through the time
and space world, and its net result. Thou standest now on a
high tower. Lean over the parapet and peer as far out into
the future as thou canst. Thou standest as did Moses on
Mount Pisgah. Strain thy eyes to catch sight of the Promised
Land. But remember that the Promised Land turned out to
be a land still of promise, not of fulfilment,—a land in which
the prophetic soul of Israel matured its visions of a fulfilment never on earth to be attained.

Remember that as thou art linked to thy ancestry, so art
thou linked to posterity. The future centuries of the human
race are like the future years of an individual. Thou art
keenly interested in what may happen hereafter to the race
with which thou art interlinked. But the race, like the individual, will be cut off and become extinct before ever the
ideal is reached. Remember, therefore, that the purpose for
which humanity exists is achieved at every moment in
everyone who appropriates the fruits of partial success and
frustration. Whosoever standing on the earth as a foundation builds up for himself the spiritual universe attains the
purpose of human existence. There is indeed progress in the
explicitness with which the spiritual ideal is conceived, and
we are immeasurably interested in the greater light to be
attained by our posterity. But the essential fruition of the
contact of the infinite that is in us with the finite world is
achievable at every moment in every human being. And this
gives an entirely new meaning to the spiritual gains
achieved in solitude, which seem vain because there are no
witnesses. But neither will there be witnesses when the last
human beings perish on earth. The spiritual bravery of the
shipwrecked man who sinks on the lonely ocean springs
from the conviction that though the sea can overwhelm him
there is that in him greater than ocean's immensity; a conviction achieved through the experience of living in the life
of others. The same is the gain achieved by the sick man who
lies in solitude like a helpless log in the darkened room. The

altruistic philosophy fails in accounting for the moral grandeur that attaches to the spiritual victories gained in silence and solitude.

Face the terrors of life before you leave life. Be resolute to the last not to cherish illusions. Face the terrors of life, the absence of observable design, the cruelties, the ferocities. Think of William Blake's poem "The Tiger": "Did he who made the lamb make thee?" In your philosophy there is no question any longer of a Creator. Creation is an attempt to explain the coexistence of the imperfect with the perfect, to account for a lower stage in terms of a higher. The ultimate inability of man to understand, to explain, is one of the principal frustrations he meets with, is the crucifixion of man at the point of his intellect.

The radical incompetence of man to grasp with his intellect the world as a "universe," is to be faced by him and accepted without qualification. It marks off this philosophy of life from those philosophies and theologies which have attempted to explain the universe, and which, while affecting humility, are the dupes of an unwarranted self-confidence. Unqualified admission of the incompetence of the human intellect to resolve the world riddle is the determining factor in the more profound humility which characterizes the religion of ethical experience. Agnosticism on the intellectual side is the very condition of the transcending ethical conviction subsequently attained. Without intellectual agnosticism there is no ethical certainty. . . .

*

Sigmund Freud (1856–1939)

Freud lived most of his life in Vienna. He was a neuropathologist, clinical neurologist, extensive writer, and the father of psychoanalysis. Following is a brief excerpt from his *Civilization and Its Discontents*, translated by James Strachey.

CIVILIZATION AND ITS DISCONTENTS

The question of the purpose of human life has been raised countless times; it has never yet received a satisfactory answer and perhaps does not admit of one. Some of those who have asked it have added that if it should turn out that life has *no* purpose, it would lose all value for them. But this threat alters nothing. It looks, on the contrary, as though one had a right to dismiss the question, for it seems to derive from the human presumptuousness, many other manifestations of which are already familiar to us. Nobody talks about the purpose of the life of animals, unless, perhaps, it may be supposed to lie in being of service to man. But this view is not tenable either, for there are many animals of which man can make nothing, except to describe, classify and study them; and innumerable species of animals have escaped even this use, since they existed and became extinct before man set eyes on them. Once again, only religion can answer the question of the purpose of life. One can hardly be wrong in concluding that the idea of life having a purpose stands and falls with the religious system.

*

Sholom Dov-Ber Schneersohn (1860–1920)

Rabbi Sholom Dov-Ber was the fifth-generation leader of Chabad. He was born in Russia and assumed the leadership upon the death of his father in 1883. The discourse that follows was translated by Zalman I. Posner and is from Schneersohn's work, *Kuntres Uma'ayon Mibais Hashem.*

KUNTRES UMA'AYON MIBAIS HASHEM

Discourse Sixteen
Chapter 1

The cause for the scholarly and the worshipper becoming arrogant and smug in his virtue is, again, folly. Arrogance is foolishness, for "the prideful are stupid." What is he so proud of? If for his intelligence, that is not his at all. It is part of what the sages meant in Avos (chapter 3), "Give Him of His, for you and yours are His." In the prayers we say, "You grant man knowledge," since it is something granted from Above. If he is proud of his assiduous study, that too might be natural for him, because he is an introvert. Even if he compelled himself to industrious study, God gave him the strength to achieve. His "service of the heart" with love and *dvekus* comes from strength given him. Why should a lowly mortal take pride in what is not his?

Therefore our Rabbis declare, "If you studied much Torah, do not claim credit for yourself" (Avos 2:9). The Mishna does give a reason there, "For you were created for this purpose," but this is an additional reason, if the first reason is challenged as insufficient. One might answer to the statement that since man's abilities to study and serve are not self-generated but given by God, therefore man should not claim credit for his achievements, but insisting that man is a free agent who is perfectly capable of choosing not to study Torah and worshipping with devotion, and in light of these options man might rightly feel proud of his positive decision. To this the Mishna continues, "For you were created for this purpose," the creation of man was precisely for this goal. To explain:

"*Breshis* (In the beginning, or as Rashi notes—for the *two* called *reshis*, beginning) God created," are the opening words of Torah. The sages interpret this as, "For the Torah called *reshis* and for Israel called *reshis* (God created . . .)." God intended for Israel to be elevated through Torah which is His intellect and will.

The Zohar declares, "Three are bound to each other. Israel are bound to Torah and Torah to God," for Torah is the instrument by which the souls of Israel are bound to Godhood. Elsewhere (III, 11b) Zohar remarks on the verse, "Ten by ten were each spoon" (Numbers 7:86) that the Ten Commandments parallel the Ten Fiats by which the world was created (Avos 5:1).

The Talmud (Shabbos 88a) tells us that God made a condition with Creation. "If Israel fulfil my Torah, good. If not, Creation shall revert to chaos and void."

Midrash (*Shmos Rabba* 48) comments on "*Eleh* (these) are the accounts of heaven and earth as they were created." *Eleh* (these, meaning heaven and earth), by whose merit were they created and in whose merit are they maintained? In the merit of "*Eleh* (these) are the names of the children of Israel" (Exodus 1:1). And *Eleh* (these, meaning people of Israel), by whose merit do they exist? In the merit of "*Eleh* are the testimonies and statutes and judgments."

Therefore the Mishna declares, "For you were created for this purpose" (*Aboth* 2:8). The primary purpose of man is Torah. "The end of the matter, when all is heard, fear God and keep His commandments, for this is all of man" (Koheles 12:13). In that case, when man does what he was created for, he has no reason for claiming credit. In references to his divine service too, when he attains *ahava* and *dvekus* (love and attachment to God), he has no cause for satisfaction, for this is the whole reason for his being in this world. Man's ultimate is that he rise through Torah and service, as we have explained (Discourse I:3 and 4) in reference to the purpose of all creation.

On the contrary, his satisfaction with his Torah study and worship make it quite clear that his service did not effect a state of *bitul*, nullification, loss of self-awareness. He has, in this case, not attained the desired fulfillment. Instead of smugness he should properly be anguished that he has fallen so short of fulfilling his purpose in life, and if so, why was he created at all, and what has he achieved?

It is conceivable that he has not been perfectly meticulous in all matters, and even trifling matters are reckoned as significant for one of his stature, as we noted in Discourse XV: 5. And if these "trifles" entailed any "profanation of the Name," God forbid, then better had he never been born. Had he never engaged in Torah and worship it would have been better, for then at least the *hilul Hashem* would have been avoided. The cause of all this is that his divine service is not true. Were it true service it would have brought *bitul* to his soul, and it would never have occurred to him that he had done anything praiseworthy. It goes without saying that he would have been scrupulous about every least "trifle."

But when the "spirit of folly" sways him, he is arrogant in his learning; he regards himself as meritorious.

Summary

Arrogance is stupid; competence and understanding in Torah study, and the ability to worship properly, come from Him, and for this was man created; his self-satisfaction indicates that he has not attained true fulfillment; the arrogant profanes the Name.

*

Albert Einstein (1879–1955)

Einstein was born in Ulm, Germany. After serving in a patent office he became a professor at the German University of Prague. Einstein left Germany in 1933, and ultimately became an American citizen. He helped raise money for various Jewish causes. Einstein was a physicist and Nobel Prize winner, and is perhaps most remem-

bered for his equation $E = mc^2$ and the Theory of Rela-
tivity. The selection that follows is from his broadcast
for the United Jewish Appeal, delivered on April 11,
1943, and reprinted in his autobiography, *Out of My
Later Years.*

OUT OF MY LATER YEARS

51
The Goal of Human Existence

Our age is proud of the progress it has made in man's
intellectual development. The search and striving for truth
and knowledge is one of the highest of man's qualities—
though often the pride is most loudly voiced by those who
strive the least. And certainly we should take care not to
make the intellect our god; it has, of course, powerful mus-
cles, but no personality. It cannot lead, it can only serve; and
it is not fastidious in its choice of a leader. This characteristic is reflected in the qualities of its priests, the intellectuals.
The intellect has a sharp eye for methods and tools, but is
blind to ends and values. So it is no wonder that this fatal
blindness is handed on from old to young and today involves
a whole generation.

Our Jewish forbears, the prophets and the old Chinese
sages understood and proclaimed that the most important
factor in giving shape to our human existence is the setting
up and establishment of a goal; the goal being a community
of free and happy human beings who by constant inward
endeavor strive to liberate themselves from the inheritance
of anti-social and destructive instincts. In this effort the
intellect can be the most powerful aid. The fruits of intellectual effort, together with the striving itself, in cooperation
with the creative activity of the artist, lend content and
meaning to life.

But today the rude passions of man reign in our world,
more unrestrained than ever before. Our Jewish people, a

small minority everywhere, with no means of defending themselves by force, are exposed to the cruelest suffering, even to complete annihilation, to a far greater degree than any other people in the world. The hatred raging against us is grounded in the fact that we have upheld the ideal of harmonious partnership and given it expression in word and deed among the best of our people.

*

Joseph Isaac Schneersohn (1880-1950)

Rabbi Joseph Isaac was born in Russia and was the sixth-generation leader of Chabad. In 1906, he traveled to Europe to intervene in the pogroms that were occurring there. Upon the death of his father in 1920, he became the leader of Chabad. Joseph Isaac was imprisoned briefly by the Soviets in 1929 for his activity in strengthening religion. Shortly after his release he moved to Poland. Upon the outbreak of World War II, he emigrated to New York where he established a chain of yeshivot and schools, the Kehot Publication Society, and the Refugee Relief and Rehabilitation Organization. The following selection is from his work, *Chassidic Discourses*.

CHASSIDIC DISCOURSES

Sefer Ha Ma'amarim—Yiddish

סוף דבר הכל נשמע את האלקים ירא

ואת מצותיו שמור כי זה כל האדם

"The end of the matter, all having been heard, fear the Almighty,

observe His commands, for this is
the whole of man." [Ecclesiastes 12:13]

This verse teaches us the ultimate lesson derived from every
matter; man's purpose in life can be accomplished only by
fearing God and observing His commandments. It was for
this reason that man was created. This concept is also alluded to in the verse: "I made the earth, and created 'man'
upon it" (Isaiah 45:12). God says that because of man, meaning the Jewish people, He created the world. [That "man"
means the Jewish people] we derive from the verse: "And
you are My sheep, the sheep of My flock, you are man"
(Ezekiel 34:31). Comments the Talmud: "You, the Jewish
people, are [referred to as] 'man'."

That God created the world because of the Jewish people,
is also explained in the *Midrash*. Commenting on the verse:
"In the beginning, — *Bereishis*, God created the heavens and
the earth," the *Midrash* says: "The word *Bereishis* indicates
that there are two "firsts," [for *Bereishis* is composed of the
two words] "*beis raishis*," [there are two matters that are
"first" and supersede all else], Torah and Jews, for whom's
sake the world was created."

The Talmud states: "God made a stipulation with heaven
and earth, 'Should the Jewish people perform the commandments then all is well. If not, I shall return you to nothingness'" (*Avodah Zorah* 3a). The continued existence of the
world is thus dependent upon the Jewish people studying
Torah and performing *mitzvos*.

The *Midrash* expounds on the verse: "These are the prog-
eny of heaven and earth" (Genesis 2:4): "In what merit do
these [heaven and earth] exist? In the merit of '*These* are the
names of the Jewish people' (Exodus 1:1). [The world exists
in the merit of the Jews.] And in what merit do *these* [the
Jewish people] exist? In the merit of, '*These* are the testimonies, statutes, and laws.'" [Jews exist in the merit of their
performing *mitzvos*.] This, then, is the meaning of the verse:
"[I made the earth,] and created, *borosi*, man upon it." The
Hebrew word *borosi* is numerically equivalent to 613. Man

was created for the express purpose of performing the 613 commandments with fear of God.

Creation of man refers not only to his body but also to his soul, which is part of Divinity. Body bereft of soul is but the flesh of man, and the soul without its body is the spirit of man. Only when body and soul unite does the name "man" properly apply. Thus, God placed the soul in the body so that man perform the *mitzvos* with fear of God.

It is written: "The Almighty, *Elohim*, made man that he fear Him" (Ecclesiastes 3:14). [The appellation used in this verse is *Elohim*], for the aspect of fearing God stems from [God as He is known by the Divine name] *Elohim* [which alludes to God as Supreme and Mighty Judge]. For this reason, the verse [quoted at the outset of the discourse] states: ". . . fear the Almighty, *Elohim*," for fear of God comes from the Divine name *Elohim*.

Summary

Man was created for the expressed purpose of performing Torah and *mitzvos*, and this was God's stipulation [with creation]. The body is flesh of man; the soul, his spirit. Man is a combination of the soul within the body. Fear stems from the Divine name *Elohim*.

*

Mordecai Menachem Kaplan
(1881–1983)

Kaplan was born in Lithuania. At the age of 9, he moved with his family to the United States, where he became a rabbi, writer, and founder of the Reconstructionist movement. Following his ordination by the Jewish Theological Seminary of America, he was appointed

dean of the school's Teachers Institute. In 1917, Kaplan
founded the first synagogue center. Later, he founded the
Society for the Advancement of Judaism, *Reconstructionist Magazine*, and the Jewish Reconstructionist Foundation. Kaplan wrote several books in which he defined
Judaism as an "evolving religious civilization." Following
is his concise definition of the purpose of Jewish existence given toward the end of his book *The Purpose and
Meaning of Jewish Existence*.

THE PURPOSE AND MEANING
OF JEWISH EXISTENCE

It is true that traditional religion has always held out a
distant prospect of such a metamorphosis. It has pictured
the Messianic era when even the ravenous beasts would
become tame. In the meantime, however, man has acquired
far more power than he possesses the ability to bring under
the control of moral responsibility. Never has Hillel's question, "And if not now, when?" been so pertinent and so
ominous, unless forthwith answered in the spirit in which it
is asked. That spirit is implied in the first two questions, the
answer to which must be the combination and coalescence of
what is true and good in collectivism with what is true and
good in individualism, in independence and in interdepen-
dence. That combination of moral forces, which the conscience has to exert, must be the answer to that which has
become the burning problem of our every-day existence:
How to outlaw war and the manufacture of armaments. If
not now, when?

The religion of moral responsibility in action can no
longer afford to confine itself to vague abstractions about
Deity and the moral law. It must be specific and concrete. It
must address itself to all civilizations and peoples in terms
of their respective memories, experiences, and problems
and hopes. In other words, it has to be indigenous and not

imported. Like the Jewish religion, the religion of active moral responsibility has to be universal in form and specific in content, speak in the name of humanity as a whole and be relevant to the particular interests of each particular nation.

The *purpose* of Jewish existence is to be a People in the image of God. The *meaning* of Jewish existence is to foster in ourselves as Jews, and to awaken in the rest of the world, a sense of moral responsibility in action.

*

Isaac Breuer (1883–1946)

Breuer was born in Papa, Hungary and moved to Frankfurt as a child. He studied history, law, and philosophy at various universities. Ultimately, he became an advocate (attorney) and notary. In 1936, he left Germany and moved to Jerusalem. Breuer was one of the founders of Agudat Israel and published a number of works relating to Judaism. Following is a section from his book *Concepts of Judaism*.

CONCEPTS OF JUDAISM

Man and the World

"God said:
 Let us make a man
 In Our form, after Our likeness."—
"Then God created man in His form—
 In God's form He created him:
 Male and female He created them."—
"God formed man, dust from the earth,
 And breathed into his face a living soul,
 And man became a living person."—[Genesis 1:26–27]

1

Heaven and earth were created. The word of creation had
summoned them from the void, the deed of creation had
molded them and the will of creation had endowed them
with permanence. Matter was no longer chaos. The meaningful hierarchy of diverse forms had already been established: in the universe—the system of orbits, on earth—
growth and life, and the Creator was already setting about
preparing the Sabbath of creation and leaving off from His
labor.

But the Creator was still alone. The magnificence of the
abundance of creation had been set out: the Creator had
already given "names" to the manifold parts of matter; they
were arrayed before the Creator in predetermined perfection. He found no satisfaction in them. Something was missing—a creature.

> "The universe, to which I have given names:
>   Only for the sake of my *revelation* have I created it,
>   Molded it, even completed it." [Isaiah 43:7]
> "Everything which God has created in His world,
>   He has created only for his revelation." [*Yoma* 38a]

Creation is revelation. Not simply existing matter pure
and simple, the incomprehensibly chaotic nameless matter,
but everything God has "created *in* His world," everything
God has "named" *in* this world, the *form* of matter, creation
completed as formed matter—this is the revelation of God.

In the account of creation there is a clear distinction
between material and form: Matter as such is an incomprehensible puzzle, an eternal secret. All that we know about it
is that it was just—created. It was created in the concealment of the Creator. It remains in concealment. The Philosophers' sagacity strives in vain to fathom its essence. It has
no name. It has not been revealed. The inconceivable is not
accessible to conception.

Matter as such is that which is capable of being given shape but which has not been shaped. Its lack of name lies in its lack of shape: in its plasticity, its capability of being given a name. It is the unrevealed *object*, on which revelation operates.

God is the absolute *"I," "Anokhi,"* the absolute *subject*. The incomprehensible puzzle. The eternal mystery. This is God in Himself. No relationship is able to penetrate to Him. Thoughts tumble into confusion, whenever they wish to approach His nature. He is the shaper who has no shape. His incomprehensibility lies in His shapelessness. In His shaping lies His revelation.

God and matter: the form-giver pure and simple, and the formable pure and simple: absolute subject and absolute object: they are as distinct as Yes and No.

Here, every step bodes danger. Here each, and the least, misunderstanding plunges one into the abyss of destruction.

Subject is not conceivable without object, so the philosophers say. The object lies intrinsically in the subject, and the subject in the object. The subject can only be subject in relationship to the object; the object only in relationship to the subject. There is no object without a subject, no subject without an object. In conception, subject and object are simultaneous. Conception is the coincidence of the conceiving and the conceivable.

But philosophers are only acquainted with the epistemological "I" of experience. The "I" of the world as nature is not the "I" of the world as creation.

God is the absolute "I"—the absolute subject. God is not the "I" of matter, but "I" pure and simple. God as the absolute subject is the unrevealed God. But even the unrevealed God is—God.

Revelation is the purpose of creation. But in creation God's essence does not purely and simply reveal itself. Otherwise God and creation would be identical. God reveals himself in creation solely as—Creator.

God is not *only* Creator, even if He has only revealed Himself as *Creator*. God existed even before there was creation. The error of pantheism lies in the identification of God with God's *revelation*.

If God wishes, however, to reveal Himself as *Creator*, then the matter of creation may not be God Himself. Therefore, before God reveals Himself in it and through it, matter is— non-God.

If revelation does not concern the essence of God, then it can only be the revelation of a relationship of God; then it requires a substratum with which God enters into a relationship: then this substratum must exist outside God; then the creation of matter is the precondition of the relational revelation of God—not of the revelation of His essence.

Not God pure and simple, but God who is revealed in the world, is the formless form-giver. The relationship into which God has entered with matter as such by revealing creation—this relationship exhausts matter, but it does not exhaust God.

It exhausts matter. Matter as absolute object is, purely and simply—non-God. God, however, in no way presupposes non-God. Otherwise, God would not be the absolute "I." Rather, God *created* non-God in order to reveal Himself as form-giver in non-God and through non-God.

As God pure and simple is incomprehensible, so non-God pure and simple is just as incomprehensible. The formless form-giver, before He gives form; the formless formable, before it assumes form: both are an eternal mystery. If the essence of non-God pure and simple were revealed, then this would not be the relational revelation of God, but the revelation of the absence of any relationship of God, the revelation of God pure and simple. Whosoever comprehends non-God pure and simple, comprehends also God pure and simple.

God in Himself as absolute subject—matter as such as absolute object; creating form-giver—created form-assumer: in the theory of revelation, both are a presupposition, a precondition of the relational revelation which is consummated in the *form* of creation; in the theory of revelation both lie beyond relational revelation.

Matter as such, shapeless material, has been created but not revealed. It is only matter which has been formed, the completed creation, that has been revealed.

Matter as such is a pure circumstance of creation. Only form becomes a revealed concept of creation. The completed creation is the unity of the circumstance of creation and the concept of creation as a unity desired by God. *The form of completed creation is the form of God revealing Himself and, at the same time, the form of revealed creation: for it is only by reason of this form that God and creation become manifest.*

Completed creation, however, given "names" by God, is in the first place only *capable* of revelation. It is still not revealed. The addressee of the revelation is still lacking. Man is still lacking. The Creator reveals Himself *through* matter. He does not reveal Himself *to* the matter. Formed matter does not give any satisfaction to the Creator revealing Himself. The Creator revealing Himself is still—alone.

Then the creating form-giver addresses the created form-assumer: *"Let us make a man in our form!"*

"Let us make": this sentence is the profoundest which is told us about the essence of man as the addressee of revelation.

"Let us make": man is the child of the form-giver and the form-assumer; child of the forming Creator and of formed creation.

"God *formed* man, dust from the earth." This is the form of the form-assumer.

"God *created* man in His form" ("He breathed into his face a living soul"). This is the form of the form-giver.

"And man became a living person." That is the likeness of God. And, at the same time, the likeness of creation.

Man as a *thinking being* is constantly referred to in these passages. All the elements of his reflective consciousness are indicated here in their totality.

"Let us make": forming Creator and formed creation combine to beget man. Forming Creator and formed creation give him their form, so that he may combine both in his consciousness. Child of the forming Creator and of formed creation, this is man.

Forming Creator-form is not the same as the formed creation-form. Forming Creator-form is the molding activity of the subject. Formed creation-form is the molded passivity of the object. The perceiving "I" of man, however, is at once subject and object.

"Let us make a man in our form": *These words, spoken by the form-giver to the form-assumer, literally characterize man's perceiving "I."*

In me there is the perceiving; and in me is the perceived. All perception is self-perception. I can perceive nothing that is *outside* of myself. How am I to perceive what is outside of myself? The perceived world is not outside of myself, but within me. Everything I conceive has the *a priori* forms of my thinking intuition. The *a priori* forms of the conceiving "I," the forms of thought and forms of intuition, are in their totality the "form of the form-giver," in which the molding Creator reveals Himself to man. By reason of these *a priori* forms, the conceiving "I" bears within itself the form-laws of molded creation, and it molds anew with every conception the matter of creation, proving itself with every conception a true child of God-Creator.

But the perceiving "I" is not God-Creator Himself. It is the child of God-Creator and of creation. It is not the absolute subject, but really only the subject of *its* object.

The object of the perceiving "I" is not creation pure and simple. Creation pure and simple is the created object of the "I"'s father—of God.

The object of the perceiving "I" is the formed "I" as the child of formed creation.

The forming while perceiving "I" is the father's child, God-Creator's child. The formed while perceived "I" is the

mother's child, creation's child. The forming Creator lives in
the "I," and in the "I" there lives formed creation. Perceiving
is in the "I" and in the "I" there is the perceived. Child of the
absolute subject and child of the absolute object, this is man
as "I"—subject-object.

Child of the form-giver and of the form-assumer: "Male
and female He created them."

It is in vain that the philosophers toil to uncover the
mystery of the "givenness" of the "object" of perception. For
them the "I" of the theory of perception is the absolute "I."
They take the child for its—father. What patent scorn! Their
omnipotent "I," in all the splendor of its forming laws, is
nevertheless blind and void! It has eyes that see nothing. It
has ears that hear nothing. It has hands that seize nothing.
It must wait until it is "given" an "object." From whence
stems the passivity of the omnipotent "I"? Why does perceiving always and constantly mean at the same time being
perceived? From whence springs this "affectedness of the
subject"? Is it affected by the "thing-in-itself"? That is a
relapse into dogmatism. Does it affect "itself"? That is an
eruption into megalomania. There is no solution here.

Only Torah can provide a solution. Man as perceiving "I"
is not absolute subject nor does it produce the absolute object
out of itself. Formed creation exists *before* man. Man, as
perceiving "I", is not the precondition of creation as such.
But he is the indispensable condition of *revealed* creation.

Creation as such is related only to the Creator. Man is the
child of the Creator and of creation. The *revelation* of the
formative power of the Creator and of creation's receptive-
ness of form is accomplished *in* him as the perceiving "I"
and *through* him as the perceiving "I."

Creation is not in man. How were it possible? But the
revelation of the forming Creator and formed creation: this
is indeed in man.

What the theory of perception calls the "world as idea,"
this is in truth the "world as revelation." Everything that
the theory of perception, with no meager degree of discern-

ment, has discovered is valid for the world as revelation. The
world as revelation exists indeed only in the reason of the
thinking "I" which, as the child of God-Creator, is endowed
with the form-laws of molded creation; which, as the child of
creation, is endowed with the formability of creation; and
which establishes within itself the unity of the revealed
world, derived from the form-laws and from formability.
The synthetic unity of the consciously existing "I"—this is
the unity of the "I" within the antithesis of molding form and
molded form; the unity of the "I" within the antithesis of its
origin in the Creator and its origin in creation; the unity of
form in itself and formed existence. The "I" comprehends
itself as existing and as existence-forming. In being conscious existence, therefore, the formed existence of creation
and the Creator's giving of form become manifest.

The "givenness" of the "object of perception" is nothing
but the "givenness" of creation. The world as revealed conception, however, is not a "replica" of creation as such. Creation as such, the absolute object of the Creator, does not
penetrate the conception of the perceiving "I," is not revealed to the perceiving "I." Merely the molded *form* of
creation in the "I" is the object of perception just as only the
molding form in the "I" is the subject of perception. Outside
of the molding form in the "I" there yawn wide for the "I"
the jaws of—the void. The path beyond revelation, beyond
the revealed world, is closed to the perceiving "I." Creation
does not crouch secretly in the "object of perception" as the
"great unknown." Nor can it be creation that the perceiving
"I" "affects" so that it perceives it more or less correctly.
Only the *form* of creation is disclosed to him; it alone is
"given" him. It is, however, completely disclosed to him.
Opposite the *a priori* molding form in its necessary general
validity there stands the empirical molded form in its concrete uniqueness. The molded form cannot possibly be anything but "given." Its "givenness" precisely marks it as—
creation-form, whilst the character of Creator-form is precisely its necessary general validity which is imposed upon
the entire creation.

The consciously existing "I," therefore, is solely the molding and molded form of creation elevated to awareness. To the perceiving "I," being is no different from being created. It is the fact that in the "I," as the child of God-form-giver, the form confronts the being-formed independently, that constitutes its awareness. It is not creation, but the being-formed of creation that is comprehensible to the perception of the consciously being-formed "I."

The form-giver in the "I" is the subject. The being-formed in the "I" is the object. The molding form conceives. The molded form is conceived. Only form is conceivable. Only that lies in the conception. Only that is the object of perception. For the *conceiving* "I," there is no answer to the pressing question as to *what* then is actually formed. For the question itself is—nonsensical. Only being-formed, as such, is conceived. There exists in the conception nothing else but concrete being-formed. There cannot penetrate the conception a "being-in-itself," which is a molded being. Only "formedness" penetrates the conception. Nothing else. A "being in itself" is not concealed behind the "formedness" in the conception of the perceiving "I." Whatever concrete "formedness" there is in creation—and only that—has creation bestowed on its child. The "formedness" of creation is "given" to him. Nothing else.

The question as to what crouches in the conception behind the significance of "formedness" is nonsensical. There is nothing behind it—absolutely nothing. "Let us make a man in our *form*": this has been literally fulfilled.

This question, however, is meaningful: how and why just *this* concrete "formedness" and not any other?

Torah indeed provides the answer to the question, which alone is meaningful. And it alone can provide the answer.

The concrete "formedness" in the perceiving "I" is precisely the "formedness" of creation, which reveals itself in the perceiving "I" just as the *a priori* forming in the perceiving "I" is the Creator's forming, by means of which he moulded the formless-formable in the work of the six days. Creator-form and creation-form are both revealed in the perceiving "I". The rest is silence.

The synthetic unity of the consciously existing "I" is en-
gendered from form and being-formed. Being-formed, however, is nothing but the fulfillment of form. Form is the
"have-to-be" of being-formed. Being-formed corresponds to
the "have-to-be" of form. The conception of the consciously
existing "I" is the pacified "have-to-be." Form and being-
formed are in conception inseparably bound. The form of
the Creator, which is revealed in the consciously existing "I,"
is the "have-to-be" of created matter, which this latter, as
the formless-formable at the Creator's behest and through
the Creator's act, has realized as the form-formable in the
six days' work. The form of creation, revealed in the consciously existing "I," its being-formed, is creation's concrete
form of existence, to which the "have-to-be" imposed upon it
by the Creator has brought it. Both—the Creator's form-
giving command and creation's form-assuming obedience—
are revealed to man as the child of the Creator and of creation. The world of the consciously existing "I" is the world of
the absolute "have-to-be" and of absolute obedience. "Have-
to-be" and "to-be" are completely identical in formed creation, since formable creation accepted utterly and completely the form which the form-giver, in fulfillment of a
predetermined pattern, commanded in word and deed. Just
so in the world of conception of the consciously existing "I," a
contrast between form and being-formed is unthinkable.
Rather, it comprises, as its two constituents, the form of the
absolute "have-to-be" and the form of being corresponding
absolutely to this "have-to-be." The consciously existing "I"
is therefore the true addressee of the revelation of the almighty laws of the Creator and of the almighty obedience of
creation. It is not the Creator who is revealed, but the laws of
the Creator. It is not creation that is revealed, but the obedience of creation. The Creator's "Let there be," spoken to
already existent creation; the "It was so" of creation by
reason of which the formable took on form: in every conception, composed of form and "formedness," the consciously
existing "I" experiences it anew.

*

Harry Waton (?1880–?1960)

Waton was a political "leftist" who also wrote about philosophy and *kabbalah*. He was the first editor of *The Marxian* and *The Marxist*. Waton was also active in the Committee for the Preservation of the Jews during the 1930s and 1940s. The following excerpts are from Waton's *Key to the Bible*.

KEY TO THE BIBLE

Key Terms

Gematria. A method of biblical exegesis based on the interpretation of a word or words according to the numerical value of its letters in the Hebrew alphabet, and the search for connections with words or phrases of equal value.

Sephirot. A technical term of kabbalistic mysticism used to designate the ten potencies or emanations through which the Divine manifests itself; God emerges from His hidden abode. The common names of the Sephirot are:

1. Keter — Crown
2. Hochmah — Rational wisdom/Intellect
3. Binah — Intuitive wisdom/Reason/Understanding
4. Hesed — Loving Kindness/Mercy/Grace
5. Gevurah — Might/the Power of God/Law/Judgment/Awe
6. Tiferet — Glory/Beauty
7. Netzach — Victory/Eternity/Triumph
8. Hod — Majesty/Glory/ Splendor
9. Yesod — Foundation
10. Malchut — Kingdom/Sovereignty

Chapter I
First Aspect of the Mathematical System

10. The Hebrew alphabet consists of twenty-two letters. Each letter has a numerical value, it represents a number. The following are the letters of the Hebrew alphabet and their numerical equivalents:

ל = Lammed	30	א = Alef	1
מ = Mem	40	ב = Bet	2
נ = Nun	50	ג = Gimmel	3
ס = Samech	60	ד = Dalet	4
ע = Ayin	70	ה = Hay	5
פ = Pey/Fey	80	ו = Vav	6
צ = Tzadde	90	ז = Zayin	7
ק = Kof	100	ח = Chet	8
ר = Resh	200	ט = Tet	9
ש = Shin	300	י = Yod	10
ת = Tav	400	כ = Kaf	11

The numerical value of a word is the sum of the numerical values of the letters composing the word. The following will show the numerical values of words:

אהיה E (Ehyeh) (I am)		יהוה D (Adonai) (God)		אלהים C (Elohim) (God)		אדני B (Adonai) (God)		שדי A (Shaddai) (Almighty)	
א	1	י	10	א	1	א	1	ש	300
ה	5	ה	5	ל	30	ד	4	ד	4
י	10	ו	6	ה	5	נ	50	י	10
ה	5	ה	5	י	10	י	10		
				מ	40				
	21		26		86		65		314

אדם J (Adam) (Man)		אברהם I (Avraham) (Abraham)		יצחק H (Yitzchok) (Isaac)		יעקב G (Yakov) (Jacob)		משה F (Moshe) (Moses)	
א	1	א	1	י	10	י	10	מ	40
ד	4	ב	2	צ	90	ע	70	ש	300
ם	40	ר	200	ח	8	ק	100	ה	5
		ה	5	ק	100	ב	2		
		ם	40						
	45		248		208		182		345

Chapter II
Second Aspect of the Mathematical System

22. Numbers do not pertain to things; numbers pertain to the mind. If I take ten apples and put them in a bag, there is nothing in the apples to tell that they are ten in number or that they are more or less than ten in number. If I arrange the apples in a row, one after another, there is nothing in the apples to tell which is the first, which is the second, and which is the last. All this is perceived by my mind, and exists only in my mind. Suppose that I count: 1, 2, 3, 4, 5, 9. My mind perceives a hiatus between 5 and 9. How does the mind come to the perception of numbers, and how does it detect a hiatus between numbers?

All realities exist in a four-dimensional continuum: three dimensions of space, and one dimension of time. Time and space are absolute condition to the existence of realities. Take away space and time, and all realities will disappear. Time is a succession of moments; the moments follow one another in an absolute order. There can be no hiatus between the moments of time; and the succession of the order cannot be changed. Space is a coexistence of spaces; the spaces coexist side by side of one another. There can be no vacuum between the spaces. Time and space are inherent in the realities of existence; they are the absolute condition to the existence of the realities; but the realities do not manifest this to the senses, because the senses cannot comprehend time and space. Like all other realities, the mind is part of existence, and partakes of time and space. Take away time and space, and the mind will cease to exist. The mind perceives time and space, and the perception of time manifests itself in the perception of numbers. And, just as the moments of time follow in succession, one after another; so the numbers in the mind follow in succession, one after another. And, just as there can be no hiatus in the moments of time, so there can be no hiatus in the numbers. Hence, when I count: 1, 2, 3, 4, 5, 9, the mind at once perceives a hiatus between the 5 and the 9.

23. We saw that the letters of the Hebrew alphabet have numerical values; they represent numbers, and are represented by numbers. We saw that the numerical values of the first ten letters follow one another in a natural order of succession. Beginning with the א (alef) whose numerical value is 1, the numerical values of the succeeding letters are: 2, 3, 4, 5, 6, 7, 8, 9, 10. But, when we come to the eleventh letter, the כ (kaf), we find that its numerical value is 20. Thus between the י (yod) and the כ (kaf) there is a hiatus, 8 numbers are missing. And the same is the case of all other letters, until we come to the last letter, the ת (tav), we find that its numerical value is 400. Thus the 22nd letter, which should have the numerical value of 22, has the numerical value of 400–378 more than 22. It is thus clear that the hiatuses between the letters must involve realities which are not disclosed by the numerical values of the letters. Hence the letters do not tell the whole story. This means that the first aspect of the mathematical systems does not reveal the whole of what the Bible contains. To comprehend what the Bible contains, we must fill up the hiatuses in the numerical values of the letters, and this we can do by filling up the hiatuses with other letters and words. But how can we find out the other letters and words? Existence already showed the way.

The realities of existence by their surface appearance, do not tell the whole story. Behind the surface appearance of things there is a long story of creation and evolution. But this long story is concealed by the very appearance of things. As the human mind grew and developed, men of thought began to penetrate behind the surface appearance of things, to find out what is behind the surface appearance of the things. In the course of time, they discovered that all material realities consist of molecules; the molecules consist of atoms; the atoms consist of electrons and protons; and the electrons and protons are nothing else than energy. This energy is the infinite and eternal substance out of which all realities were carved out. Thus all material realities revealed themselves to be only energy, and energy revealed itself to be the material realities. A reality, as it appears, is a very complex thing, the result of a long process of creation and evolution. To comprehend a reality, we must resolve it into the elements out of which it was created, and these elements themselves we must reduce to their ultimate substance. Only now can we comprehend a reality. We do the same in mathematics—the key to the understanding of the realities of existence. A large number is a complex reality. To comprehend a large number, we reduce it to its lowest terms. And now we can comprehend the large and complex number. Existence itself taught mankind the way to the discovery of the story hidden behind the surface appearance of things. And this method we have to use to comprehend the Bible. The first thing we must do is to reduce the complex numerical values of the letters to their natural and lowest terms. This will give us the following numerical values of the letters of the alphabet:

ל	12	א	1
מ	13	ב	2
נ	14	ג	3
ס	15	ד	4
ע	16	ה	5
פ	17	ו	6
צ	18	ז	7
ק	19	ח	8
ר	20	ט	9
ש	21	י	10
ת	22	כ	11

In the Second Aspect of the Mathematical System we shall use these numerical values of the letters of the alphabet. And we shall see the relation between these two aspects of numerical values.

24. It is clear that a word in the second aspect will have a lower numerical value than the same word will have in the first aspect. An illustration will make it clear. Take the first word in the Bible: *Bereshit*—In the beginning (Genesis 1:1).

The First Aspect			The Second Aspect
2	ב	ב	2
200	ר	ר	20
1	א	א	1
300	ש	ש	21
10	י	י	10
400	ת	ת	22
913			76

Thus we see that the same word, in the first aspect has the numerical value of 913, and in the second aspect it has the numerical value of 76. It is therefore clear that, when we use the second aspect, we shall need more words to make up the numerical value in the first aspect. And this means that the first aspect implies, but [does] not express, many words which are concealed behind the numerical value of the first aspect. Let us begin, as before, with the consideration of the names of God. Since the name ‏יהוה‎ (Adonai) consists of the letters of the first half of the alphabet, which have the numerical values of the second aspect, we shall get the same numerical values in both aspects. Hence we shall begin with the name ‏אלהים‎ (Elohim). We saw that in the first aspect this name has the numerical value of 86. And now let us see what its numerical value will be in the second aspect. The following will show this:

א	1
ל	12
ה	5
י	10
ם	13
	41

Thus the numerical value of the name ‏אלהים‎ (Elohim) in the second aspect is 41. What does the number 41 symbolize? We must then return to the first aspect to find a word that has the numerical value of 41. And this word is ‏אם‎ (Ima), Mother. We saw that Elohim is the Mother of Creation, the

Mother of all living beings. The word אלהים (Elohim) did not tell this. But the second aspect reveals this. Now, we have mathematical proof that Elohim is the Mother of creation and of life. But what is mother? We seem to know what mother is; but this is only a surface knowledge. What really is mother? The real mother is a creator. The mother receives from the father the seeds which contain life in its primordial state, and creates out of that life a living being. This is what constitutes a mother. But how does the mother create out of a primordial state of life a living being? Between life in its primordial state and a living being there is an infinite process of creation and evolution. How does the mother accomplish this? For this purpose mother must be a creator. But with what can mother create? With what do we create things? We create things with the hand. The hand with the five fingers is the absolute basis of human intelligence, knowledge and understanding, and the absolute basis of all creation accomplished by man. Without the hand, man would remain a mere animal. The hand, is the mother of creation. The numerical value of אם (Eim) in the second aspect is 41; but 41 is not yet the lowest term. We must reduce it to a lower term. This we accomplish by reversing the order of the digits. Instead of 41, we shall get 14. Now, what does this number symbolize in the first aspect? It symbolizes the hand. The Hebrew word for hand is יד (Yod), and its numerical value is in both aspects 14. Why is the hand symbolized by the number 14? Because the hand consists of five fingers, and the five fingers consist of 14 phalanges. 14 is not yet the lowest term. The number 14 consists of 1 and 4. 1 and 4 are 5. Thus the hand is symbolized by 5, the number of fingers. That the five fingers may constitute a hand, they must cooperate with one another. It is only when the five fingers cooperate with one another do they constitute a hand, and then can create. Cooperation is the basis of all creation and progress. Cooperation brings out a power for creation, which without cooperation cannot be brought out. Man was called into existence to create a world for himself; and for this purpose man needed power to create. For this reason, man was given two hands. The numerical value of hand is 14; and the numerical value of two hands is twice 14, or 28. 28 is the numerical value of the word כח (Koach) power.

Introduction to the Kabbalah

61. The Bible tells us, in the first chapter of Genesis, that Elohim created the world: לעשות (La'asot), to be completed. Elohim performed the first stage in the process of creation: בריאה (Beriah) and part of the second stage of the process יצירה (Yetzirah); but the third and final stage of creation remained yet to be performed. The third and final stage is: עשיה (Asiyah) Elohim created the world on the basis of law; but the completion of the world required also mercy. Elohim is Law, Jehovah is Mercy. Hence in the next chapter of Genesis the Bible tells us that now both Jehovah [and] Elohim completed the world upon the basis of law and mercy. The completion of the world upon the basis of law and mercy is called: תיקון העולם (Tikkun Ha-Olam); it is the moral and spiritual completion of the world. The supreme purpose of God in creating the world was to bring into the world mankind who shall recognize, honor and love God, and honor and love one another. And this is the destiny of mankind. Mankind are destined to become rational, morally autonomous, recognize Jehovah as God, identify themselves with His will and purpose, to love and honor Jehovah, love and honor one another, live in peace and enjoy the good of the עץ החיים (Etz Ha-Hayyim), the tree of life. To realize this purpose, Jehovah chose the Jews—the first that recognized Jehovah, and who by this became the sons of Jehovah—to be the means through whom Jehovah will redeem the rest of mankind, so that like the Jews, they shall become the sons of Jehovah. This will be the Kingdom of Jehovah on earth.

Three times a day—morning, afternoon and evening—the Jews conclude their prayers (Alenu) as follows:

Therefore we hopefully look unto Thee, Jehovah our God, in the near future to see the Glory of Thy power; that all abominations shall be banished from the earth, and that all idols shall be utterly exterminated: לתקן עולם במלכות שדי (L'Tikkun Olam B'Malkhut Shaddai) to complete the world with the Kingdom of Shaddai; so that all dwellers on earth shall recognize and know that only unto Thee they shall submit, and only unto Thee they shall give honor and that all may assume the yoke of Thy Kingdom, and that Thou shalt reign over them forever. For the Kingdom is Thine, and wilt reign in glory forever. As it is written in Thy Torah: Jehovah will reign forever. In that day Jehovah will be One and His name will be One.

This is the תיקון העולם (Tikkun Ha-Olam). This is the purpose of God in creating the world. The supreme concern of the Kabbalah is this: תיקון העולם (Tikkun Ha-Olam). The Kabbalah reveals explicitly what is implicit in the Bible. Just as existence manifests itself in a phenomenal form which conceals the infinite and eternal nature of existence; so the Bible manifests a phenomenal form which conceals the infinite and eternal story of creation and destiny. Since an idea must precede the creation of anything, it is clear that in the very account of creation given by the Bible in the first chapter of Genesis there must also be contained the idea of the: תיקון העולם (Tikkun Ha-Olam). It is therefore our next task to consider this.

62. And, first, what is the: מלכות שדי (Malkhut Shaddai), the Kingdom of Shaddai? Why do the Jews hope that Jehovah will complete the world morally and spiritually with the Kingdom of Shaddai? This we will presently see. For this purpose, we must resort to the mathematical system.

The numerical value, in the second aspect, of the words: מלכות שדי (Malkut Shaddai) is 99; and 99 is the numerical value, in the second aspect, of the words עולם עשיה (Olam Asiyah), the world of completion; and 99 is also the numerical value, in the second aspect, of the words: שם יהוה אלהים

(Shem Adonai Elohim), the name of Jehovah thy God. The name of Jehovah becomes manifest in the completed world, in the עולם עשיה (Olam Asiyah).

Next, the above prayer speaks of במלכות שדי (B'Malkut Shaddai) with the Kingdom of Shaddai. The numerical value of the words: במלכות שדי (B'Malkut Shaddai), in the second aspect, is 101; and 101 is the numerical value, in the second aspect of the words: אנכי יהוה אלהיך (Anochi Adonai Eloheha) I Jehovah am thy God. Since the Jews attained to the recognition of Jehovah, they became the sons of Jehovah, and through them Jehovah completes the world morally and spiritually. Again, 101 is the numerical value of: בינה ומלכות (Binah V'Malkut). We saw that בינה (Binah) is the second sephiroh, it is Elohim: and מלכות (Malkut) is the tenth sephiroh, it is the earth and all that dwell on the earth, where the Kingdom of Jehovah will be realized. We saw that originally both these sephiroth were one; they were separated, and their destiny is to become reunited and become like חכמה (Hochmah), the first sephiroh. This means that the earth and all that dwell on it will become rational and morally autonomous, for בינה (Binah) is Reason, and the Mother of all creation.

And now let us consider the whole statement: לתקן עולם במלכות שדי (L'Tikkun Olam B'Malkut Shaddai). The numerical value of the whole statement, in the second aspect, is 215; and 215 is the numerical value of the following words: נעשה אדם בצלמנו כדמותנו (Na'aseh Adam B'tsalmaynu Kidmutaynu). Let us make man in our צלם (Zelem) and as our דמות (Demut). Great scholars tried to determine the meaning of these two words: צלם ודמת (Zelem V'Demut), but they failed. When we come to the study of the Bible we shall consider the meaning of these two terms. For our present purpose, we must consider the following. Elohim began with the statement נעשה אדם בצלמנו כדמותנו (Na'aseh Adam B'tsalmaynu Kidmutaynu). Let us make man in our צלם (Zelem) and as our דמות (Demut). And right in the next sentence the

Bible tells us: Vayivrah Elohim Et Ha-Adam B'tsalmo
B'tselem Elohim Bara Ohto, בצלם, בצלמו האדם את אלהים ויברא.
אתו ברא אלהים Elohim *created* the man in the אלהים צלם (Zelem
Elohim). What became of the דמות (Demut)?

And now turn to Genesis: 5, 1. Here the Bible tells us
the following: אתו עשה אלהים בדמות אדם אלהים ברא ביום (B'Yom
B'ro Elohim Adam B'demut Elohim Bara Ohto). In the day
that Elohim *created* man, He *made* man in the אלהים דמות
(Demut Elohim). It is thus clear that, in the first instance,
man was *created*, but not yet completed. Man will become
completed when he will be *made* in the אלהים דמות (Demut
Elohim). The *making* of man in the אלהים דמות (Demut Elohim) this is the העולם תיקון (Tikkun Ha-Olam), the completion
of the world.

And now take the whole statement: שדי במלכות עולם לתקן
(L'Tikkun Olam B'Malkut Shaddai), to complete the world
with the Kingdom of Shaddai. The numerical value, in the
second aspect, of this whole statement is 215: and 215 is the
numerical value, in the second aspect, of the words: נעשה
כדמותנו בצלמנו אדם (Na'aseh Adam B'tsalmaynu Kidmutaynu).
Let us *make* man in our צלם (Zelem) and as our דמות
(Demut). This was the primordial idea of God, to realize
which He created the world. Thus right in the very *creation*
of man, his destiny was already announced.

The foregoing gives an idea what the Kabbalah is and
what it teaches. The Kabbalah is not merely a philosophy of
existence. No philosophy crystallized by all the philosophers
that lived, put together, contain a fraction of what the Kabbalah reveals; but the supreme aim of the Kabbalah is the
העולם תיקון (Tikkun Ha-Olam). The idea of the העולם תיקון
(Tikkun Ha-Olam) is not merely a wish; it is the intellectual
perception of the supreme purpose of God in creating the
world and mankind. Such intellectual perception was attained only by Moses and the Prophets. And it is the task of
the Kabbalah to make manifest what Moses and the Prophets had intellectually perceived.

*

Yehuda Ashlag (1886–1955)

Ashlag was born in Warsaw and emigrated to Palestine in 1920. He wrote numerous kabbalistic texts, including works on Vital's *Etz Hayyim* and the *Zohar*. Following is an excerpt from his work *An Entrance to the Zohar*, edited by Philip S. Berg.

AN ENTRANCE TO THE ZOHAR

Chapter 2
Purpose of Creation

The best way of understanding all these questions and inquiries would be to consider the ultimate objective of the action, I mean by that, the purpose of the Creation. For it is impossible to understand anything while it is still being made, but only after it has been completed. It is quite obvious we are not dealing here with actions that were committed without any purpose, for only unbalanced minds act without any purpose. Now I know that there are some would-be scholars, who have thrown off the yoke of the Torah and of its Commandments, who claim that the Creator created the world and then abandoned it to its fate. The reason for this, they say, is that it does not befit the Creator in all His Exaltedness, to watch over their petty and despicable ways. However, the claim that they put forward is not based on knowledge, for it is not possible to decide that we are base and worthless unless we decide that it is we who created our own selves together with all these imperfect and despicable characteristics that we possess. But when we decide that the Almighty Creator, in His Supreme Perfection, is the craftsman who created and designed our bodies with all their good and bad tendencies, then it follows that no bad or contemptible or imperfect work could ever leave

the hands of a perfect craftsman, but rather every single
piece of work will be evidence of the high quality of its
maker. Is it the fault of a ruined coat if it has been made by
an inept tailor? A similar idea is expressed in a story related
in the Talmud (*Ta'anit*, 20): "It happened once that Rabbi
Eliezer, son of Rabbi Shimon, met by chance a man who was
extremely ugly . . . and he said to him: 'How ugly this man
is!' . . . He replied 'Go and say to the craftsman who made
me: How ugly is this vessel which You have made!'"

Therefore those would-be scholars who say that because of
our baseness and worthlessness, it does not befit the Almighty to watch over us and so He has abandoned us, are
merely proclaiming their own ignorance. Imagine meeting
a man to whom it had occurred to create creatures with the
intention at the very outset that they should be tortured and
made to suffer all their lives just like us, and then after that
he decided to fling them behind his back without any desire
at all to watch over them, or help them even a little. How
deeply would you censure and despise him! Is it then possible to conceive of such an idea applying to the Almighty
Who brought all being into existence?

Common sense demands that we should understand the
opposite of what is superficially apparent. And we should
decide that we are really such good and exalted creatures
that there is no limit to our importance, which is exactly as
befits the craftsman who made us. For all the short-comings
and defects that you may care to think up about our bodies,
even after you have answered them all away, are still only to
be related to their Creator who created us together with all
our inherent natural characteristics. It is clear that it is He
who made us and not we ourselves, and that He also knew of
all the consequences which would continue to result from all
the characteristics and evil tendencies that He implanted in
us. However, as we have said, we must look at the ultimate
objective of the action, and then we will be able to understand everything. There is a well-known proverb that goes
"Do not show a fool a job half-done."

Our Sages of blessed memory taught us (Etz Hayyim, the

section on vessels, at the beginning of the first chapter), that
the Holy One, Blessed be He, created the world only to give
pleasure to those whom He created. So it is in this direction
that we should concentrate all our attention, for this is the
ultimate intention and purpose of the creation of the universe. Consider this: since the Thought of Creation was to
give pleasure to those whom He created, it follows that He
created within the Souls a very large measure of the "will to
receive" that which He thought to give them. For the
amount of any enjoyment and pleasure is measured by the
amount of the "will to receive" them. The greater the "will to
receive" is, the greater the pleasure will be, and the less the
"will to receive" is, the amount of pleasure taken in receiving will also be proportionately less. And so the actual
Thought of Creation necessarily requires the creation
within the Souls (*Neshamot*) of an extremely large amount
of the "will to receive" which would be appropriate for the
large amount of pleasure which the Almighty thought of
giving to the Souls. For tremendous enjoyment and a large
"will to receive" go hand in hand.

When we know this, we will then be able to fully understand our second inquiry. We wanted to know what there
was that did not exist at all in the Essence of the Almighty,
but could be called a completely "new" creation of something from something non-existent. But now we know quite
clearly that God's Thought of Creation, whose whole purpose
was to give enjoyment to those He created, created out of
necessity the "will to receive" from Him all the goodness and
pleasantness that He thought for them. Obviously this "will
to receive" was not contained in the Essence of the Almighty
before He created it in the souls, for from whom could He
have received anything? Therefore He created something
completely "new" that was not contained within Him. In
addition to this, it is clear that in accordance with the
Thought of Creation there was no need at all to actually
create more than this "will to receive," for this "new" creation was sufficient means through which the Almighty
could fulfil the entire Thought of Creation, which was to

give us enjoyment. All that was contained in the Thought of Creation, namely all those benefits that He thought for us, proceed directly from the Essence of the Almighty, therefore there is no need at all to create them anew, since they proceed as substances created from other substances already in existence, to the large "will to receive" that is within the soul. It should now be absolutely clear to us that the "will to receive" was the only substance in the entire creation, from beginning to end, that was actually created as something new.

*

Isadore Epstein (1894–1962)

Epstein was born in Kovno, Lithuania. In 1911 he moved to England and became a rabbi and scholar. Epstein was a lecturer and librarian at Jews' College in London. Between 1935 and 1952 he was editor of the English translation of the Talmud by the Soncino Press. Following are multiple excerpts from Chapter 12 of Epstein's book, *The Faith of Judaism*.

THE FAITH OF JUDAISM

Chapter XII
Divine Purpose in Creation

Judaism, as we have seen, emphasises its particular doctrine of creation, not because of the doctrine itself, but because of its tremendous practical consequences. The doctrine of creation as taught by Judaism preserves, as has been shown, alike the freedom and the transcendence of God, the denial of which would involve the rejection of the whole Torah.

But there is another practical consequence which makes this doctrine fundamental to Judaism. In the Jewish doc-

trine of creation, as already stated, there is no real distinction between God's creation of the world and His preservation of it. Both are aspects of His creative activity. The same
divine activity which brought the world into existence preserves it from collapsing into non-being. God's concern with
the world is not to be thought of as relating merely to the
provision of the world with its initial impulse to come into
being, but as an incessant and intimate care for the beings to
which God has given all they have and all they are. This is
the truth which the Bible is never tired of asserting. 'I have
graven thee upon the palms of my hands' (Isaiah 49:16). 'He
hangeth the earth upon nothing' (Job 26:7), and it is a truth
which forms the theme of that grand Nature Hymn, the
104th Psalm. This universal teaching of the Bible is equally
confirmed by the Talmudic Sages: 'God created and He
provides; He made and He sustains'; and the Jew affirms
this, his faith in God's sustenance and maintenance of existence, daily in his prayers, in the words: 'He reneweth daily
the work of the Beginning.' Were God for a single moment to
withdraw His providence the whole of existence would col-
lapse into non-being. 'Thou hidest Thy face, they are con-
founded' (Psalm 104:29). Thus are excluded not only all
pantheistic doctrines that would seek to confuse God with
Nature, but also the notion of an absentee God, so fashion-
able in a past age, under the name of Deism—a notion which
would conceive God's relation to the world as that of a
watchmaker to a watch which he has constructed and
which, having been set going, continues to function for some
time, at any rate without any need for the continued presence or attention of its maker.

This belief in God's preservation of the world is a natural
corollary to the Jewish doctrine of creation. The idea of
'creation out of nothing' (as explained) carries with it inevitably the idea that the world depends on God's immediate
will and power for its existence. This close connection between the two notions has been well brought out by Rabbi
Shneur Zalman Ladier (1747–1812), the famous Chassidic
teacher and leader, in his classic work, 'Tanya.' There he

points out the error of those who would compare the work of
God, the maker of heaven and earth, to the doings of man,
and imagine 'that just as a vessel emerging from the smith
does not require any more the attention of its maker, but is
able to retain its shape and form even after he withdraws his
hand from it, so, these fools think, it is with the work of God.
But their eyes are shut and they are unable to see the great
difference which exists between the work of man, who
merely makes something out of something else (as for example when a smith makes from a bar of silver the form of a
vessel), and the creative act of God, which brought something into being out of nothing . . . and that consequently the
withdrawal of the power of the Creator can only result in
the creature relapsing into nothing. Thus must the power of
the Creator remain indispensable for the continued existence and being of the creation.'

The relationship between God and the world, both as its
Creator and Preserver, lays the foundation for the Biblical
emphasis upon the significance of human existence and
human life. Contrary to the notion that human life is meaningless, because it is shaped by blind forces, and that man is
a puny and helpless creature because he is dependent entirely upon a physical organism, Judaism affirms the creative and life-giving action of an Eternal Spirit, Who is ever
at work in His Universe, guiding the whole of human existence towards the fulfilment of a purpose that has been with
Him from the very beginning, for the individual, the nation
and the human race.

The conception of divine purpose constitutes the essential
nature of the religion which Israel gave to the world. Af-
firming the existence of a Divine Sovereign behind the
scheme of things, it discerns in the events of the day the unfolding of a divine process directed towards a goal. The full
scope of the divine purpose has never been claimed to be
comprehensible to our state of human knowledge; but that
such a purpose exists and that it is being worked out
through the domain of human existence has ever been a
fundamental principle of Judaism.

'Of all things the Holy One, blessed be He, created in His world, He did not create a single thing for no purpose,' declared our Rabbis (*Shabbat* 77b). Similarly Maimonides in his *Guide* writes, 'No intelligent person can assume that any action of God can be in vain and purposeless. . . . According to our view,' he continues, 'and the view of all that follow the Torah, all actions of God are exceedingly good: "And God saw everything that he had made, and behold, it was very good"' (Genesis 1:31).

Elsewhere in chapter 13 of the same book, Maimonides quotes the verse from the Proverbs 16:4: '"Everything that the Lord made is for Himself"—that is, for His purpose.'

. . .

But although the knowledge of the full significance of the divine purpose has not been given to man, we can discern part of this purpose in studying man. Made in the image of God, man, as we have seen, is possessed of unique attributes that are divine—reason, freedom, creativeness and moral goodness. And these attributes were not bestowed on man in vain, but in order to enable him to participate in the work of God. Thus it is that Judaism conceives the relation of man to God as that of a *Shuttaf* (a co-worker), co-operating with God in the fulfilment of His purpose.

The beginning of this co-operation is clearly indicated in Genesis. There we see God's creative power calling the world and man into existence under the figure of a brooding bird seeking to bring into being the promise of life beneath its wings. But the creative process does not end when the world and man have been created. That which had been created had to be maintained, developed and fostered. 'God established the earth, He created it not in vain, He formed it to be inhabited' (Isaiah 45:18).

This task was entrusted to man. Adam, the first man, is described as a self-active, labouring and creative being, charged by the Divine Creator to develop the resources and the potential wealth of the earth which had come to him as a

gift from God. In the words of the *Zohar Hadash*, 'God said
to Adam, Hitherto I alone was engaged in the work; hence-
forth you (also) must work.' And so every man, in his own
way, must work, must create. Made in the image of God, he
must make God's standards his own; and because God
creates, he, too, must work and co-operate with Him in
developing the world which has been committed to his care.
'A man', declared our Sages, 'is in duty bound to love work
and occupy himself with work, which God calls His own, as
it is said, God rested from all His work which He did' (*Aboth*
de Rabbi Nathan 21). If man fails to exercise these creative
powers, the wrath of God manifests itself against him by
causing him to lose them. In the physical organism, neglect
of functions results in decline and final atrophy, and the
same law operates in the world order over which man has
been placed in charge. To refuse to work is to forfeit the
blessing of God. 'For the Lord has blessed thee in all the
work of thy hands' (Deuteronomy 2:7)—'If man does work',
comments the Midrash, 'he receives the Divine blessing; if
not he loses it.' Significant in this connection is the Midrashic passage: 'When Abraham was travelling through Aram
Naharaim and Aram Nahor, he saw its inhabitants eating
and drinking and revelling, and he exclaimed: "May my
portion not be in this country." But when he reached the
promontory of Tyre and saw them engaged in weeding and
hoeing at the proper seasons, he exclaimed: "Would that my
portion might be in this country"' (Genesis *Rabbah* 39:9).
Still more significant is the passage in the Jerusalem Talmud: 'Great is work, for the generation of the Flood was
destroyed only because of robbery, whereas a workman may
perform work and is exempt from the law of robbery'
(*Maaserot* 2:6)—an allusion to the Biblical law which permits the labourer to eat of the produce on which he happens
to be engaged (Deuteronomy 23:25–26).

The implication of this passage is that the nation or society which destroys the principle of creativeness or productivity brings about its own dissolution and destruction.

God's attribute of creativeness is allied to His attribute of
goodness. His creative activity springs from His character
of goodness, of which His tenderlove, grace (*hesed*), is the
highest expression. God, as the Torah describes Him (Exodus 34:6; Numbers 14:18), is 'full of tenderlove' (*rab hesed*).
The world, in Jewish thought, was created in response to
divine tenderlove: '*Olam hesed yibbaneh.*' The tenderlove of
the Lord, according to the Psalmist, fills the earth (Psalm
33:5); and it is this divine tenderlove with which, in the
words of the Jew's thrice-repeated daily prayers, 'God sustains the living.' Here, too, the attributes of God are to serve
as a pattern for man. True human creativeness, like the
creativeness of God, must be allied to goodness, otherwise
creativeness ends in destruction, of which the atomic bomb
is the latest manifestation. It is this conformity with the
character of the creative activity of God, this obedience to
Him, which lies at the basis of man's creative co-operation
with Him. Without obedience to God, the human creative
effort is bound to end in frustration and failure. This lesson
too is already taught in Genesis. By reason of disobedience to
God, Adam, we read, is cast out of the Garden, to toil by the
sweat of his brow to subdue a thankless soil, which often
rewarded him with nothing but thorns and thistles. But this
is only the beginning of the sad story of human misery.
Disobedience and sin that parted man from God end in
parting man from man. Adam disobeyed the command of
God, and his son, under the sway of a grasping and domi-
neering spirit, disregards his brother's rights and kills him.
The same story is repeated in the generations that follow.
Human arrogance erects high towers for the glorification of
self and in defiance of God, and the design fails, with disas-
trous effects. Society is torn asunder by discord, dissension
and strife, and human unity is broken up into a number of
diverse and warring classes and nations speaking different
languages and thinking different thoughts.

Coming down to our own times, we have witnessed the
repetition of the same old story, but on a larger and more

tragic scale. Modern trade and industry, in pursuit of material wealth and power, have been dominated too much by selfish interests to be concerned with principles of right and wrong. Thus has human creative activity been perverted from the divine purpose which was to inspire it, and become the source of universal discord, ruin and death.

Creativeness and goodness are thus essential elements in the divine purpose, which is dependent for its fulfilment on man's co-operation; and Man, selected by God to be His agent, is called upon to co-operate with Him in the work of creative goodness.

. . .

This principle of co-operation has its parallel in the world of nature. The seed produces fruit only when it falls into good ground, that is, into ground which has been prepared, and so is receptive and able to contribute its own dynamic quality to the creative end which is the purpose of the union. Here we see the soil is as important as the seed. Neither is complete without the other. The preparation of the ground is thus the essential contribution which human effort must make towards the fruitfulness of the seed. In the same way, it is man's active co-operation which conditions the fulfilment of God's purpose of creative goodness in His work.

This idea of the need of human co-operation for the realisation of divine purpose in terms of creative goodness has much bearing on the problem of evil. When we consider the age-long process of creation as disclosed by modern science, we may well shrink back in horror. The Creator who made the world so beautiful has not made it good. There is indeed goodness among men, but it is always imperfect and, side by side with it, there is evil without end—lust, cruelty, selfishness, greed and treachery. Is then God who made the world so beautiful careless of the happiness of His creatures and regardless of the sin and crime which darkens human lives? If not, why is the world so full of evil?

The conception of the need of human co-operation helps us

to answer the question briefly in this way. God made the world beautiful, because He loves the beautiful and can produce it without the intervention and co-operation of man. He has not made the world wholly good because goodness can only come about through the co-operation of men with one another and with God. Goodness cannot be produced by compulsion. It must be the free offering of the will, recognising the laws of goodness and yielding to it. Goodness throughout the Universe is impossible, apart from the willing denial of selfish inclinations on the part of the individuals who form its social content. It takes man as well as God to make the world good. To have the world uniformly good would have meant to deprive man of his free will, which is his glory and distinction. The freedom to choose good involves the freedom to do evil. This freedom meant the coming into existence of a countless multitude of individuals in competition with one another, each striving towards the realisation of its own potentialities, and thus common life became inevitably a struggle with pain, disappointment and slaughter. The struggle for existence, the sacrifice of one another—all became inevitable. Yet these elements became the means of an upward movement towards higher forms of life and therefore towards the full realisation of the purpose of God. While we are no nearer comprehending why this should be the nature of existence, there is no longer any initial contradiction between divine power and divine goodness. If the world waits upon man's co-operation for its perfection, the evil we see in it is all due to the absence of man's share in this co-operative work with God; and the question why God did not make the world uniformly good becomes as little perplexing as the question why He did not make loaves to grow out of the earth, and why He did not equip the world with engines, motor-cars and wireless-sets. It is all a question of co-operation, which is basic to all creative activity, whether in the domain of physical nature or of moral endeavour. And it is only when every individual being in the Universe will participate in this co-operation, with all it implies of willing self-denial and self-surrender, that the world will become good as it is beautiful.

At the basis of the co-operation in creative goodness is the harmony which must exist between God and man and between man and his fellow-man, as partners in this co-operative work. Harmony involves the perfect co-ordination of the parts which together make up the whole. Failure in such co-ordination in the physical world means friction, jarring and ultimate breakdown; in the spiritual world it means discord, strife and destruction. Harmony is therefore an essential element in that process of fulfilment in which man has been charged to co-operate.

. . .

'The Lord of Hosts hath spoken, who shall annul it?' (Isaiah 14:27). Human beings must at all costs learn to co-operate with one another and with God. If human obduracy of heart and obstinacy of will bar the way, there are divine judgments that now and then are made manifest in the form of visitations of diverse sorts, from wars to social upheavals, to teach mankind the lessons of co-operation and righteousness. 'For when thy judgments are on earth, the inhabitants of the world learn righteousness' (Isaiah 26:9). And these visitations will recur over and over again until mankind shall have at long last taken well this lesson to heart. If, after six years of 'blood, sweat and tears,' which this generation has passed through, mankind still refuses to co-operate with God's righteous purpose and the world continues to be torn, distracted, and bewildered, with passions of hatred and cruelty raging unchecked in so many places—what else is mankind to expect, but another manifestation of divine judgment, in the form of a much more cruel and more devastating war, upon their apostasy from Him? Yet, the world is safe in the hands of God, who, as Creator, will not allow it to drift to shipwreck and irremediable ruin; and, no matter how much it might 'zigzag', God will surely bring it home at last in fulfilment of His righteous purpose for His creation.

*

Joshua Adler (ND)

Joshua Adler was the author of a work entitled *A Philosophy of Judaism*, published by Philosophical Library. Like many other writers, Adler contends it is impossible to comprehend the purpose of creation. Unfortunately, no biographical background was available on this writer.

A PHILOSOPHY OF JUDAISM

This section is written only to pacify those who crave diligently to find the reason for creation, and to show the limitations of inquiry into this field. The answer to the first will demonstrate the second.

Man cannot find the goal in nature. Nature and its equilibrium of action can have no ulterior motive. It cannot state what is accomplished in its incessant movement of diversified functions. Nature can at best be explained to the human mind as means towards an end. The means is not a very docile functioning and certainly demands much attention. But when the analysis thereof reaches into crucial stages one can find nothing more to say about nature except that it is what it is.

Our goal can only be in something which is above nature and not subject to its meaninglessness. It cannot be either ephemeral, or multilateral or contradictory in its fulfillment. It must contain eternalness, unitedness and infiniteness in order to be a destination which will satisfy the human spiritual drive. It is within this context that man seeks to solidify his diversified knowledge and seeks a monolithic substance which is at the foundation of all other knowledge. He seeks therein to establish the identity of the truly unified and infinite existence which is not to be found within nature. He seeks to grasp the eternal fountainhead and to become connected with it.

Only in these terms can we begin to secure insight into the true goals of human existence. The ultimate answer to this question must remain one based upon our experiences and our extant insights. The goal of the human being is to fulfill the potentialities given to him in creation. This is his raison d'etre as indeed it is of the rest of creation. What we can do to extend this statement is only to clarify how and what are man's potentialities and what are his capabilities. From our survey of man's intentions and from a survey of the creation narrative we came to a similar conclusion. That man is the product of two distinct and mutually divergent tendencies; that his need is for fulfillment within both; that this can only be accomplished if he uses his own potentialities in each field correctly; and that it becomes necessary for the maintenance of a complete being for man at times to limit some of his excessive natural drives.

Within this formula, man's amount of possible fulfillment remains manifold. For me to attempt to delimit what areas constitute spiritual success and which segments of existence are for natural accomplishments would be to set finite limits on infinite phenomena. For man has the infinite stretches of all creation to manipulate within. Thus wherever and whenever he touches infinite universality and transcends his own finite existence he is fulfilling his creative abilities. When he lives within his nature and does not become overwhelmed thereby, becoming an animal of drives worse than any other animal, he is also fulfilling his Divinely given attributes. This is the sum total of our explanation of the goal.

It is always possible to find some who will not be satisfied with such an explanation. They ask the question, Why creation? What is the purpose for having created a world with all its responsibilities? To this we must admonish that it is an illicit inquiry. We cannot attempt to comprehend the "Why of Creation." Several important reasons are within the possi-

bility of one to present for this fact. In the first place it is not
possible to enlighten thereupon since the Divine has not
given us the reason. In the final summation it remains for
the Divine to state what his intention is and not for us to
impose our various theories, and as far as one can surmise, it
has not been revealed. For a second point we must state that
we could not possibly apprehend an explanation, for it
would necessarily entail an understanding of what is non-
creation; or shall we say what did not exist before existence
came into being. This is logically beyond our possibilities for
we ourselves are part of existence and that which exists
cannot understand that which doesn't exist. It is quite analogous to the problem of demonstrating fire to a fish. The fish
cannot grasp the concept since he has no possibility of both
witnessing fire and remaining alive. We, in our own right,
have no possibility of witnessing non-existence and remaining alive. We, however, at times feel that if our spiritual
faculties were well used we could answer this question to
our contentment and then the above logical impasse would
be beyond that which we seek. Here we arrive at still
another reason for our inability to respond to the question,
why creation. This is that that explanation would entail at
least a possibility to transcend our material being. Since this
still remains an impracticality, and our material existence
would countermand the singleness which such an explanation would imply, we cannot even grasp such a definition of
the why of creation, if it were offered. We cannot remain
corporeal entities and attempt to deal with non-corporeal
ideas at the same instant. The answer in natural terms can
only be in relation to fulfillment of function. In spiritual
terms it may be more satisfactory, but it cannot be dealt
with in these terms while we maintain our natural being
which contradicts the spiritual terms of unity.

Some once explained the task of the philosopher within
the analogy of a puppet show. He said that most people see
the movement of the puppets, but cannot know how they
operate. The philosopher walks around the curtains to the

posterior of the show and seeks to uncover and explain the process of how the puppets operate. Why the puppets exist, however, he cannot explicate. This is all that we have been able to accomplish here. The logical impasse is not a small one, and is in my opinion the true reason for the illegality of this question. Even the other reasons at best give possibility for an answer only after one's physical demise from the earth. If that is so then we must be thereto resigned.

We have attempted to bring the world of the Biblical creation tale into comprehension within the terminology of modern man. The reinterpretation of this segment of the Jewish consciousness leads to a concurrence of similar ideas and concepts in both. It also leads, in my opinion, to a more adequate explanation of the meaning of that much perplexing opening section of the Bible.

*

Menachem Mendel Schneerson (1902–   )

Schneerson is from a family of chasidic leaders and is a descendant of Schneur Zalman of Lyady. He was born in Russia, moved to Warsaw in 1929, and later studied in Paris. In 1941, he moved to New York, and three years later became the head of the Kehot publishing house. Schneerson became the leader of Chabad upon the death of his father-in-law in 1950. The Rebbe, as he is universally known, has devoted himself to the development of the kabbalistic philosophy of Chabad Hasidism and the spreading of Jewish learning throughout the world. Following is Schneerson's preface to *Tanya*, and two pieces of correspondence from *Letters by the Lubavitcher Rebbe*.

TANYA

Preface by the Lubavitcher Rabbi שליט״א

Chassidus in general, and Chabad Chassidus in particular, is an all-embracing world outlook and way of life which sees the Jew's central purpose as the unifying link between the Creator and Creation. The Jew is a creature of "heaven" and of "earth," of a heavenly Divine soul, which is truly a part of Godliness, clothed in an earthly vessel constituted of a physical body and animal soul, whose purpose is to realize the transcendency and unity of his nature, and of the world in which he lives, within the absolute Unity of God.

The realization of this purpose entails a two-way correlation: one in the direction from above downward to earth; the other, from the earth upward. In fulfillment of the first, man draws holiness from the Divinely-given Torah and commandments, to permeate therewith every phase of his daily life and his environment—his "share" in this world; in fulfillment of the second, man draws upon all the resources at his disposal, both created and man-made, as vehicles for his personal ascendancy and, with him, that of the surrounding world. One of these basic resources is the vehicle of human language and communication.

As the Alter Rebbe, author of *Tanya*, pointed out in one of his other works, any of the "seventy tongues" when used as an instrument to disseminate the Torah and Mitzvoth, is itself "elevated" thereby from its earthly domain in the sphere of holiness, while at the same time serving as the vehicle to draw the Torah and Mitzvoth, from above downward, to those who read and understand this language.

LETTERS BY
THE LUBAVITCHER REBBE שליט״א

By the Grace of God
First Day of Selichoth
5713. Brooklyn, N.Y.

To my brethren, everywhere
God bless you all

Greeting and Blessing:

On the threshold of the New Year, may it bring blessings to us all, I send you my prayerful wishes for a good and pleasant year, materially and spiritually.

Rosh Hashanah marks the beginning of a new year—5714—since the Creation, a new date in the cycle of time, and everyone hopes and prays that it will also be the beginning of a new era in one's personal life, one that is "good and sweet" materially and spiritually.

It is significant that the anniversary of the Creation is not celebrated on the first day of Creation, but on the sixth, the day when Man was created. Although all other living things making up our vast universe—the inanimate, vegetable and living creatures—preceded the creation of Man, as is related in the Torah, in the first chapter of Genesis, nevertheless it is on the anniversary of Man's creation that we celebrate Rosh Hashanah, and on this day we say, "This is the day of the beginning of Thy works!"

Herein lies a profound lesson for every one of us:

Man, the microcosm ("small world") contains within him all the "Four Kingdoms" into which the macrocosm, the universe at large, is divided. In the course of his life man passes through the stages of inanimate, vegetable and animated existence until he reaches maturity and begins to live a rational and spiritual life of a human being. Even then, in his daily life, he may experience a varied existence, as reflected in his deeds and actions: Part of the time he may be regarded in the category of the inanimate; at other times he may vegetate, or live an animated existence; but a true human being he is when his activities give evidence of his intellect and spiritual qualities. Moreover, the name "man" is justified only then, when also those areas of one's life and activities which correspond to the animal, vegetable and even inanimate "kingdoms" are sublimated, elevated and sanctified to the level of human quality.

Rosh Hashanah, and the Ten Days of Repentance introducing the new year, is the time for self evaluation and mature reflection on the profound lessons of these solemn days:

Just as the world, *all* the world, begins its true existence, an existence befitting the purpose of its creation, from the day Man was created, who immediately after coming to life proclaimed the sovereignty of the Creator to all the universe: "Come, let us worship, let us bow down and kneel before God our Maker" inspiring the whole universe with this call (Zohar I, 221b; Pirkei d'Rabbi Elazar, ch. 11), thereby making all the universe an abode for the Divine Presence and carrying out the inner purpose of the Creation.

So each and every individual must realize that his whole essence and purpose consists in the predominance of the true human element of his being and the 'humanization' of the inanimate, vegetable and animal parts of which he is composed. It is not enough, not enough at all, if part of his time and effort correspond to the behavior of a true human being; it is absolutely necessary that the "man" should inspire, sublimate, elevate and sanctify all his component parts, including the animal, vegetable and inanimate, in order that they too, respond to the call, "come, let us worship, let us bow down and kneel before God, our Maker." Such a life in accordance with the commands of the Creator, a life in accordance with the Torah and Mitzvoth which

God, our Maker, has given us, and only such a life, justifies one's own existence, and justifies thereby also the Creation.

With the traditional blessing of Kesivo VaChasimo Toivo

I remain
Cordially yours,
/signed: *Menachem M. Schneerson*/

By the Grace of God
In the Days of Selichos
5715. Brooklyn, N.Y.

To the Sons and Daughters
of our people Israel, Everywhere,
God bless you

Greetings and Blessing:

On the eve of Rosh Hashanah I extend my prayerful wishes to my brethren, every Jew and Jewess in the midst of our people Israel, the time hallowed traditional blessing of "Shono toivo umesuko"—a good and sweet year.

The celebration of Rosh Hashanah, the beginning of the year, has been ordained by our Torah to take place on the anniversary of the Creation, but not on the first day of Creation. It has been made to coincide with the sixth day of Creation, the day when Man was created.

The significance of this day, and of this event, is not in the fact that a new creature was added to Creation, a creature one plane higher than the rest of the animal kingdom, as the animal is superior to plant, and plant to mineral.

The significance lies in the fact that the new creature— Man—was essentially *different* from the others.

For it was man who recognized the Creator in and through Creation, and, what is more, brought about the elevation of the entire Creation to that recognition and thus to the fulfillment of its Divine design and purpose.

Since such recognition and appreciation of the Creator is the ultimate purpose of the Creation.

* * *

One of the main distinguishing features which set Man apart from all other creatures, is the free choice of action which the Creator bestowed upon him.

Man can use this special Divine gift in two opposing directions. He may, God forbid, choose the way leading to self-destruction and the destruction of everything around him; or, he can choose the right way of life, which would elevate him and the Creation with him to the highest possible perfection.

And to help us recognize and choose the right path, we were given the Torah, which is Divine and eternal, hence, its teachings are valid for all times and in all places.

* * *

It is not possible for man to make his choice unaided, merely by virtue of his intellect, for the human intellect is limited. The intellect can only serve to discover and bring forth that inner absolute intuition and faith in things which lie beyond and above the realm of the intellect; the faith and intuition which are the heritage of every Jew, therewith to illuminate his entire being and to guide him in his daily living to a life inspired by Torah and Mitzvoth.

* * *

On Rosh Hashanah man stands not only before the Divine Judgment, but also before his own.

The verdict of his own judgment, with regard to the future, must be: that he takes upon himself to fulfill his duty, that is, to work for the fulfillment—in himself and in his surroundings—of the call:

"Come, let us worship, bow down and kneel before God our Maker", a call for absolute submission to God first sounded by the first man, Adam, on the day of his creation, on the first Rosh Hashanah.

This can be attained only through a life inspired and
guided by the Torah.

And that he must once and for all abandon the opposite
road, which can only lead to destruction and doom.

* * *

Let no one think: who am I and what am I to have such
tremendous powers of building or destruction.

For we have seen—to our sorrow—what even a small
quantity of matter can do in the way of destruction through
the release of atomic energy. If such power is concealed in a
small quantity of matter—for destructiveness, in denial of
the design and purpose of Creation, how much greater is the
creative power entrusted to every individual to work in harmony with the Divine purpose, for in this case one is also
given special abilities and opportunities by Divine Providence to attain the goal for which we have been created: the
realization of a world in which

"Each creature shall recognize that Thou didst create
him, and every breathing soul shall declare: 'God, the God of
Israel, is King, and His reign is supreme over all.'"

With the blessing of Kesivo vachasimo toivo,
/signed: *Menachem Schneerson*/

*

Abraham Joshua Heschel
(1907–1972)

Heschel was a United States scholar and philosopher.
He descended from a famous line of hasidic rabbis, and
earned a doctorate at the University of Berlin. In 1938,
he was deported by the Nazis to Poland and eventually
came to the United States via England. From 1940 to

1945 Heschel taught at Hebrew Union College in Cincin-
nati. Following this period he began teaching at the Jewish Theological Seminary of America in New York. Heschel wrote numerous books and articles, and was active
in the civil rights movement and the dialogue between
Jews and Christians. Heschel is considered one of the
greatest Jewish thinkers of this century. Following is an
excerpt from his work *Man Is Not Alone.*

MAN IS NOT ALONE

43 The People Israel

The Meaning of Jewish Existence

There is a high cost of living to be paid by a Jew. He has to
be exalted in order to be normal in a world that is neither
propitious for nor sympathetic to his survival. Some of us,
tired of sacrifice and exertion, often wonder: Is Jewish existence worth the price? Others are overcome with panic; they
are perplexed, and despair of recovery.

The meaning of Jewish existence, the major theme of any
Jewish philosophy, is baffling. To fit it into the framework of
personal intellectual predilections or current fashions of our
time would be a distortion. The claim of Israel must be
recognized *before* attempting an interpretation. As the
ocean is more than what we know about it, so Judaism
surpasses the content of all philosophies of it. We have not
invented it. We may accept or reject, but should not dis-
tort it.

It is as an individual that I am moved by an anxiety for
the meaning of my existence as a Jew. Yet when I begin to
ponder about it, my theme is not the problem of one Jew but
of all Jews. And the more deeply I probe, the more strongly I
realize the scope of the problem: It embraces not only the
Jews of the present but also those of the past and those of the
future, the meaning of Jewish existence in all ages.

What is at stake in our lives is more than the fate of one generation. In this moment *we*, the living, are Israel. The tasks begun by the patriarchs and prophets, and carried out by countless Jews of the past, are now entrusted to us. No other group has superseded them. We are the only channel of Jewish tradition, those who must save Judaism from oblivion, those who must hand over the entire past to the generations to come. We are either the last, the dying, Jews or else we are those who will give new life to our tradition. Rarely in our history has so much depended upon one generation. We will either forfeit or enrich the legacy of the ages.

Thinking Compatible with Our Destiny

Understanding Judaism cannot be attained in the comfort of playing a chess-game of theories. Only ideas that are meaningful to those who are steeped in misery may be accepted as principles by those who dwell in safety. In trying to understand Jewish existence a Jewish philosopher must look for agreement with the men of Sinai as well as with the people of Auschwitz.

We are the most challenged people under the sun. Our existence is either superfluous or indispensable to the world; it is either tragic or holy to be a Jew.

It is a matter of immense responsibility that we here and Jewish teachers everywhere have undertaken to instill in our youth the will to be Jews today, tomorrow and for ever and ever. Unless being a Jew is of absolute significance how can we justify the ultimate price which our people was often forced to pay throughout its history? To assess Judaism soberly and farsightedly is to establish it as a good to be preferred, if necessary, to any alternative which we may ever face.

The task of Jewish philosophy today, is not only to describe the essence but also to set forth the universal relevance of Judaism, the bearings of its demands upon the chance of man to remain human. Bringing to light the lonely splendor of Jewish thinking, conveying the taste of eternity

in our daily living is the greatest aid we can render to the
man of our time who has fallen so low that he is not even
capable of being ashamed of what happened in his days.

We were not born by mere chance as a by-product of a
migration of nations or in the obscurity of a primitive past.
God's vision of Israel came first and only then did we come
into the world. We were formed according to an intention
and for the sake of a purpose. Our souls tremble with the
echo of unforgettable experiences and with the sublime expectation of our own response. To be a Jew is to be committed to the experience of great ideas. The task of Jewish
philosophy is to formulate not only these ideas but also the
depth of the commitment in vivid, consistent thinking. The
task of Jewish philosophy is *to make our thinking compatible
with our destiny.*

Life appears dismal if not mirrored in what is more than
life. Nothing can be regarded as valuable unless assessed in
relation to something higher in value. Man's survival depends on the conviction that there is something that is worth
the price of life. It depends upon a sense of the supremacy of
what is lasting. That sense of conviction may be asleep, but
it awakens when challenged. In some people it lives as a
sporadic wish; in others it is a permanent concern.

What we have learned from Jewish history is that if a
man is not more than human then he is less than human.
Judaism is an attempt to prove that in order to be a man, you
have to be more than a man, that in order to be a people we
have to be more than a people. Israel was made to be a "holy
people." This is the essence of its dignity and the essence of
its merit. Judaism is a link to eternity, kinship with ultimate
reality.

A sense of contact with the ultimate dawns upon most
people when their self-reliance is swept away by violent
misery. Judaism is the attempt to instill in us that sense as
an everyday awareness. It leads us to regard injustice as a
metaphysical calamity, to sense the divine significance of
human happiness, to keep slightly above the twilight of the
self, enabling us to sense the eternal within the temporal.

We are endowed with the consciousness of being involved in a history that transcends time and its specious glories. We are taught to feel the knots of life in which the trivial is intertwined with the sublime. There is no end to our experience of the spiritual grandeur, of the divine earnestness of human life. Our blossoms may be crushed, but we are upheld by the faith that comes from the core of our roots. We are not deceived by the obvious, knowing that all delight is but a pretext for adding strength to that which is beyond joy and grief. We know that no hour is the last hour, that the world is more than the world.

Israel—A Spiritual Order

Why is our belonging to the Jewish people a sacred relation? Israel is a *spiritual order* in which the human and the ultimate, the natural and the holy enter a lasting covenant, in which kinship with God is not an aspiration but a reality of destiny. For us Jews there can be no fellowship with God without the fellowship with the people Israel. Abandoning Israel, we desert God.

Jewish existence is not only the adherence to particular doctrines and observances, but primarily the living *in* the spiritual order of the Jewish people, the living *in* the Jews of the past and *with* the Jews of the present. It is not only a certain quality in the souls of the individuals, but primarily the existence of the community of Israel. It is neither an experience nor a creed, neither the possession of psychic traits nor the acceptance of a theological doctrine, but the living in a holy dimension, in a spiritual order. Our share in holiness we acquire by living in the Jewish community. What we do as individuals is a trivial episode, what we attain as Israel causes us to grow into the infinite.

The meaning of history is to be a sanctuary in time, and every one of us has his part in the great ritual. The ultimate meaning of human deeds is not restricted to the life of him who does these deeds and to the particular moment in which they occur.

Religious living is not only a private concern. Our own life is a movement in the symphony of ages. We are taught to pray as well as to live in the first person plural. We do a mitsvah "in the name of all Israel." We act both as individuals and as the community of Israel. All generations are present, as it were, in every moment.

Israel is the tree, we are the leaves. It is the clinging to the stem that keeps us alive. There has perhaps never been more need of Judaism than in our time, a time in which many cherished hopes of humanity lie crushed. We should be pioneers as were our fathers three thousand years ago. The future of all men depends upon their realizing that the sense of holiness is as vital as health. By following the Jewish way of life we maintain that sense and preserve the light for mankind's future visions.

It is our destiny to live for what is more than ourselves. Our very existence is an unparalleled symbol of such aspiration. By being what we are, namely Jews, we mean more to mankind than by any particular service we may render.

We have faith in God and faith in Israel. Though some of its children have gone astray, Israel remains the mate of God. We cannot hate what God loves. Rabbi Aaron the Great used to say: "I wish I could love the greatest saint as the Lord loves the greatest rascal."

Israel exists not in order to be, but in order to cherish the vision of God. Our faith may be strained but our destiny is anchored to the ultimate. Who can establish the outcome of our history? Out of the wonder we came and into the wonder we shall return.

The Dignity of Israel

Belonging to Israel is in itself a spiritual act. It is utterly inconvenient to be a Jew. The very survival of our people is a *kiddush hashem*. We live in spite of peril. Our very existence is a refusal to surrender to normalcy, to security and comfort. Experts in assimilation, the Jews could have disappeared even before the names of modern nations were

known. Still we are patient and cherish the will to perpetu-
ate our essence.

We are Jews as we are men. The alternative to our existence as Jews is spiritual suicide, disappearance. It is *not* a
change into something else. Judaism has allies but not sub-
stitutes. Jewish faith consists of attachment to God, attachment to Torah, and attachment to Israel.

There is a unique association between the people and the
land of Israel. Even before Israel becomes a people, the land is
preordained for it. What we have witnessed in our own days is
a reminder of the power of God's mysterious promise to Abraham and a testimony to the fact that the people kept its
promise, "If I forget thee, O Jerusalem, let my right hand
wither" (Psalm 137:5). The Jew in whose heart the love of Zion
dies is doomed to lose his faith in the God of Abraham who
gave the land as an earnest of the redemption of all men.

The people of Israel groaned in distress. Out of Egypt, the
land of plentiful food, they were driven into the wilderness.
Their souls were dried away; there was nothing at all: no
flesh to eat, no water to drink. All they had was a promise: to
be led to the land of milk and honey. They were almost ready
to stone Moses. "Wherefore hast thou brought us up out of
Egypt, to kill us and our children and our cattle with
thirst?" they cried. But, after they had worshipped the
golden calf—when God had decided to detach Himself from
His people, not to dwell any more in their midst, but to
entrust an angel with the task of leading them out of the
wilderness to the Promised Land—Moses exclaimed: "If
Thou Thyself dost not go with us, take us not out of the
wilderness" (Exodus 33:15). This perhaps, is the secret of
our history: *to choose to remain in the wilderness rather than
to be abandoned by Him.*

Israel's experience of God has not evolved from search.
Israel did not discover God. Israel was discovered by God.
Judaism is *God's quest for man.* The Bible is a record of
God's approach to His people. More statements are found in
the Bible about God's love for Israel than about Israel's love
for God.

We have not chosen God; He has chosen us. There is no concept of a chosen God but there is the idea of a chosen people. The idea of a chosen people does not suggest the preference for a people based upon a discrimination among a number of peoples. We do not say that we are a superior people. The "chosen people" means a people approached and chosen by God. The significance of this term is genuine in relation to God rather than in relation to other peoples. It signifies not a quality inherent in the people but a relationship between the people and God.

Harassed, pursued with enmity and wrong, our fathers continued to feel joy in being Jews. "Happy are we. How good is our destiny, how pleasant our lot, how beautiful our heritage." What is the source of that feeling?

The quest for immortality is common to all men. To most of them the vexing question points to the future. Jews think not only of the end but also of the beginning. As parts of Israel we are endowed with a very rare, a very precious consciousness, the consciousness that we do not live in a void. We never suffer from harrowing anxiety and fear of roaming about in the emptiness of time. We own the past and are, hence, not afraid of what is to be. We remember where we came from. We were summoned and cannot forget it, as we wind the clock of eternal history. We remember the beginning and believe in an end. We live between two historic poles: Sinai and the Kingdom of God.

> Upon thy walls, O Jerusalem,
> I have set watchmen,
> All the day and all the night
> They shall never be silent.
> Ye that stir the Lord to remember,
> Take no rest,
> And give Him no rest
> Till He establishes Jerusalem,
> And makes it a praise in the earth.
>   Isaiah 62:6–7

*

Robert Gordis (1908–   )

Gordis was born in Brooklyn, New York. He is a biblical scholar, rabbi, educator, author, and editor. In 1929, Gordis earned his Ph.D. from Dropsie College, and soon thereafter was ordained at the Jewish Theological Seminary. Between 1931 and 1969 he was the rabbi at Rockway Park Hebrew Congregation in New York. Gordis has written over twenty books and numerous articles, and he has been the recipient of many awards. Following is an article by Gordis that appeared in *Midstream* magazine.

THE TRUTHS OF GENESIS

That the Bible is not a science textbook is generally recognized. Genesis is not intended to teach 20th-century man astronomy, geology, and biology, let alone astrophysics or biogenetics. But the importance of Genesis for the history of science should not be overlooked. Actually, the creation narrative in the first chapter of Genesis rests upon a profound scientific insight. It is true that the ancient Hebrews, unlike the Greeks, evinced no outstanding talent for scientific thought. Yet incredibly, it was Genesis rather than the Greek philosophers and scientists that arrived at the concept of a "uni-verse" created by one will and hence governed by universal laws of nature.

Tribute has widely been paid the creation story for its literary qualities. The Latin writer Longinus (in *On the Sublime*) cited the first chapter of Genesis as a supreme example of sublimity in literature. In our day, a contemporary writer in a religious journal seeking to "defend" Genesis voiced faint praise when he declared "the biblical account of creation is not science, but it is good literature."

Nevertheless, neither the literary greatness of the creation narrative nor its profound scientific insight is as significant as the basic truths it contains. More precisely, the literary power of Genesis is the instrument for the transmission of its truths.

To be sure, the creation narrative seeks to buttress its insights and affirmations by utilizing the scientific knowledge of its own day, but the conclusions are impervious to the shifting sands of scientific theory. Their religious and ethical validity does not depend upon the doctrine of a special creation in six days, which was entirely plausible to the ancients, nor are they impugned by the modern view of evolution, which commends itself to us today and which will undoubtedly undergo modification in the future. In fact, if all the rest of the Bible were to be lost, it would be possible to reconstruct the fundamentals of religion and ethics from the opening chapter of Genesis.

I. Religious Truths

The religious truths in Genesis are imbedded in the biblical text itself. The ethical imperatives implicit in Genesis are spelled out by the ancient rabbis in the Mishnah, but their scope is universal and their concern all of humanity. The basic religious affirmations of Genesis are six in number:

1. *The world has a plan and a purpose known only to God.* "In the beginning God created heaven and earth" (verse 1). The world is the handiwork of one God who created the world in accordance with His will. The universe is not an accidental concatenation of atoms or subatomic particles, the result of a fortuitous "big bang" in outer space. Whatever the process involved, the world is the product of a divine Intelligence which we call God, working out a plan and purpose. The world is cosmos, not chaos.

Regarding that purpose, mortals can only speculate, but the order and rationality of nature, from the microcosm of the atom to the macrocosm of outer-space systems, testifies to the existence of a plan. Maimonides declared that the existence of God's plan was beyond human power to fathom. Supreme court Justice Oliver Wendell Holmes used a military metaphor, "We are soldiers in a great campaign, even if we are not privy to the battle-plan."

At the root of the metaphysical angst of the biblical thinker Ecclesiastes was his deep distress at man's inability to fathom the purpose of creation, but he did not waver in his conviction that such a purpose existed: "He has made everything beautiful in its proper time, and also put the love of the world in men's hearts, except that they may not discover what God has done from beginning to end" (Ecclesiastes 3:11. My translation—R.G.).

Most religious spirits have found contentment and serenity in the conviction that a beneficent Will is at work in the world though hidden from humanity. But whether these limitations on human knowledge are congenial or not, the sense of a cosmic plan and purpose remains the foundation for a religious worldview.

2. *All life is holy and integral to the Divine order of creation.* "So God created the great sea monsters and every living creature that moves, with which the waters swarm, according to their kinds, and every winged bird according to its kind. And God saw that it was good. And God blessed them, saying, 'Be fruitful and multiply and fill the waters in the seas, and let birds multiply on the earth'" (verse 28). The process of creation underscores the unity and holiness of all life, for the Creator blessed the so-called lower orders of creation in words identical with the benediction pronounced upon the human race.

One of the ethical consequences of this insight into our unity with the animal world is the horror at inflicting unnecessary pain upon any creature. At the one end of the spectrum is the prevention of cruelty to animals, for which the rabbis coined a poignant phrase, "the pain of living creatures." At the other end of the spectrum is the doctrine of vegetarianism, the avoidance of the use of animals for food. Though espoused by a small minority, vegetarianism has excellent biblical warrant in its favor. In verse 29, God permits only the eating of fruits and vegetables. Not until Noah emerges from the Ark after the Flood, are he and his descendants allowed to eat meat, with the proviso that blood is not to be ingested (Genesis 9:8-9). The pouring out of the blood after the slaughter of an animal for food is enjoined by biblical law (Leviticus 17:13,14). Since blood is the seat of life, the act constitutes a symbolic sacrifice, a recognition that all life is sacred.

3. *Men and women are equal in God's plan.* "God created the human being (*ha'adam*) in his image, in the image of God He created him, male and female did He create them" (verse 29). For generations men read the words, but remained blind to their clear intent. Not the male alone, but the female as well is fashioned in the Divine image. Every human being is endowed with the gifts of the spirit that make him or her, in the words of the Eighth Psalm, "little lower than God." If both sexes are equally sacred, they are— or should be—equal in status.

4. *Every human being is fashioned "in the Divine image."* There is no richer metaphor in literature than "the image of God." Early thinkers derived from it the immortality of the soul or man's authority to rule over animal creation. It has been equated with the striving for justice or with the quest for truth. Some have related it to the presence in man of a conscience, a monitor of his actions. Others have called attention to man's faculty of consciousness, his awareness of self. Man is the only creature that can laugh and cry, that possesses a sense of time and a knowledge of his own mortality.

The relation of an image to the original suggests the basic intent of the metaphor. Man is endowed on a small scale with the attributes which God possesses in plenitude: for man they are, preeminently, the power of reason and the capacity to create. However interpreted, the "image of God" is the plus in man over and above all other living creatures with whom he is otherwise linked in countless ways, and by that token, the patent of his dignity and value.

The marvels of space exploration, thus far at least, have not succeeded in discovering another being to challenge the uniqueness of man in the cosmos.

5. *Man is the responsible ruler of the created world.* "God blessed them, and God said to them, 'Be fruitful and multiply, and fill the earth and subdue it; and have dominion over the fish of the sea and over the birds of the air and over every living thing that moves upon the earth'" (verse 21). Man's special position in the cosmos endows him with special responsibilities, both to his own species and to all living creatures. He has an obligation to preserve the life he has been endowed with and to order his society so that it promotes the life and well-being of its members. His dominion over the earth and its inhabitants is not a license to destroy, but a responsibility to conserve.

To read into this passage permission for man to ride rough-shod over other living creatures or to despoil the earth of its treasures, or to pollute the air and water, is to pervert the glory of creation clearly indicated in the closing verse of the creation account.

The meaning of man's mastery of creation is spelled out in the second chapter of Genesis. Man is placed in the Garden of Eden with the explicit mandate *l'ovdah uleshomrah,* which the New English Bible renders properly, "to till it and to care for it." Possessing a superior endowment, man is empowered to be not a ruthless tyrant, but a responsible ruler of the world of nature.

6. *The world is good.* "And God saw everything that he had made, and behold, it was very good" (verse 31). Here the basic judgment "God saw that it was good," which is repeated on each day of creation, reaches its triumphant climax. The Hebrew phrase *tobh me'od,* "very good," is also read by the ancient rabbis as *tobh mot,* "even death is good"; in spite of all the tragedies and frustrations in human experience, the world is good, and life is a blessing.

Later generations, confronted by massive difficulties, were not always able to sustain so optimistic a view of life and the world. The Talmud (*Erubin* 13b) informs us that for two and a half years a controversy between two schools of rabbis on the value of life persisted. The School of Shammai maintained, "Better for man not to have been created than to have been created." The contrary view was upheld by the School of Hillel who declared, "Better for man to have been created than not to have been created." The darker view of Shammai prevailed, but with a characteristic ethical addition: "The decision was 'better for man not to have been created; but now that he has been, let him carefully examine his actions.'"

The biblical and the rabbinic views are not irreconcilable. It is man who has perverted creation. The world is good; man often is not. His duty is to guard against the evils of cruelty, greed, and ignorance. Thus he can help redeem the world and restore it to its pristine goodness and beauty.

II. Ethical Principles

Fundamental as these affirmations of religion are, equally basic postulates of ethics are derived from the first chapter of Genesis. These truths the ancient rabbis set forth in a homily, at once naive and profound, that deserves to be quoted in full:

> 1. Mankind was created through Adam alone to teach that one who destroys a single human life is regarded as though he destroyed an entire world, and one who saves a single human life is regarded as though he saved an entire world.
> 2. The human race began with a single individual for the sake of peace among all men, so that no man might say, "My ancestor is greater than yours."
> 3. Beginning the human race with Adam alone makes it impossible for heretics to say, "There are many heavenly powers."

4. Moreover, the creation of humanity through one ancestor proclaims the greatness of the Holy One, Blessed Be He. For a human mint-master strikes off many coins from a single mould and they are all identical. But the King of Kings, the Holy One, Blessed Be He, stamps each man in the mould of Adam, and yet no one is identical with his fellow.

5. Finally, the creation of Adam teaches that each human being is obliged to declare, "For my sake was the world created." (Mishnah, *Sanhedrin* 4:5)

An ancient supplemental rabbinic work, the Tosefta (*Sanhedrin* 8:3), which is contemporaneous with the Mishnah, adds another significant inference from the creation of Adam:

Mankind has a single ancestor, so no sinner may say, "I am a sinner by inheritance, being a descendant of sinners," and no saint may say, "I am a saint by virtue of my descent from saints."

Only Section 3, which negates dualism and polytheism and affirms the existence of a universe which is the product of one beneficent and purposive God, is theological in theme. The remaining sections of the passage are ethical, containing all the fundamentals of man's social relationships flowing from his God-given nature.

It should be noted that the structure of the passage is the key to its contents. Section 1, which proclaims the dignity of every human being, is the basis for Section 4, which establishes man's right to freedom, basically the right to be different from others. Section 2, which enunciates the equality of all people, is the foundation for Section 5, which sets forth the right of every human being to share in the blessings of the world that God created and pronounced good. *In sum, the inherent dignity of all human beings is the source of their inalienable right to liberty and their innate equality is the basis for their claim to justice.*

Some important observations on the Mishnah's teaching on freedom and on justice should be spelled out. The differences among people are God-given and hence not superficial or unimportant. They are not the artificial invention of priests or tyrants or the products of the corruption by civilization of the original innocence of the human race, as some 18th-century thinkers believed. Nor are these distinctions among people an unfortunate aspect of human nature with which society must struggle and which it would be better to eliminate. The ancient sages saw more truly into human nature when they recognized the physical and spiritual differences among people as God-given, innate, integral features of personality. In other words, human differences are not merely legitimate but, when properly utilized and expressed, valuable resources for the enrichment of human life and culture.

The right to justice inheres in all individuals, whatever their ethnic origin or racial character. The right and the duty to enjoy God's world and its blessings are inalienable, having been conferred upon them by God and not by the state or a social contract. These rights, which should be enforced and protected by a just government, cannot be abrogated by human fiat.

The final section, added from the *Tosefta*, underscores man's moral freedom and responsibility. It declares that individuals cannot take refuge in their heredity, either to arrogate superior virtues to themselves or to excuse major vices. Determinism, whether theological or scientific, cannot overturn the indispensable principle that human beings are accountable for their actions. Only this axiom makes possible a viable society, resting on individual responsibility, without which the world returns to chaos.

Thus the first chapter of Genesis, standing majestically at the opening of the Book of Books, sets forth the fundamentals of religion and the essentials of ethics for humanity. Genesis is true—*that* is its enduring message.

*

Eliezer Berkovits (1908–   )

Berkovits, a leading philosopher–theologian and talmudic scholar, was born in Oradea, Transylvania. He was
ordained in 1934 and five years later left Germany for
England. Between 1946 and 1958, Berkovits officiated in
Sydney, Australia, and in Boston. In 1958, he became
chairman of the Department of Jewish Philosophy at
Hebrew Theological College in Chicago. Currently he
resides in Israel. A portion of his *Crisis and Faith* follows.

CRISIS AND FAITH

4   Meaning, Value and Person

1

We saw that from the purely scientific point of view the
world is an unplanned, inexplicable chance event that is
because it happens to be. We also showed that such a universe lacks meaning and value. The insignificance of our
globe in purely materialistic terms is explained by Edding-
ton, to quote him once again, with the help of the following
example. Imagine, he says, New York's Grand Central Station filled with particles of dust from the floor to the ceiling
and from one end to the other. Concentrate on one particle of
dust. That particle of dust represents the size of the earth in
relationship to the universe. In quantitative terms, this
earth of man is as ridiculously insignificant in its comparative smallness as the rest of the universe is idiotic in its
limitless vastness. There is nothing more stupid than mere
quantitative size. The mathematically quantified and scientifically objectified universe lacks quality; because of that it
is without meaning and value.

Yet, there is meaning in the world, for man knows about

meaning. He searches for it. Even when he denies it, he
affirms it. If he reaches the conclusion that there is no
meaning to life, he must have some idea of what that meaning ought to be and looking around in the world he cannot
find it. Only in the light of some expectation of meaning can
he reach the judgment that existence is meaningless. Of
course, where there is meaning, there is value; that which is
meaningful is valuable, and only that which is valuable can
be meaningful. What is the significance of the fact that man
asks about meaning and searches for it?

Camus was of the opinion that the universe was meaningless; only man in it knew about meaning, only he can intro-
duce meaning into it. Notwithstanding the high esteem in
which one holds Camus, this kind of reasoning is clearly
fallacious. If the universe were meaningless, a chance event,
how could man know about meaning? He is part of that
same universe, formed by the same impersonal forces. It
would be the mystery of all mysteries, the miracle of all
miracles, if an unplanned, purposeless, indifferent universe
had produced meaning in that tiniest little lump of matter
that owed its very existence to a failure of "antiseptic precaution" in Nature. It would be an even deeper mystery than
God's creating the universe *ex nihilo*. Meaning cannot be a
chance event; it has to *be meant*, intended, willed.

That the world is God's creation is not a statement about
cause and effect. Creation is essentially different from causation. Causation is an event; creation is of the spirit. Creation introduces the idea of intention into the universe. The
world is intended: planned, purposed. The world is because
it is meant to be. This is, of course, not a scientific statement.
But no statement about meaning can be scientific. Yet,
meaning is of the very essence of man. To say that the world
is divine creation is affirmation of its quality. Creation is the
qualitative dimension of reality. The fact that reality issued
from the will of God, that it is purposed by God, gives value
to being as its essential quality. The world is valuable because of its creation. Creation redeems existence from the
nausea of "Istigkeit" (to use a term of Meister Echhart),

from the dumbness of mere being. The scientific-quantitative description is an attempt at showing how the world appears: it cannot deal with what it is. The world as creation dwells in the dimension of ends: its quantitative interpretation represents one of its aspects that has meaning only because it provides the means for the realization of ends. Without the reference to the dimension of ends, a scientifically objectified being drowns in absurdity.

If Camus' Meursault found redemption for his alienation when, in the absurdity of his own existence, he discovered brotherhood with the meaninglessness of our indifferent universe, the man who lives in the created world is not in need of such desperate solutions at which one grasps in order to overcome the dread of a prison's death row. The man of creation knows himself as part of a cosmos that comprehends all in the unity of a divine plan. He knows that his existence is intended like the being of everything else that surrounds him. He knows of no cosmic alienation. As God's creature he belongs in God's creation. He is not crushed in his physical insignificance by the vastness of the universe. He is meant like everything else. He has his place within the whole and holds it. The innumerable galaxies do not frighten him. The cosmos is his home, no less than it is theirs.

The man who knows himself as part of creation is distinct from the rest of the universe in that he knows. He who knows of plan and meaning is responsible. Facing the world as creation, man faces God. That is the foundation of his being as a person. To be a person is to be responsible. God's call to man calls him from the realm of "thinghood" into personal life.

2

The Jew who lives in the presence of God knows that the world is purposed and that, therefore, it is valuable and meaningful. But what is the purpose, what is the meaning? The more fundamental question is, why creation at all?

The most common answer found in philosophical as well as kabbalistic writing is: "It is the nature of the Good One to

do good." Rabbi Schneur Zalman in the *Likutei Amarim*
maintains that God created with His attribute of *gedulah*,
which is the attribute *of ḥesed*. In other words, He created
out of lovingkindness. But lovingkindness toward whom?
There is no answer to the question. Prior to creation, there is
nothing apart from God. Toward whom, then, is God exer-
cising lovingkindness when He creates? All such and similar explanations are of no avail. In order to act kindly, there
must already be something in existence to be the recipient of
kindness. But nothing needs nothing, one cannot be kind to
nothing.

The only acceptable explanation seems to be that of
Maimonides, who maintains that all we can say in reply to
the question why God created is: It was His will to create.
Obviously, He must have willed this world, otherwise He
would not have brought it into being. The point Maimonides
makes is that, no matter what reason we may think we have
found for God's creating, we shall always be able to ask:
What for? Did He create the universe to reveal His mighti-
ness? What for? Did He wish to reveal Himself to man, to
give him the Torah, the commandments? What for? An infinite being like God, possessing perfection, could not be in
need of anything. To want anything would be desiring something. But why should God desire anything? What could He
be lacking? Therefore, all we know is that the world is the
result of an act of divine volition; but there is no answer to
the "why?"

We might go one step farther. The purpose of the act of
creation must have been a divine one. On account of that, its
knowledge is inaccessible to man. Even if God desired to
communicate to man His own divine reason for wanting to
create, our finite minds would not be able to grasp it. He
would have had to bestow upon us His divine intellect in
order to inform us of the meaning of creation unto Himself.
It is, of course, an impossibility to be man, equipped with
God's mind.

One thing, however, is certain. Since the world is creation, there is purpose to it; there must be meaning in existence. Victor Frankl, in his *Man's Search for Meaning*, disagrees with those psychologists who are of the opinion that man is determined by his drives, such as the desire for pleasure or for power, or whatever else the case may be. According to him the importance of the drives is exaggerated. What is decisive for human existence is man's will for meaning. In the concentration camps, Frankl found that it was not the physically fittest people who had the best chance for survival, but those who, in spite of everything, were still able to retain some sense of meaningfulness in existence.

Martin Buber maintains that one of the results of a revelational experience is that man comes out of it with the conviction of life's meaningfulness, with the certainty that from now on nothing can be meaningless. However, what the meaning is according to Buber is not revealed. Revelation has no content according to him. With the certainty that life is meaningful, man has to go into the world and discover the meaning for himself. Sartre believes that man has to create his own values. As we saw earlier, Buber, in disagreement, maintains that values cannot be created; they exist, they are given; they have to be discovered. Similarly, there is meaning; one has to discover it for one's personal life. In essence, Frankl says the same. One cannot tell anyone what the meaning of one's existence is; but meaning confronts man and he has to respond to it. There is a serious problem inherent in such a position. If man alone can discover the meaning of his life, if he has to find it, to choose it from among many other possibilities, then clearly everyone is to choose the meaning of his own existence. But if it is up to man, to everyone individually to choose, who is to decide on right or wrong? Every choice of each person is as valid as that of any other. There are then no objective standards by which to choose and to decide. While the practice of human kindness toward all may be meaningful for one person, genocide may be equally meaningful for another. Yet meaning must be personal, it has to be the meaning of my own life; it cannot but be subjective. But if so, the distinction between right and wrong disappears. The floodgates of anarchy, everyone doing his own thing, have been opened on mankind.

The solution to the problem would seem to be that the subjectively chosen meaning has to be found or discovered or created within an objectively given frame of reference. For a Jew this objective frame of reference is the Torah and the *Mitzvot* (commandments), which determine for all Jews in common the meaning of being Jews, to live in accordance with the will of God as revealed in His Torah. Outside of this objectively given frame of reference there can be no meaning in being a Jew. In fact, even a person who does not practice Judaism can only be a Jew if he is qualified to be one in conformity with the objective standards that determine what it means to be a Jew.

However, while the objective frame of reference determines the meaning of being a Jew, it does not determine the specific meaning in the life of this specific Jew or of the other. In other words, that subjective meaning which is essential for every individual in his own personal, unique life situation is not determined by Torah and *Mitzvot*. It is here and here alone, that Buber and Frankl come into their own. It is up to every individual to discover the subjective meaning of his own personal life, what to do with his life within the objective frame of reference. Others may advise him, may help him, but ultimately the choice must be his own, the decision must be his.

No one can really tell anyone else what the meaning of his life should be. This is just as well; only a puppet could be so instructed. It is of the very essence of human existence to search for this personal meaning to one's personal existence, to formulate it, to discover it. It is of the very essence of life's adventure and man's creativity. It may even be that, while the meaning of one man's life is something very tangible and definite, that of another is the search for it. It is told of Rabbi Israel Baal Shem Tov that, lying on his death bed, he was heard to say: "Now I know what I have lived for."

As far as a Jew is concerned, despite the fact that he might often feel frustrated, depressed, or dejected at not being able to discover the subjective, personal element within the meaning of his existence, his life can never be completely meaningless. For he shares with all other Jews in the objective meaningfulness to be found within the frame of reference of Torah.

*

Will Herberg (1909–1977)

Herberg was born in New York City and was an educator, philosopher, social critic, lecturer, and writer. During the 1920s, he was active in the Young Communist League and edited Communist Party publications. In 1932, he earned his Ph.D. from Columbia University. By the 1940s, he had abandoned communism and turned his attention once again to Jewish concerns. Following is a brief excerpt from his work *Judaism and Modern Man*.

JUDAISM AND MODERN MAN

The Mystery of Israel

On a naturalistic basis, no other conclusion is possible.

Jewish existence acquires meaning only in terms of the categories that emerge from the biblical-rabbinic faith. In the normative biblical-rabbinic view, as we have seen, Israel is not a "natural" nation; indeed, it is not a nation at all like the "nations of the world." It is a *supernatural* community, called into being by God to serve his eternal purposes in history. It is a community created by God's special act of covenant, first with Abraham, whom he "called" out of the heathen world and then, supremely, with Israel corporately at Sinai, Jewish tradition emphasizes the unimportant and heterogeneous character of the People Israel apart from God's gracious act of election, which gives it the significance it possesses in the scheme of world destiny. The covenant of election is what brought Israel into existence and keeps it in being; apart from that covenant, Israel is as nothing and Jewish existence a mere delusion. The covenant is at the very heart of the Jewish self-understanding of its own reality.

We miss the entire meaning of the covenant as understood in biblical-rabbinic thought if we imagine it as something that depends for its power and reality upon the voluntary adherence of the individual Jew. The covenant, in biblical-rabbinic faith, is not a private act of agreement and affiliation; it is not a contract that becomes valid only when the individual Jew signs it. Indeed, the individual Jew would not be a Jew at all in any intelligible sense were he not *already* under the covenant. The covenant is an objective supernatural fact; it is God's act of creating and maintaining Israel for his purposes in history.

What are these purposes? What is the vocation of the covenant-folk? These questions bring us to the heart of the "mystery of Israel."

"You shall be unto me a kingdom of priests and a holy nation" (Exodus 19:6): that is the basic formula in which the election and vocation of Israel are defined. Taken in its fulness, as it is developed in subsequent thought, this commission may be seen to imply a triple task: to receive and to cherish the Torah of God; to hear and to obey his voice in loving service and thus to live a holy life in a holy community under his kingship; and to be a "light to the gentiles" by showing forth God's greatness and goodness as well as by an active effort to bring peoples of the world to acknowledge the Holy One of Israel. In a word, in inward life, corporate existence and outgoing service, to "sanctify the Name" and to stand witness to the Living God amidst the idolatries of the world.

*

Alexandre Safran (1910–   )

Rabbi Safran was born in Bacau, Rumania. In 1940, he was elected Chief Rabbi. During World War II, he took an active role to improve Jewish conditions in his country. In 1948, Safran moved to Switzerland. He has taught at Geneva University, written numerous works, and been active in many organizations. The following excerpt is from his work *The Kabbalah*.

THE KABBALAH

From Existence to the Void

The purpose of the creation *'yesh me-ayin'*, the creation *'ex nihilo'* is to correlate the *'yesh'*, that which exists, with the *'ayin'*, that which does not exist, the void. This plan can be executed only by man who, indeed, lives in the *'yesh'* but is also capable of living in the *'ayin'*.

The *'yesh'*, the material life, springs from the *'ayin'*, the source of life, and also returns to the *'ayin'* of true life. Because of its transitory character the *'yesh'* even acquires a full, lasting value, "persists" and accomplishes its *'kiyyum'*. Man, who has departed from the source of life "despite himself", tries—as soon as he is able—to return to it of his own, free will and in pure love.

In fact, man is the personification of the *'yesh'*. If he considers it to be an autonomous, lasting truth, if he divorces it from its source and neglects its high aim, then he is committing a sin. Thus it was that Adam separated the tree of *'yesh'*, the tree of the knowledge of good and evil, from the tree of *'ayin'*, the tree of life. He believed himself capable of managing the *'yesh'* in his own way and in this way condemned himself to death, that is, to taste the bitter "flavour" of death.

When man succeeds in distinguishing the 'yesh' from the 'ayin', from which he comes "despite himself" but to which he can go of his own, free will, he liberates himself from the fear of death. He learns that his entry into the 'yesh' bears witness to God's love for him: it is God's Will that man should live in the 'yesh', not only that he should exist and not die in it but that he should return to Him alive of his own accord.

The distinction which man is to make between the 'yesh' and the 'ayin' is fundamentally the same as the distinction which he should make between existence and life (and between death and life), between the apparent and the real, between the false and the true, between servitude and freedom.

This distinction is related to the knowledge of good and evil, which is itself connected with the will to perform a creative work. But it cannot be a clear distinction because the 'yesh' does not allow absolute clarity. It is a product of the pluralistic will of the Creator because it is made up "of good and evil", of the good which can be transformed into evil and of an evil which can be transformed into good. Without a certain amount of confusion in the 'yesh', the attraction of sin would be diminished and man's freedom would be abolished because there would no longer be any possibility to choose.

The dividing line between 'yesh' and 'ayin' is thus far from clear: "every creature is made up of 'ayin' and 'yesh'". Man must not confuse them; he must not allow the 'yesh' to absorb the 'ayin' nor the 'ayin' to destroy the 'yesh'. The 'yesh' must be purified in the 'ayin', the body must be purified in the soul, so that it acquires the value of the soul and so that the 'yesh' consents in love to be imbued with the 'ayin'.

The 'yesh' does not arouse an attitude of contempt in the man of the Kabbalah. It does not cause him to adopt either a pessimistic attitude to life or an ascetic tendency. The 'yesh' is a temporary state. Man must regard it as such in order to make better use of it. It corresponds to a phase of prepara-

tion for the *'ayin'* and must work for the good because it is
included in God's plan.

The *'yesh'* is not an "illusion" as in the Hindu view. But it
can become so if man keeps it separate from its origin and
its goal. The *'yesh'* has no reality apart from its relationship
with the *'ayin'*. Indeed, the *'ayin'* is always more real, more
'yesh', than all the realities of the world. The *'ayin'*, the
'kelum', the "nothing", is the *'kol'*, the "whole", whereas the
'yesh', that which exists, is merely a particular, ephemeral
form of the *'ayin'*.

Thus the "destruction of the *'yesh'* in the face of the *'ayin'*"
corresponds to a true evaluation of the *'yesh'* which is restored to its true dimensions and to its intermediate position
between the two "poles" of the *'ayin'*.

The *'yesh'*, which was conceived by God, remains good
even when man makes bad use of it, even when he separates
it from the *'ayin'* (65) and thus disturbs not only the *'yesh'*
but also the *'ayin'*. In order then to make good the damage
done by man, God frees the *'yesh'* from its temporary occu-
pant so that the *'yesh'* can return to the *'ayin'*.

Nevertheless, when God created the world in love and for
the sake of the good, He put His trust in man, the righteous,
to whom He gave the title of creator. God created the *'yesh'*
and set it in opposition to the *'ayin'* in order to allow man in
his freedom to unite the *'yesh'* with the *'ayin'*. The creative
and redemptive action which God has assigned to man consists of restoring the *'yesh'* to its original *'ayin'*—condition: in
this way the plurality of the *'yesh'* merges into the oneness of
the *'ayin'*.

Thus man is to perform an act of *'teshuvah'*, of "return", of
cosmic "healing". As soon as he has left the *'ayin'*, he is
drawn back to it. Therefore he tries to find particles of the
'ayin', which constitute manifestations of the original will,
in the *'yesh'* itself. In his search for harmony, man gathers
the "fragments" of the divine will which are scattered in the
world, unites them as one whole and restores them to their
origin: to the supreme, universal Will. Thus he unites and
completes God's original work, and so performs a work of

redemption. He establishes in the world the mastery of the one divine Will. He restores perfect order to the universe.

The work of salvation is the culmination of a long 'avodah', a "labour" which man performs with persistence. Man is the servant of God who directs his thoughts, words and deeds to the one goal of redemption. Daily "labour" and daily "prayer" are complementary. Together they constitute the 'avodah' which God demands.

Thus man restores God's work which had been reduced in value not only by man's sin but also according to God's own will. He reunites the 'yesh' with the 'ayin'. But as the personification of the 'yesh' he does not abandon his own individuality, his own "ego". He returns to the 'ayin' but he still retains his 'ani'.

At His first meeting with man, God came forth from the 'ayin' and took on the form of an 'ani' who offers Himself to man. Man, for his part, transformed himself from an 'ani' into an 'ayin'. He "annihilated" himself before God. But he only becomes aware of his "annihilation" because of the reinforcement of his 'ani'. He was not submerged by God; he has not surrendered his own personality, nor has he abandoned his earthly responsibilities.

Every meeting with God renews man who then returns to his 'yesh' profoundly marked by the spirit. As long as he exists, as long as he remains in his transitory state of existence, he has no right to neglect his supra-temporal task. This task consists of transforming his existence into a life, of preparing a certain "quantity" of life which he can then take with him from this earth to incorporate it in eternal life, when the time comes for him to leave this world. In the future, death will not signify disintegration or punishment or compulsion or defilement because the 'yesh' will be absorbed by the 'ayin' although it will continue to exist within it.

In the present, not only does man need the 'yesh', the 'yesh' also needs man. Man enables the light of the 'ayin' to shine through the 'yesh'. In the Messianic age 'ayin' and 'yesh' will be surrounded by the same radiance, as they were before the Fall.

*

Samuel Belkin (1911-1976)

Samuel Belkin was born in Swislocz, Poland. He was an educator, rabbi, and scholar. In 1928, he was ordained and the following year immigrated to the United States. In 1935, Belkin earned his Ph.D. from Brown University. Between 1943 and 1976 he served as president of Yeshiva University. The following is from his work *The Philosophy of Purpose*.

THE PHILOSOPHY OF PURPOSE

In order to properly understand Judaism, it is important to distinguish between two different approaches to a consideration of man and the world. One we may call a philosophy of reason; the other, a philosophy of purpose. The first is the approach of the pure rationalist; the second, is the traditional Jewish attitude.

The rationalistic philosopher is concerned primarily with origins and causes. He begins by asking: Who or what caused the universe to come into being? Having reached the conclusion that creation in itself is proof of the existence of a Creator, the rationalist speculates further. Is creation the result of divine design, divine will, or divine goodness? Did God create the world *ex nihilo* or from pre-existent matter, and if from the latter, was pre-existent matter itself created or is it eternal? The chief aim of rationalistic philosophy is to find a rational explanation of creation. It is not concerned with the purposefulness with which God animates creation in general and man in particular. It is a philosophy of reason, not a philosophy of purpose.

The "purposeful" philosopher, on the other hand, is concerned not with the origins and causes of creation, but with its meaning for man. He may search for explanations of how things came into being, but chiefly he considers those things which are already in existence. He attempts to define their meaning for man and to divine the purpose which is fulfilled by their proper utilization. Even those Jewish philosophers who were trained in Aristotelian rationalism have, in the main, endeavored to create a harmony between the philosophy of reason and the philosophy of purpose. For in Judaism if a philosophy of reason is to be spiritually meaningful even for the rationalist, it must always be accompanied by a philosophy of purpose.

Philosophers of reason may question why and how God created the world. The Torah does not speculate about such matters. It merely states concerning the things created, "God saw that it was good." There is a continuous process of creation, and in this continuous renewal of creation, which determines man's relation to the Creator, is revealed the wonder and goodness of God: "He is the Lord of Wonders who in His goodness reneweth the creation every day continually." For example, the Almighty's provision of man's daily sustenance demonstrates the ever-present and never-ending goodness of God. Therefore, in the *Birkat Hamazon*, (the Grace recited after meals) we thank God "Who feedest the whole world with Thy goodness" and declare that "He is both good and bestows goodness" (*hatov vehamativ*). But the goodness of God has definite ethical and spiritual purposes and is dependent on man's willingness to live in accordance with the will of God.

That our Sages were not concerned with the cause of creation but with man's relationship to God, is clearly demonstrated in the following statement found in the *Beraita*:

For two and a half years the School of Shammai disputed with the School of Hillel. The former contended that it would have been better had man not been created. The latter claimed that it is better

that man was created than if he had not been
created. The two Schools finally decided that it
would have been better for man had he not come
into being. But since he has been created, it be-
hooves him to search his deeds. Others record the
tradition thusly: Let him weigh the consequences
before he performs his deeds. [*Erubin* 13b]

This is probably the only purely academic and theoretical
dispute among the Tannaim for which a final decision is
recorded in the Talmud, and the conclusion reached has a
direct bearing on human conduct.

The Shammaites held that since man is endowed with an
evil inclination, which he follows when he sins against man
and God, it would have been better if he had not been
created at all. Since this was their view, the School of Shammai was faced with the question why God did create man?
The answer they gave was that we, being mortal, can never
comprehend the divine reason, the "*why*" of God. The School
of Hillel, on the other hand, held that the creation of man
was good. Obviously then, it was in His goodness that God
created man.

The agreement of both Schools, that it would have been
better for man had he not been created, is a declaration that
we do not understand the *why* of human creation. Their
conclusion that since man has been created he must examine
his actions and avoid sin, implies even more. It teaches that
if man can never learn the cause of creation, he is duty-
bound to strive to uncover the divine purpose in creation. It
is the judgment of our Sages, that man cannot comprehend
the divine cause, but he can, and must discover for himself
the moral and spiritual purpose which give meaning to his
creation. Similarly, we may not always know the divine
reason for many laws of the Torah, but we do know the
divine purpose a man fulfills by observing the Torah. By
keeping the divine ordinances and living up to the moral
obligations contained in them, man serves his Creator.

God the Creator and Overseer

The philosopher of purpose, as against the rational philosopher, searches for spiritual values and seeks unity with God.
The difference between the two can be illustrated by examining philosophic proofs of the existence of God. Among the
better known of these proofs is the teleological argument
that the order of the universe makes it self-evident that the
world was brought into being by a Creator. This argument,
which the Stoics used to prove the existence of God as imma-
nent in the world, Philo Judaeus explained with the following analogy:

> Should a man see a house carefully constructed
> with a gateway, colonnades, men's quarters, wom-
> en's quarters, and other embellishments, he will
> get an idea of the artificer, for he will be persuaded
> that the house never reached that completeness
> without the skill of the craftsman. The same holds
> true for the building of a city or a ship or any other
> construction. By the same token, anyone entering
> this world, as if it were a vast house or a city and
> beheld the sky circling around and embracing
> within it a variety of phenomena; the planets, and
> fixed stars without any variation, moving in rhyth-
> mical harmony and with advantage to the whole
> . . . will surely argue that these have not been
> wrought without consummate art, but that the
> Maker of this universe was and is God. [*Leg. All.*
> III:27]

Assuming that such philosophic arguments are scientifically valid, they are evidence merely of the origin of the
world. They offer neither a rational explanation for, nor
faith in, the continuing relationship between the Creator
and His creation, which faith is the very quintessence of the
religious belief that God rules and directs the world He has
created. According to our Sages, Abraham, too, saw the

wonders of creation as evidence of the existence of God. His
aim, however, was not to prove the existence of God through
creation, but to pose a fundamental religious question: "Is it
conceivable that the world be without an overseer" (*man-
hig*)? And the Holy One, Blessed Be He, looked out and said:
"I am the Overseer and the Sovereign of the Universe"
(Genesis *Rabbah* 39). In other words, Abraham was concerned with establishing the continuous sovereignty of God,
and not with proving philosophically that the existence of an
artifact demonstrates the existence of an artificer.

In the same way, our Sages were not drawn to speculative
discussions as to whether the world was created through the
will of God or the goodness of God. Their main concern was
the purpose behind creation. Hence, at the marriage cere-
mony which symbolically affirms God's perpetual act of
creation, we pronounce the blessing, "Blessed art Thou, O
Lord, King of the Universe Who created all things for His
glory." It is not the origin of creation, but rather the purpose
of creation which is important. Man was created for the
purpose of fulfilling the Law of God. It is this principle
which is behind the assertion of our Sages that the Holy One,
Blessed Be He, created the entire world for the sake of man,
who observes the Law (*Yoma* 38b; *Berakhot* 6b).

Creation, in the Jewish view, is not merely an act of the
past. Anyone who acknowledges God as his guide and master becomes His associate in the continuous process of creation. God said to Abraham: "My Name was not known
among my creatures, and thou hast made It known among
them. I will regard thee, therefore, as though thou wast
associated with Me in the act of creation" (Genesis *Rabbah*
43:7).

Hence, in searching for the purpose of creation, our Sages
developed not a philosophy of the *original why* but a religious philosophy of *what for*; a spiritual design for purposeful living; a faith based on the intimate relation between
man and the living God who is greatly concerned with the
conduct of men. One of the most striking verses in the Torah
reads: "And ye shall keep My commandments and do them; I

am the Lord. And ye shall not profane My Holy Name, and I will be sanctified among the children of Israel. I am the Lord who sanctifies thee" (Leviticus 22:31–32). It has been properly noted that in this verse lies the essence of Judaism. God confers sanctity on the people of Israel but Israel hallows God by observing His Torah. Hugh Bergmann has aptly written:

> If God is holy, why is it written that He is to be sanctified through man? To understand this, we must enter more deeply into the notion of God which characterizes the Jewish religion. This notion is fundamentally different from any that is familiar in the conceptual world of Western culture. In that world, God and the universe exist as given once and for all and earth and man are separated from God. Judaism also separates God and the world, but it so integrates the fate of both that not only is the world dependent on God but (this being our central point), the fate of God is dependent on that of the world. The contrast between the strictly Western and the Jewish notion can perhaps best be characterized by saying that according to the former, the relation of God to the world is static and according to the latter, it is dynamic. [Quoted in *Rebirth*, ed. L. Lewisohn, p. 137]

Our Sages, in their own way, make the same point: "Before our father Abraham arrived in this world, if it may be permitted to say so, the Holy One, Blessed Be He, was King only of Heaven, but when our father Abraham came into the world he crowned Him as King over heaven and earth." (*Sifre* Deuteronomy 213) It is man, through his pious actions, who sanctifies God and crowns Him as King of the world. This religious philosophy of purpose gives a *raison d'etre* to man's continued existence. God created and sustains the world for the sake of man, whom He made in His image and sanctified by giving him the Laws of the Torah and the purpose of man's existence is to sanctify God by observing His Law, which makes him an associate of God in the continuing process of creation.

God is of course holy regardless of man's actions. But, say our Sages, it is the duty of man to hallow the name of God if he desires to maintain a proper relationship with God. Hence, they taught: "If you make yourself holy, I impute it upon you as though you hallowed Me, and if you do not make yourselves holy, I impute it upon you as though you did not hallow Me. Is it possible then that if you make Me holy then I am holy, otherwise, I am not holy? Does not the Torah state, 'for I am holy'—I remain in My holiness, whether you hallow Me or not?" (*Sifra* on Leviticus 19:2). Obviously then, God's holiness is not dependent upon man's action, but through man's actions God becomes holy in relation to His creation. While man cannot comprehend God's essence since "God is the place of the world, but the world is not His place," (Genesis *Rabbah* 68) yet through His Torah, God teaches us His divine purposes and His need of the human response. . . .

Rationalism and Moral Purpose

To sum up then, the religious rationalistic philosopher is primarily concerned with finding the reason for the divine law. Why did God ordain or prohibit the performance of certain acts? Why were particular persons enjoined by God to perform certain functions and others prohibited from performing them? Maimonides averred, for instance, that persons who assume that the commandments and prohibitions have no rational basis are "weak-minded" and lack a true understanding of the Torah. Of course, Maimonides himself admitted that for some laws he could find no rational explanation. He argued, however, that this does not mean that there is no explanation for those laws; it rather proves the limitations of the human mind which is incapable of discovering a reason for all the revealed laws.

There are, however, other approaches, besides the rational one to the Torah. Some of the Jewish philosophers, as well as many of the Palestinian Sages, strove to uncover the religious and moral motives and purposes of the Torah. Fundamental to this method of interpreting the Torah is the belief that in addition to the literal meaning of the Torah, which requires observance of mitzvot in compliance with the will of God, there is often a hidden meaning, a deeper purpose, often purposely obscured, imbedded within the revealed Word. To use an analogy, mitzvot may be said to have a body, which is their performance, but they also possess "souls," that is, invisible moral and spiritual purposes, which reveal themselves to man only when he attains a deeper understanding of God's moral and spiritual motives. The purposeful interpretation of the Torah never conflicts with the literal meaning of the Torah. It simply seeks to uncover just a little more, to discover a deeper level of meaning, not immediately apparent, in the teachings of the Torah.

*

Adam Schaff (1913-   )

Schaff, born in Lvov, in the Ukraine, is a philosopher and sociologist. In 1945 he earned his Ph.D., and from 1948 to 1970 he was a professor of philosophy at the University of Warsaw. Schaff has authored numerous books and contributed a large number of articles to various publications. He has been a member of many organizations. During the period of active pressure against Jews in Poland in 1968, the scope of his responsibilities at the Polish University Academy was greatly reduced. At the same time, Schaff resigned his membership in the Central Committee of the Communist Party of Poland. Following is a portion of his work A Philosophy of Man.

A PHILOSOPHY OF MAN

6
The Meaning of Life

Faced with such a hazy question as "What is the meaning of life?" it is necessary first of all to try to make the question more precise. There are perhaps two main interpretations of this question. He who asks about the meaning of life questions first of all the value of life: is life worth living? And secondly, he questions the aim of life.

"Is life worth living?" is a common question, whether the questioner seriously proposes to draw practical conclusions from a negative answer, or whether he asks in the hope of cheering himself up. The Stoics maintained that it is not necessary to console people over the inevitability of death; on the contrary, they must be persuaded that it is worth while to go on living.

However that may be, death—the threat of one's own death and the death of near ones—is often the chief incentive for reflections on the meaning of life. For besides peoples' dread of dying, they experience the tragedy of separation in the actual deaths of those close to them. People fear dying as a possibility, and experience the death of someone near to them as an actuality. We are only sometimes reminded of the inevitable approach of our own death; if it were otherwise, if people lived with the continual consciousness of death inevitably approaching, they would surely go mad. We feel the passage of time, like the flow of blood in the veins, only occasionally. Nikolaj Kuzmicz, in Rilke's *Laurid Brigge's Malta Notebook*, could live no longer once he became conscious of the passage of time.

But the question "Is life worth living?" is suggested not only by death. Physical as well as moral suffering—particularly when it seems undeserved—prompts the same question. How can such a question be answered? And how can we explain our answer to others?

We would like to answer: although death is inevitable, although suffering is unavoidable, life is still worth while, life has a meaning. But why? We are obliged to say why, if we are to convince anyone and if our answer is to express anything more than an individual opinion.

The ground we are moving on now becomes excessively slippery, and a different mode of approach is needed from that adopted towards problems in the exact or empirical sciences, or towards epistemological and ontological problems arising from the sciences. We can speak of certainties in deductive sciences and probabilities in empirical sciences which differ in degree but are always based on hard data. This also applies, though in a different way, to propositions of the philosophy of science. But with the questions we are now discussing it is not a matter of ascertaining the truth or falsity of propositions, but of assessing, evaluating. It is doubtful whether there can ever be a valid transition from description to evaluation. It is doubtful whether a description of life, however true and well founded, would automatically justify any evaluation of life.

At this point a Neo-Positivist may interject that evaluations cannot express facts and cannot be verified, so that all evaluation is subjective. He would undoubtedly be right. But he would at the same time be wrong if he concluded that questions of evaluation were pseudo-questions and so refused to deal with them. In that case he would simply be assuming what has to be proved; he would be assuming a criterion of meaningfulness and scientific character which would prejudge the problem from the start.

Actually, in examining questions such as the meaning of life, the philosopher must proceed quite differently from any procedure of the natural sciences. He must proceed differently because the subject that interests him demands a different procedure. But it does not follow that his method is impermissible, or necessarily unscientific. He, too, generalises from the facts of experience; he too bases himself on the findings of specific sciences, such as sociology or psychology. But he proceeds differently, because he does not simply describe but assesses, evaluates. And where an assessment or evaluation is being made, some scale of assessment, some chosen system of values, enters into his calculations. Of course, the selection of this scale or system is not made arbitrarily: it is socially conditioned. But social conditioning is not the only factor. Other factors come into play as well, both psychological and physiological, which belong to the individual's own personality. In one way or another such factors will always make themselves felt whenever there is a question of choice, including choice of a world view. And not only intellectual factors are involved here, but emotional factors. Hence subjectivity does play its part.

Consequently, the process of generalisation is also different. The gap between established empirical facts and their philosophical generalisation is greater; and therefore the possibility of varied interpretation is also greater. In this field the philosopher resembles the ancient sage musing over human life, rather than the experimental natural scientist. This is so, simply because the procedures of the natural scientist are useless here. The philosopher who devotes himself to questioning the meaning of life is not proceeding scientifically—but that does not imply that he is unscientific. The alternative "scientific-unscientific" does not apply here, and to call the philosopher "unscientific" would, logically, be like concluding that love is not rectangular from a negative answer to the question whether love is rectangular.

A wise man is not the same as a scholar, though scholarship and wisdom may often go together. A scholar is one who possesses a fund of knowledge in some field; he is erudite in that field. But one is wise to the extent that he is intelligent and experienced, particularly in his dealings with others. Some people are scholars in some special field but are not wise, either in the sense of general intelligence or of experience of life and knowledge of how to get on with other people. And vice versa, some people are wise without possessing erudition. The philosophy of one who engages in the problems we are concerned with should be classed as "wise" or "unwise," as suitable or unsuitable, but not as "scientific" or "unscientific." In certain situations it is a person wise in the ways of life who is most needed. So a philosopher should be not only a scholar but a wise man too. This does not contradict the requirement that he should be scientific. Scientific knowledge, the scientific approach, helps with reflections on human life and with defining an attitude towards life. The answer proposed to problems such as "What is the meaning of life?" depends, as we have seen, on various factors, but primarily on the world view of the person reflecting on the question; and such a world view may be scientific or unscientific.

For the religious believer, the question whether life has a meaning and is worth living is answered very simply, because even suffering, pain and death are in accord with the will of a higher being, who has prepared rewards in the hereafter for the faithful and punishment for transgressors. For the believer, the most difficult problems appear very simple. But a high price has to be paid for this convenience; it is bought only at the cost of a scientific attitude.

It is not possible from a lay standpoint to provide any kind of categorical and universal answer to the question whether life is worth while. Whether it is worth while or not for a given individual depends upon his actual conditions and perspectives of life—and the individual concerned has the last word here. He can draw up a kind of balance sheet, recalling everything in his life which he evaluates positively, and reminding himself of what he may easily forget under emotional strain—that he lives only once, that time alleviates suffering, that he has responsibilities to those close to him and to society, and so on. But only he can sum up the balance. For if one does not accept absolute standards, which are in essence religious, one cannot prejudge the answers for each individual. That would mean making a choice for him, which only he can make.

But he who asks whether life is worth while asks at the same time about the aim of life. What do we live for? This question is put by everyone harassed by the problem of how he should live. For our behaviour, especially in situations of conflict, depends on what we consider to be the aim of life. This remains true whether we have consciously formulated for ourselves an aim of life or not; for an idea of the aim of life, induced by education in the broadest sense of the word, is implicit in human behaviour. This applies alike to the hero who dedicates his life to the defense of some ideal, the traitor who collaborates with the enemy for money, the conscientious man who sacrifices his own interests to what he considers to be right, or the opportunist who accommodates himself to his superiors despite his own convictions.

From a religious standpoint the question of the aim of life is answered very simply. Man is subject to an external purpose, that of God, which he should obey. The only problem is to find out what this purpose is—which is done by study of the scriptures or other records of revelation. The argument against this standpoint must seek to demonstrate scientifically the human origin of these revelations, to show that God does not create man but man creates God in his own image. But of course, there can be no argument against a believer who will not accept the canons of scientific demonstration.

Lay answers to the question of the aim of life are various, and have long since been classified within the history of philosophy. So far as general approach is concerned, it is now difficult to think of anything new, except for new names. It is an "eternal question," concerning the answers to which we may feel inclined to agree that "there is nothing new under the sun." Yet the moment we stop limiting ourselves to merely abstract and general characterisation of views, and begin to penetrate deeply into the social conditions required for realising one or another aim of our activity, the situation changes. Marxist theory, like several very different ontological and epistemological theories, leads to the general position that may be called "social hedonism"— the view that the aim of human life is to secure the maximum happiness for the broadest masses of the people, and that only within the compass of this aim can personal happiness be realised. But taking into account the social condi-

tions required to realise this aim, the Marxist avows socialist humanism as his supreme principle. Socialist humanism
is indeed a variety of "social hedonism." But it is a concre-
tised conception so closely connected with all the other
tenets of Marxism that its admission implies the acknowl-
edgement of the whole system.

The propositions of socialist humanism and its precepts
for behaviour flow from the theory of Historical Materialism, and in particular: (1) the specific understanding of the
individual as a social product—as a product of "the totality
of social relations," of which we shall say more later; (2) the
specific understanding of the relation of the individual to
society on the basis of the historical materialist conception of
social development; (3) the recognition that ideals can be
realised only under given social conditions, without which
recognition they degenerate into utopias. All this leads, not
to abstract ideal, but to scientifically based concepts from
which flow definite and practical conclusions in the form of
precepts for behaviour.

The socialist humanist is persuaded that he can find personal happiness only through the happiness of society. For
only broader horizons for personal development and enlarged
possibilities for the satisfaction of human desires on a social
scale create the necessary foundations for realising personal
aspirations. He does not limit himself to seeking relations of
friendship or love with those near him—although that is clos-
est to his heart. He understands that the realisation of his
aspirations demands struggle, that the cause he serves is
socially conditioned and requires definite changes in social
relations. In a society based on social antagonism he understands that the realisation of his aspirations demands changes
in property relations and in the class relations based on them.
He advocates the class struggle in the name of the love of near
ones and of universal friendship, and he proclaims his hatred
of the exploitation of man by man in the name of love of man.

The socialist humanist knows that man is the product of
social conditions, but he also knows that these conditions
were created by man. He is a dialectician, and, precisely

because of that, fights while proclaiming peace. His ideal of socialism is at one with his humanism. As an ideal, socialism is the consistent expression of humanism; at the same time, socialism is the material realisation of the ideal of humanism. For this cause, the socialist humanist is ready to make the greatest sacrifices, and to appeal to others to do the same. He accepts the precept of "love thy neighbour," and has only contempt for those who proclaim this beautiful precept in words and betray it in deeds. For socialist humanism not only proclaims certain ideals but calls for struggle to implement them in life, and to convince other people of the necessity of joining this struggle.

*

Meir ben-Horin (1918–   )

Ben-Horin, an educator and theologian, was born in East Prussia and emigrated to the United States. Between 1943 and 1946 ben-Horin served in the U.S. Army, and continued in the reserves from 1948 to 1974 as a commissioned officer with the rank of colonel. At the same time, ben-Horin pursued his studies and earned his Ph.D. from Columbia University in 1948. During the years 1951–1957 he was an assistant professor at Boston Hebrew Teachers College. He then was named head of the Department of Education at Dropsie College. Following is an excerpt from a review of M. Kaplan's book, *The Purpose and Meaning of Jewish Existence*.

THE PURPOSE AND MEANING OF JEWISH EXISTENCE

The *purpose* of Jewish existence is to be a People in the name of God. The *meaning* of Jewish existence is to use the means

of Jewish civilization for the release of the Jewish people's
mind and love, to the end that its thinking and doing may
contribute to the purpose of mankind—to be a species in the
image of God.

*

Abraham J. Twerski (1930–   )

Twerski is from a long line of hasidic rabbis. He was
ordained in 1951, and eight years later earned his medical degree in psychiatry. In 1972, Dr. Twerski became
the founder and director of the Gateway Rehabilitation
Hospital in Pittsburgh. He has written numerous works.
Following is a selection from his book *Let Us Make Man*.

LET US MAKE MAN

Chapter 21
Self-Esteem and Purpose

"B'reshis bara Elokim"; "In the beginning God created"
(Genesis 1:1). The Rambam (Maimonides) cites this passage
as the cornerstone of the Jewish faith, to know that there is a
God and that He created the universe (Foundations of Torah
1:1).

In his monumental *Guide of the Perplexed*, the Rambam
goes to great lengths to disprove the Aristotelian position of
the eternity of matter. Rationally, we find ourselves stymied
by the concept of the eternity of anything, since we cannot
have a logical grasp of concepts beyond our experiential
contact.

Eternity, which refers to something which had no beginning, is completely beyond human experience and consequently beyond human comprehension. Whether referring

to eternity of matter or of God, eternity is a concept not accessible through rational philosophic thought. *Emunah* transcends logic and its limitations, and it is only via *emunah shlema* that we believe in an eternal God that brought the universe into being.

Torah teaches that the world was created for a purpose, and that purpose was Divinely revealed to be the observance of Torah by mankind. The nontheologic position assumes the eternity of matter, with a series of cosmic accidents resulting in a complex chain of events that produced, among other things, rational man. According to the latter point of view it is meaningless to talk of an ultimate purpose for which man was designed, inasmuch as there was no designer. Laws governing human behavior, according to this position, are essentially socially adopted rules that enable people to live together. With the exception of these rules, everyone is free to set their own goals for living, since there is no transcendental purpose to life.

The latter philosophy naturally leads to any of the varieties of hedonism. One is free to try to get the maximum pleasure out of life, and woe is to him whose pleasures are few. Suffering, like all else in the universe, is purposeless. Absolute accountability for one's behavior does not exist, since one is accountable only to one's society.

Torah philosophy stands in sharp contrast to this. The universe *does* have an ultimate purpose, man has a purpose in the universe, and each individual has a unique mission in his existence. His existence is not a biologic accident, and the particular mission which he must fulfill in life is uniquely his, and cannot be accomplished by even billions of other humans.

The Talmud states that a person is obligated to say, "The world was created for me" (*Sanhedrin* 37a). Young or old, strong or frail, bright or dull, everyone has a reason for existence. If a person is old or sick and takes much more from his environment than he has given or will ever give to it, he still has value. The principle that life *per se* has an intrinsic value regardless of one's productivity is clearly stated in the halachos of Shabbos, wherein the prohibitions of Shabbos may be abrogated when necessary for the preservation or extension of life. No distinction is made whether the life at stake is that of the community's most important and productive citizen, or a severely mentally handicapped person, or someone in irreversible coma.

Humanists say that the value of life is measured by the degree of service we provide for other people. This reminds me of the anecdote of two loiterers who were arrested and brought before the judge.

"What were you doing when the officer arrested you?" the judge asked the first man.

"Nothing," the man answered.

The judge then turned to the other man. "And what were you doing when you were arrested?" he asked.

The man pointed toward his friend. "I was helping him," he said.

It should be obvious that when one is helping someone who is doing nothing, one is doing nothing himself.

Torah provides an ultimate which gives intrinsic meaning to all life regardless of an individual's capabilities or limitations. The world was created for an ultimate purpose fully known only to God, and man has the mission of fulfilling the will of God as revealed in the Torah. Above and beyond whatever value the culture may assign to life, there is a value to life that emanates from God and which is not subject to modification by man.

Every person is obligated to fulfill the will of God by following the teachings of the Torah *to the maximum of his ability*. Over and above the intrinsic value of life, even if one's capacities have been severely compromised by illness or other causes, one can nevertheless maintain self-esteem by virtue of the fact that one is obligated only to the extent of one's capacities.

*

Aryeh Kaplan (1934–1983)

Kaplan was born in New York, educated in the Torah Voda'as and Mir yeshivas in Brooklyn, and ordained in Jerusalem. He also earned a Master's degree in physics and is listed in *Who's Who in Physics* in the United States. Aryeh Kaplan was a leading Orthodox rabbi and one of the foremost scholars of our time. In just twelve years, he had written and translated almost fifty works, several of which are included in this book. In addition, he was editor of *Jewish Life*, a frequent contributor to *The Jewish Observer*, a popular speaker, and a prime mover in the teshuvah (return to Judaism) movement. Kaplan died at the age of 48. The first excerpt is from the introduction to *The Infinite Light—A Book about God*, and the second selection is from Chapter 3 of *The Handbook of Jewish Thought*.

THE INFINITE LIGHT— A BOOK ABOUT GOD

Part One
Foundations

In order to speak about Judaism, we must speak about man and about life in general. Judaism is, first of all, a way of life, and its depth touches upon the very foundations of human existence. If you truly understand Judaism, you know the ultimate secret of life's purpose.

One of the most important elements of life is purpose. There is an old song that asks, "Why was I born, why am I living? What do I get, what am I giving?" These are questions that man has been asking himself ever since he first began using his mind. Have you ever stopped and asked yourself such questions?

Why was I born?

What meaning does my life have?

Why am I myself?

How should I live this one life of mine?

What do I have to offer life?

When we are young, such questions often bother us. Among the problems of growing up, we try to find a philosophy of life to follow. But then, caught in the business world, the market place, and the toil of raising a family, we often forget these questions. And sometimes we are rudely awakened. When tragedy strikes, the questions are thrown at us like buckets of ice water. When we grow old—and we all do grow old—we may gaze back at a lifetime and wonder. "What did I live for?"

We have but one life and must make the most of it. We all want to do what is "right." We want somehow to justify our lives. Rare indeed is the person who can say, *"This is wrong, but I will do it anyway."*

We all have a feeling that some things are right and others are wrong. We have a feeling that there is meaning to life. But many of us go no further. Even when we ask the questions, we do not go very far in seeking answers.

A very wise man once said, "The unexamined life is not worth living."

People can spend their lives seeking pleasure, fame and riches, and never once stop to ask themselves if these things are really important. But unless one gives this serious thought, he will never know whether or not he is doing the right thing. He may spend his entire life pursuing useless and even dangerous goals.

The most fundamental principal of Judaism is the realization that the universe is purposeful, and that man has a purpose in life.

Our sages thus teach us, "A person must have the wisdom . . . to know why he is and why he exists. He must look back at his life, and realize where he is going.

Both man and nature have purpose because they were created by a purposeful Being. We call this Being God.

It is impossible to imagine the world as having purpose without a Creator. Without God, the universe would be purposeless and human existence pointless. All life would be completely without meaning or hope.

For the sake of argument, let us look at the negative viewpoint more closely. Let us look at the world through the eyes of a man without belief and see it as the absolute atheist would. Since his world has no purposeful Creator, there is no purpose in existence. Mankind becomes nothing more than an accident, with no more consequence than a bacterium or a stone. Man can even be looked upon as a vile infection and a disease on the surface of this planet.

If there is no purpose to existence, all our hopes, desires and aspirations are nothing more than the mechanizations of the molecules and cells of our brain. We would have no alternative than to agree with a noted cynic who declared, "Man is a sick fly, taking a dizzy ride on a gigantic flywheel."

In a world without purpose, there can be neither good nor evil, since both of these concepts imply purpose. Without a belief in some ultimate purpose, all values become completely subjective, subject to the whim of the individual. Morality becomes a matter of convenience, to be discarded when it does not serve one's immediate goal. One's philosophy of life can simply be, "If you can get away with it, do it."

If existence has neither purpose, meaning nor depth, our attitude toward the world, toward our fellow man, and toward society in general need be little more than "so what."

If there is no God, there is no purpose. And if there is no purpose, all man's endeavors are in vain. The Psalmist alludes to this, when he says, "If God does not build the house, in vain do the builders toil; If God does not watch the city, in vain do the sentries wake" (Psalm 127:1).

But we can also look at the other side of the question and gaze at the world through the eyes of true faith. If we believe in God as Creator of the universe, then creation has a mighty purpose and life has an infinitude of depth. If man is to find meaning in life, he must seek God's purpose in creation and spend his days trying to fulfill it. The existence of man, a creature who can search for purpose in life, is no longer a mere accident, but the most significant phenomenon in all creation. The concepts of good and evil take on awesome proportions. That which is in accordance with God's purpose is good, while that which goes against it is evil. We are nothing less than partners with God in fulfilling His purpose.

Deep down, no one really feels that everything is meaningless. But many of us lose sight of the true Root of all meaning, often hiding behind a facade of cliches and excuses. Deep down, however, all of us know that there is purpose in life, and ultimately, in all creation.

The old fashioned materialist who was convinced that human life was without goal or purpose and that man is an irresponsible particle of matter engulfed in a maelstrom of meaningless forces, was a man without wisdom. A great philosopher once summed up the folly of this way of thinking by saying, "People who spend their lives with the purpose of proving that it is purposeless, constitute an interesting subject of study."

The Bible flatly says that the nonbeliever is a fool. The Psalmist thus said, "The fool says in his heart, there is no God" (Psalm 14:1).

What the Bible is saying is that one who does not believe is both stupid and blind. He does not see what there is to see. Not only is he blind, but he is also likely to act blindly. He does not recognize any purpose in existence, and is therefore likely to act without direction. He does not recognize Truth, and is apt to do everything wrong. He is so unperceptive that he cannot be trusted. He says that there is no God because he is a fool. He is too blind to see God all around him; or else he is too selfish to share his own world with its Creator.

In the entire Bible, you will not find a single philosophical argument for the existence of God. It is simply assumed. The Bible does not waste time trying to convince the atheist that he is wrong. He is considered a fool, too dull to understand, or too wicked to want to.

Belief, like beauty, is in the eye of the beholder. For over three thousand years, the existence of God was self-evident to the Jew. He needed no proof or demonstration.

The very existence of a universe implied a creator. The Psalmist thus said, "The heavens declare the glory of God, and the skies proclaim His handiwork" (Psalm 19:2). Their very existence is a hymn declaring the glory of their Creator.

The Prophet speaks of this most lucidly when he says (Isaiah 40:21, 26):

> Do you not know?
>   Have you not heard?
> Was it not told to you from the beginning?
>   Do you not understand how the earth was founded?
>
> Lift up your eyes to the stars
>   And see Who has created them
> He numbers them all like an army
>   He calls them all by name . . .

THE HANDBOOK OF JEWISH THOUGHT

Chapter Three
Man

For man to fulfill the purpose of creation, he must be aware of that purpose.

Understanding the purpose of creation obviously does not mean fathoming God's internal reasons. Since we cannot understand God, we certainly cannot understand His motivations.

Still, we can look at God's creation, and seek to comprehend the reason for its existence. We can also study what
God Himself has taught about the purpose of creation.

Since God is absolutely perfect in Himself, it is obvious
that He had no inner need to create the universe. It must
therefore be concluded that God's creation of the universe
was a most perfect act of altruism and love. It is thus written, "The world is built of love" (Psalm 89:3).

God thus created the world to bestow good to His handiwork. It is thus written, "God is good to all; His love is on all
His works" (Psalm 145:9). God Himself called His creation
good, as it is written, "God saw all that He made, and behold
it was very good" (Genesis 1:35).

Even things that appear contrary to this purpose are all
part of God's plan. It is thus written, "God has made everything for His own purpose, even the wicked for the day of
evil" (Proverbs 16:4).

God's ability is limitless, and it therefore follows that His
love and altruism are unlimited, resulting in the greatest
benefit for all creation.

God defines all good. Therefore, the greatest possible benefit is that which comes most directly from God Himself.

In order for something to be appreciated, or even de-
tected, some degree of contrast is required. Thus, in order
for the universe to experience God's presence, it must first
experience His absence. In order to provide the greatest
possible contrast, God thus created the universe as an environment where His essence would be undetectable.

To fulfill His goal, God created the universe as an environment for a creature capable of partaking of His goodness.
The creature would be capable of understanding, joy, and
happiness, as well as of communing with God. This creature
is man.

Everything in the world is thus a means through which
man becomes able to attain God's goodness. It is thus taught
that upon completing His creation, before creating man,
God said, "If there are no guests, what pleasure has the King
with all the good things He has provided?"

Man was therefore created as a creature capable of to some degree understanding, and ultimately experiencing, the greatest possible good, which is God Himself. It can therefore be said that God's purpose in creation was to allow Himself to be experienced by a creature far removed and much lower than Himself. It is thus taught that God created the universe because "He desired an abode in the lower world."

God caused man to have a psychological makeup with which he would experience the greatest possible pleasure in doing something that he knew to be good and beneficial. This pleasure is enhanced according to the importance of the authority declaring that a given action is good. Since God Himself is the highest possible authority, there can be no greater pleasure in performing a job well done than in knowingly obeying the expressed will of God.

For this reason God revealed His will to man. God thus said, "I am God your Lord, who teaches you for your profit, who leads you by the way you should go" (Isaiah 48:17).

Obedience to God's will therefore fulfills His altruistic purpose in creation. The Psalmist thus said, "You let me know the path of life; in Your presence is the fullness of joy, in Your right hand, eternal bliss" (Psalm 16:11).

In order to enjoy the pleasure of such accomplishment, it is imperative that man know that his accomplishment is a matter of his own free choice, and not the result of his nature of compulsion. So that all choices of action be up to the individual, God gave man absolute free will.

Free will is required by God's justice. Otherwise man would not be given or denied good for actions over which he had no control. Beyond this, however, it is also required by the very purpose for which He created the universe, namely, that He give man good through the pleasure of his own accomplishment.

Since the ultimate good is God Himself, the greatest possible good that he can bestow is Himself. There is no greater good than achieving a degree of unity with God, the Creator of all good. Since God desires to give man the greatest good possible, He gave him the ability to resemble Himself.

This is another reason that God gave man free will. Just
as God acts as a free Being, so does man. Just as God acts
without prior restraint, so does man. Just as God can do good
as a matter of His own free choice, so can man. Man is
therefore spoken of as being created in the image of God.

In order for man to have true free choice, he must not only
have inner freedom of will, but also an environment in
which a choice between obedience and disobedience exists.

So that such a choice can exist, God created a world where
both good and evil can freely operate. He thus said, "I form
light and create darkness; I make peace and create evil; I
am God, I do all these things" (Isaiah 45:7).

God made man's psychology so that the more difficult an
accomplishment, the more satisfaction there is in doing it.
God then created the world so that it should present man
with the greatest possible challenge.

The world was therefore created as a place where it would
be possible, but very difficult, to obey God. God allows evil
and temptation to exist, even though they may cause people
to abandon Him and ignore His teachings. Although some
may stray through their own choice, this is the price that
must be paid so that the reward for those who choose good
will be maximized. It is thus taught that for the sake of the
righteous the world was created.

Therefore even the evil and temptations of the world serve
the divine purpose of enhancing the satisfaction of accomplishment of those who overcome them. They thus serve an
important function in man's ultimate reward, and hence, in
God's purpose.

The greater the barriers that must be overcome, the
greater the satisfaction and reward in overcoming them. It
is thus taught, "Reward is according to suffering."

God may have created the possibility of evil, but He
created it in order that man should overcome it. It is thus
written, "Behold, the fear of God, that is wisdom, and to
depart from evil, that is understanding" (Job 28:28).

There is an important dichotomy between the environment required to serve God, and that required for the satisfaction and reward for such service. In order to gain the maximum satisfaction of accomplishment, one must obey God's will in an environment which presents the maximum allowable challenge for the individual. It must therefore be an environment in which neither God Himself, nor the divine nature of God's commandments is obvious. On the other hand, both God and the divine nature of His commandments must be as obvious as possible in the environment where man is to enjoy the fruit of his deeds. The more obvious this is then, the greater will be the satisfaction and reward for man's accomplishment.

God therefore created two levels to existence. He created the present world (Olam HaZeh, עוֹלָם הַזֶּה), as an environment of challenge and accomplishment, where man earns his ultimate reward. He also created a second level, the World to Come (Olam HaBa, עוֹלָם הַבָּא), as the world of ultimate reward. This will be a world where the true nature of all our deeds is perfectly obvious.

The existence of these two worlds thus resolves the dichotomy. This present world exists as the place of maximum challenge, while the World to Come is the environment of the greatest possible realization of accomplishment.

*

Adin Steinsaltz (1937–   )

Steinsaltz was born in Jerusalem, the son of a far-left socialist and early Zionist. He is a rabbi, scholar, teacher, and writer. Steinsaltz studied mathematics at Hebrew University in Jerusalem. At the age of 27 he decided to create a modern Talmud, and in 1967, the first volume appeared. Today, Steinsaltz is recognized as one of the greatest talmudists. He is currently the head of the Israel

Institute for Talmudic Research, presides over two yeshivas, and is a popular lecturer and radio speaker. Following is a chapter from his work *The Long Shorter Way: Discourses on Chasidic Thought.*

THE LONG SHORTER WAY: DISCOURSES ON CHASIDIC THOUGHT

49
Man as the Purpose of Creation

The Kabbalah of the Ari has outlined for us an enormously complicated and even detailed scheme of Creation. Without going into the complexities of this system, we may note that "there are three levels of powerful and comprehensive 'contractions,' giving rise to three comprehensive worlds. These are the Worlds of Briah (Creation), Yetzirah (Formation), and Asiyah (Action). The fourth known World of Atzilut (Emanation), which is higher than these, is Godliness itself." To be sure, there are myriads of contractions within each world itself, levels upon levels of potential that have to make room for realities of all kinds. The fourth and highest of the worlds, Atzilut, is not included in the above because it is beyond our grasp. Even the World of Briah, which is the world of the spirit, of angels, and of higher beings, is accessible to us only with difficulty. Nevertheless, something of this world is available in some degree at least, because the angelic orders function through the Sefirot of Chochmah (Wisdom), Binah (Understanding), and Daat (Knowledge), and these man can contact at his own highest level.

It should be remembered, too, that the contractions between one world and the next are so great that, for all intents and purposes, they are infinite. Not only is this true for the transition from the totally transparent world of Atzilut, which is the Godhead, to the world of Briah, but it is also true for the transition from Briah to Yetzirah and from Yetzirah to our own world of Asiyah. Thus, even the smallest particle of light that comes down from Atzilut to Briah is of the nature of the infinite, and this is similar for each world. There is something so unfathomable and wondrous about anything that descends from an upper world that it cannot be absorbed; it is virtually "infinite."

What is most incredible about all this is the role of man. Placed at the end of the series of contractions, together with gross matter and the evil impulse, man is also the purpose of it all. Having been granted a Divine Soul in a material body, man stands between light and darkness, between good and evil; and in choosing the light and the good, he raises himself to holiness. By doing so he justifies the emanation of all the worlds; he gives the creative process a meaning. Because in themselves, the higher worlds are, to a large degree, totally dependent on God; they are built and are made to function, according to set laws of Divine unfolding. Only man has the freedom to choose and to change the otherwise fixed course of events. It is in this respect, then, that we can be guided by the saying, "As water mirrors the reflection of a face." We surmise that God has put aside His infinite light and concealed it, so to speak, in the three great contractions that brought forth the knowable worlds; and He did this out of a love for man and in order to bring man to a knowledge of God. Thus, all the contractions and withdrawals were meant to provide a place for man in this world, and he is, therefore, the purpose of it all. For the existence of man is possible only if the Divine light is hidden, because His love transcends all flesh, and we could not survive in its effulgence. It is as though God pushes Himself aside in order to make room for man to exist. So does man, in response, have to go toward God and even to abandon all else in order to cleave to Him— "as water mirrors the reflection of a face."

In other words, in response to God's unremitting graciousness to man, His reduction of Himself to enable man to grow

freely, man should abandon all else and hold fast to whatever he knows of Divine reality. Nothing should prevent him
from devoting himself to God. Neither body nor soul, neither
inner nor outer forces should interfere with his acts of gratitude to God; even one's wife and children, money and honor
should be regarded as having no value in themselves, compared to that which is God.

With this in mind, it may be possible to appreciate the
profound insight exhibited by the Sages who fixed the order
of prayer before and after the daily recitation of the Shema
(Hear oh Israel, the Lord is our God, the Lord is One). The
first of the blessings before the recitation is an expression of
thanksgiving for the creation of the world, to Him who
created light and made darkness. But somehow neither this
nor the next blessing seems to have any direct relation to the
Shema. There doesn't appear to be a connection, as there is
in most blessings, before a mitzvah is performed. Nevertheless, we do feel that it is an intrinsic part of the recitation,
because the principal part of the prayer following the
Shema lies in the statement, "And thou shalt love the Lord
thy God with all thy heart and all thy soul and all thy being."
As the Sages have explained: "With all thy heart" means
with all of your impulses and desires, with all your capacity
to love, which includes the love of wife and children, the
strongest of the impulses of the heart. The peripheral loves
of a man are easily given away to God; the truly important
and central ones, those to which the heart of man is bound by
nature and his very life, like wife and children, are surrendered only with much difficulty and are, therefore, more
significant. Similarly, "all thy soul and all thy being" means
to offer up one's very life force and money and livelihood to
God.

Everything, then, has to be given to the Divine, life and
love, well-being and wealth. The obvious objection is that it
is too much to ask of material man. This may help to explain
the preceding blessings, addressed to Him who creates the
light, and so forth. They provide the necessary background,

including, as they do, the passages on the angelic orders who proclaim the glory of God, and who at the same time nullify themselves in His light. "In dread and awe they all do the bidding of their Lord, and they open their mouth in holiness and purity with song and psalm, and they bless and praise and glorify and declare the power and holiness and majesty of the name of God."

In other words, the angels do not see God as close to them but at some distance, as "filling the earth with His glory." And what is that which fills the earth with glory if not man, or Knesset Yisrael, the Divine Soul in the body of the Jewish person? This interpretation of the declaration "Holy, holy, holy, the whole earth is filled with His glory" intimates that for the angels, the seraphs, and the holy creatures on high, God is a transcendental being. His glory is not necessarily in them, but it fills the earth, the nether world of material substance, where God saw fit to place Israel, and from where Israel communes with Him. Hence the angelic orders say: "Blessed is the glory of His name from His place." Why from His place? Because the angels do not know, nor do they have access to, His place. They praise Him and His glory wherever it may be, in whatever place. As it is written: "He alone is great and holy." He is beyond all that can be perceived, even by the higher spiritual beings. At the same time, it is in us (human beings) and between us, that God dwells.

The second of the blessings preceding the recitation of the Shema emphasizes the theme of "great and abundant compassion with which you have loved us, O Lord our God. . . ." It is a love that exceeds "the nearness of God" in relation to all the hosts above who proclaim His glory aloud with reverence, in unison. God thus confers His holy spirit on man, who is thereby able to say "our God," the God who is ours, just as we say the God of Abraham, Isaac, and Jacob. This mode of address betokens a state of belonging, and God, it seems, allows us to assume this possessive attitude and to say "our God" and not the God of the angels.

The love of God for man, and for Israel in particular, like all love which overcomes the flesh, has the capacity of superseding the self of the lover. So that the Divine contracts His light; His boundless love is brought down to the dimensions of man in order to include Israel in the blessedness of His unity and oneness. The very words of the blessing bring attention to this overwhelming compassion—the word "Yetzirah" describing it indicates "more" than the great and abundant love for all created things and points to the fact that "You have chosen us." Israel is chosen as a physical entity as well as a spiritual one, "to render homage to God and with love to be in union with Him."

If one stops to consider this thoughtfully, to meditate on it ever more deeply, it becomes apparent that the blessings were meant to be more than verbal utterances of readiness for the Shema recitation. They are expressions of the "reflection of a face in water," the urge of a soul to respond to God in like manner to His infinite graciousness and to cleave to Him and to be at one with His light. This urge is manifested as a longing for His embrace like that of lovers, of mouth to mouth, of spirit to spirit. The further expressions of this love in the following passages express the readiness to render to God all that one is and all that one possesses: "And thou shalt love the lord thy God with all thy heart and all thy soul and all thy being."

What is behind such an exorbitant declaration? Is it more than a manner of speaking? How is it to be done? For there is no doubt about the sincerity of the urge to cleave to God, to unite with Him in love, spirit to spirit. The answer is given immediately after: "And these words which I command you this day shall be in your heart. And you shall teach them diligently to your children and you shall speak of them when you sit in your house and when you walk by the way, when you lie down and when you rise up" (Deuteronomy 6:5–7).

As it is written in the book, *Etz HaChaim*, this loving embrace is accomplished by the union of the Divine Chochmah, Binah, and Daat with the corresponding Chabad in a person; and this means the study of Torah. For man cannot otherwise unite with the Divine Wisdom, Understanding, and Knowledge. This is what is intimated by the phrase "mouth to mouth, and spirit to spirit." For from the mouth the spirit comes forth and is articulated in words; words of Torah that speak of God and with God. Thus is accomplished, insofar as man is able, the Divine union. For "man shall live by every word that proceedeth out of the mouth of God" (Deuteronomy 8:3), and when spirit meets spirit in this manner, it is called the kiss of Divine love.

However, this is still not the realization of man's life on earth; it does not yet fulfill the final phase of the many contractions of God and His worlds. In order for man to keep the flow going, he has to make his physical body participate in it: The mineral and vegetable substances which he consumes as food and become his body and life force have to be raised to the Divine. "And the glory of God shall be revealed, and all flesh shall see it together" (Isaiah 40:5). The purpose of Creation is the revelation of His glory and that "all flesh shall see it." The emphasis is on filling this earth of ours with His glory, to "change darkness into light and bitterness into sweetness." This is the direction given to man's labors, to help draw the infinite light down. And this can only be done by first raising the "feminine waters," of receptivity, by offering up his own soul and his whole being to God. Thus, the purpose of all Divine worship is not the expression of human desires and needs, nor even the uplifting of man himself; rather, it is the drawing down, or extension, of Divine glory into the world. This is the final goal of spiritual work, even though this work cannot be done without raising the "feminine waters." That is, if man does not make his effort to raise and rise, he cannot make the connection. The contact must be established properly in order for the Divine light to flow. But the essence of the matter and the purpose of man's labors is really to be a channel for the Divine light, that through man this light should be able to illuminate all of the reality of the physical and the spiritual world.

*

Robert Nozick (1938–   )

Nozick was born in Brooklyn, New York. He earned his Ph.D. from Princeton University in 1963 and has taught at a number of institutions. Currently, Nozick is the chairman of the Department of Philosophy at Harvard University. He has written numerous articles and books. The following selection is from his text *Philosophical Explanations*.

PHILOSOPHICAL EXPLANATIONS

Chapter Six
Philosophy and the Meaning of Life

God's Plan

. . . One prevalent view, less so today than previously, is that the meaning of life or people's existence is connected with God's will, with his design or plan for them. Put roughly, people's meaning is to be found and realized in fulfilling the role allotted to them by God. If a superior being designed and created people for a purpose, in accordance with a plan for them, the particular purpose he had for them would be what people are *for*. This is distinct from the view that finds meaning in the goal of merging with God, and also from the view which holds that if you do God's will you will be rewarded—sit at his right hand, and receive eternal bliss—and that the meaning and purpose of life is to achieve this reward which is intrinsically valuable (and also meaningful?).

Our concern now is not with the question of whether there is a God; or whether, if there is, he has a purpose for us; or whether if there is and he has a purpose for us, there is any way to discover this purpose, whether God reveals his purpose to people. Rather, our question is how all this, even if true, would succeed in providing meaning for people's lives.

First, we should ask whether any and every role would provide meaning and purpose to human lives. If our role is to supply CO_2 to the plants, or to be the equivalent within God's plan of fixing a mildly annoying leaky faucet, would this suffice? Is it enough to be an absolutely trivial component within God's grand design? Clearly, what is desired is that we be important; having merely some role or other in God's plan does not suffice. The purpose God has for us must place us at or near the center of things, of his intentions and goals. Moreover, merely playing some role in a central purpose of God's is not sufficient—the role itself must be a central or important one. If we describe God's central purpose in analogy with making a painting, we do not want to play the role of the rag used to wipe off brushes, or the tin in which these rags are kept. If we are not the central focus of the painting, at least we want to be like the canvas or the brush or the paint.

Indeed, we want more than an important role in an important purpose; the role itself should be positive, perhaps even exalted. If the cosmic role of human beings was to provide a negative lesson to some others ("don't act like them") or to provide needed food for passing intergalactic travelers who *were* important, this would not suit our aspirations—not even if afterwards the intergalactic travelers smacked their lips and said that we tasted good. The role should focus on aspects of ourselves that we prize or are proud of, and it should use these in ways connected with the reasons why we prize them. (It would not suffice if the exercise of our morality or intelligence, which we prize, affects our brain so that the intergalactic travelers find it more *tasty*.)

Do all these conditions guarantee meaning? Suppose our ingenuity was to be used to aid these travelers on their way, but that their way was no more important than ours. There was no more reason why we were aiding them (and perishing afterwards) than the other way around—the plan just happened to go that way. Would this cruel hoax leave us any more content than if there were no plan or externally given role at all?

There are two ways we individually or collectively could be included in God's plan. First, our fulfilling our role might depend upon acting in a certain way, upon our choices or cooperation; second, our role might not depend at all upon our actions or choices—willy-nilly we shall serve. (In parallel to the notion of originative value we can say that under the first our life can have originative meaning.) About the first way we can ask why we should act to fulfill God's plan, and about both ways we can ask why fitting God's plan gives meaning to our existence. That God is good (but also sometimes angry?) shows that it would be good to carry out his plan. (Even then, perhaps, it need not be good *for us*— mightn't the good overall plan involve sacrificing us for some greater good?) Yet how does doing what is good provide meaning? Those who doubt whether life has meaning, even if transparently clearheaded, need not have doubted that it is good to do certain things.

How can playing a role in God's plan give one's life meaning? What makes this a meaning-giving process? It is not merely that some being created us with a purpose in mind. If some extragalactic civilization created us with a purpose in mind, would that by itself provide meaning to our lives? Nor would things be changed if they created us so that we also had a feeling of indebtedness and a feeling that something was asked of us. It seems it is not enough that God have some purpose for us—his purpose itself must be meaningful. if it were sufficient merely to play some role in some external purpose, then you could give meaning to your life by fitting it to my plans or to your parents' purpose in having you. In these instances, however, one immediately questions the meaningfulness of the other people's purposes. How do God's purposes differ from ours so as to be guaranteed meaningfulness and importance? Let me sharpen this question by presenting a philosophical fable.

TELEOLOGY

Once you come to feel your existence lacks purpose, there is little you can do. You can keep the feeling, and either continue a meaningless existence or end it. Or you can discover the purpose your existence already serves, the meaning it has, thereby eliminating the feeling. Or you can try to dispose of the feeling by giving a meaning and purpose to your existence.

The first dual option carries minimal appeal; the second, despite my most diligent efforts, proved impossible. That left the third alternative, where, too, there are limited possibilities. You can make your existence meaningful by fitting it into some larger purpose, making yourself part of something else that is independently and incontestably important and meaningful. However, a sign of really having been stricken is that no preexisting purpose will serve in this fashion—each purpose that in other moods appears sufficiently fructifying then seems merely arbitrary. Alternatively, one can seek meaning in activity that itself is important, in something self-sufficiently intrinsically valuable. Preeminent among such activities, if there are any such, is creative activity. So, as a possible route out of my despair, I decided to create something that itself would be marvelous. (No, I did not decide to write a story beginning "Once you come to feel your existence lacks purpose." Why am I always suspected of gimmicks?)

The task required all of my knowledge, skill, intuitive powers, and craftsmanship. It seemed to me that my whole existence until then had been merely a preparation for this creative activity, so completely did it draw upon and focus all of my experience, abilities, and knowledge. I was excited by the task and fulfilled, and when it was completed I rested, untroubled by purposelessness.

But this contentment was, unfortunately, only temporary. For when I came to think about it, although it *had* taxed my ingenuity and energy to make the heavens, the earth, and the creatures upon it, what did it all amount to? I mean, the whole of it, when looked at starkly and coldly, was itself just an object, of no intrinsic importance, containing creatures in a condition as purposeless as the one I was trying to escape. Given the possibility that my talents and powers were those of a being whose existence might well be meaningless, how could their exercise endow my existence with purpose and meaning if it issued only in a worthless object?

At this point in my thoughts I came upon the solution to my problem. If I were to create a plan, a grand design into which my creation fit, in which my creatures, by serving the pattern and purpose I had ordained for them, would find their purpose and goal, then this very activity of endowing their existence with meaning and purpose would be my purpose and would give my existence meaning and point. Also, giving their existence meaning would, retroactively, make meaningful my previous activity of creation, it having issued in something that turned out to be of value and worth.

The arrangement has served. Only occasionally, out of the corner of my mind, do I wonder whether my arbitrarily having picked a plan for them can really have succeeded in giving meaning to the lives of the role-fulfillers among them. (It was necessary, of course that I pick some plan or other for them, but no special purpose was served by my picking the particular plan I did. How could it have been? For my sole purpose then was to give meaning to my existence, and this one purpose was insufficient to determine any particular plan into which to fit my creatures.) However, lacking any conception of a less defective route to meaningfulness, I refuse to examine whether such a symbiotic arrangement truly is possible, whether different beings can provide meaning and point to each other's existence in a fashion so seemingly circular. Such questions press me toward the alternative I tremble to contemplate, yet to which I find my thoughts recurring. The option of ending it all, by now familiar, is less alien and terrifying than before. I walk through the valley of the shadow of death.

To imagine God himself facing problems about the mean-

ingfulness of his existence forces us to consider how meaning attaches to his purposes. Let us leave aside my fancy that
since it is important that our lives be provided with meaning, God's existence is made meaningful by his carrying out
that task, so that—since his plans for us thereby become
meaningful—our meaning is found in fitting those plans.
For if it were possible for man and God to shore up each
other's meaningfulness in this fashion, why could not two
people do this for each other as well? Moreover, a plan whose
only purpose is to provide meaning for another's life (or the
planner's) cannot succeed in doing the trick; the plan must
have some independent purpose and meaning itself.

Nor will it help to escalate up a level, and say that if there
is a God who has a plan for us, the meaning of our existence
consists in finding out what this plan asks of us and has in
store for us. To know the meaning of life, on this view, would
consist in our knowing where we came from, why we are
here, where we are going. But apart from the fact that many
religions hold such knowledge of God's purposes to be impossible (see, for example, *Ecclesiastes* and *Job*), and condemn
various attempts to gain such knowledge (such as occult
techniques and necromancy), and apart even from the fact
that this seems too much a metapurpose, no more satisfying
than saying "the purpose of life is the quest for the purpose
of life", this view merely postpones the question of wherein
God's plan itself is meaningful.

What is it about God's purposes that makes them meaningful? If our universe were created by a child from some
other vast civilization in a parallel universe, if our universe
were a toy it had constructed, perhaps out of prefabricated
parts, it would not follow that the child's purposes were
meaningful. Being the creator of all we see is not sufficient
to endow his purposes with meaningfulness. Granted, the
purposes of God are the purposes of a powerful and important being (as compared to us). However, it is difficult to see
why that suffices for those purposes to ground our existence
in meaning. Could the purposes of scientists so give meaning
to artificially created short-lived animal life they main-

tained in a controlled laboratory environment? The scientists, creators of the animals' universe and life, would be as gods to them. Yet it would be unbearably poignant if the most intelligent animal, in a leap of intuition, did its equivalent of worshiping the absent scientist.

Various gnostic doctrines have held that our world (or universe) was created by a being who was not the supreme divine being, or who was not the only aspect of the divine being. These doctrines envisaged an even more supreme God above the creator of our universe. If some people were fulfilling (and were committed to fulfilling) the local Lord's commands and plans, would it follow that their lives had meaning? How are things different if it is the plan of the top God (must there be a top to the levels?) which we are fulfilling, and how is it to be determined which lead to follow?

Such speculations about levels, perhaps hidden, beneath levels are bewildering, especially since we shall never be able to claim with certainty of some religious doctrine or scientific theory that it has identified the "ground floor", that there cannot be, underneath the fundamental processes or entities E it identifies, even more fundamental hidden ones of a very different character which give rise to the reality or appearance of E. In his novel *The Magus* John Fowles depicts this: each time the central character comes to a view of what is occurring, this is undercut by a new and different deeper view.

I don't say there is no ground floor (would it be better if there were not?), just that we wouldn't know it if we reached it. Even infinite reflexiveness could have a level underlying it, giving rise to it. My purpose is not to emphasize our limits as knowers but to note the power of our imaginations. We can always imagine a deeper reality, deeper even than what turns out to be the deepest; if we cannot imagine its precise character, nevertheless, we can imagine that there is such a thing. There are or can be mysteries within and behind mysteries. To mention only religious views, the Hindus speak of parabrahman which is beyond even Brahman, and gnostic views posit a God beyond the creator of this universe.

Once we are embarked there is no sure stopping; why not a God who created that God, and so forth?

Not only can we not be certain about the ground floor; *it*, if it is the sort of thing that is conscious, cannot be either. For perhaps underneath or apart from everything it knows, is something else that created or underlies it, having carefully covered its tracks. Philosophers have sometimes searched for indicators of a conscious Absolute, in the hopes of making us "at home" and unalienated in the universe, akin to its fundamental character, or somehow favored by it. If there were such an Absolute, it too must occasionally look over its shoulder for a glimpse of a yet deeper, and perhaps not fully friendly, reality. Even the Absolute is a little bit paranoid—so how alien from us can it be?

Yet "like us" does not mean it likes us and is supportive of us and our aspirations, as provided in the vision of a personal God who cares. Is the universe at its fundamental level friendly to our seeking of value; is there some cosmic undergirding so that values, in the phrase of William James, "throw the last stone"? Some have woven science-fiction fantasies of a level that is thus supportive—emissaries from intergalactic civilizations who watch over and guide our progress—and apparently find this comforting. This is not the "ground floor", though. But how important is it anyway that there be a force for value at that level, if it is so distant as effectively to have nothing to do with us? It is not difficult to imagine structures about levels that undercut other levels of reality and their support (or non-support) of value. It is less important, though, whether the ground floor exerts a force for value, than whether we do.

There also might turn out to be fewer levels than appear. The gnostic theorists, for example, whatever their evidence for multiple deities, would have had no way to exclude the possibility that there was but one deity who was schizophrenic or possessed different personalities which he alternately showed. On this view, rather than taking sides in a cosmic clash, the task of man for which he was created (by which personality?) might be to act as therapist to bring together the different personalities of God (unifying them or eliminating one?)—the task might be to heal God. This would certainly give man a central mission and purpose in the cosmic structure, but one might question the meaning-fulness of harmonizing *that* structure. Another similar theory would see man not as therapist but as therapy, functioning as do patients' drawings in psychological treatment, produced with conflicting impulses to express its maker's nature. When such a deity's products come to think of their maker as psychotic and in need of help and integration, is that a sign of a breakthrough of insight in *it*? (This would provide an ironic version of Hegel's view that in his philosophy Geist comes to full self-awareness.)

These diverse possibilities about the intentional and purposeful creation of our universe—by a child in another dimension, by one of a hierarchy of gods, by a schizophrenic God—press home the question of how, or in virtue of what, a religious view can ground the meaning of our lives. Just as the direct experience of God might unavoidably provide one with a motive to carry out his wishes, so it might be that such an experience (of which type of creator?) always would resolve all doubts about meaning. To experience God might leave one with the absolute conviction that his existence was the fountain of meaning, watering your own existence. I do not want to discount testimony reporting this. But even if we accepted it fully, it leaves unanswered the question of how meaning is possible. What is it about God, as usually conceived, in virtue of which he can ground meaning? How *can* there be a ball of meaning? Even if we are willing to treat the testimony in the way we treat accurate perceptual reports, there still remains the problem of understanding how meaning can be encountered in experience, of how there can be a stopping place for questions about meaning. How in the world (or out of it) can there be something whose nature contains meaning, something which just glows meaning?

In pursuing the question of which aspects of God can provide meaning to our existence, we have presented examples of other more limited imaginable beings who do have those aspects (for example, creator of our universe) yet who obviously fail to give meaning. Perhaps it is in that very step to these examples that we lose the meaning. Perhaps the intrinsic meaningfulness of God's existence and his purposes lies in his being unlimited and infinite, in his being at the ground floor and not undercut or dwarfed or put in a smaller focus by any underlying level or being or perspective. No wonder, then, that the meaning disappeared as we considered other cases that purported to isolate the salient meaning-producing aspect of God. (Still, there would remain questions about why only certain ways of being linked—as creation, worshiper, role-fulfiller, or whatever—transmit meaning to people from God.) If the plausibility of seeing God as providing a stopping place for questions about meaning is grounded in his very infinitude and unlimitedness, in there being no deeper level or wider perspective, we can ask what this shows about the notion of meaning. How must the notion of meaning be structured, what must be its content, for (only) unlimitedness to provide a secure basis for meaning and a stopping place for questions about meaning?

*

Mattis Kantor (1943–   )

Mattis Kantor is a prominent Australian rabbi and educator. He was ordained in 1966 at Yeshivah Tomechei Tmimim. Four years later he completed his Master's degree at Fordham University. Kantor is a Lubavitcher hassid and one of the leading authorities on the philosophy of Lubavitch/Chabad. He has written many articles in various journals. Following is a brief excerpt from his work *Chassidic Insights.*

CHASSIDIC INSIGHTS

The Purpose

The speech of God, the creation, conceals the existence of God from us—the created.

Although, as the *human-body* develops, the *human-essence* reveals itself (accordingly), the *development* of our created *existence* (through our activities in the proper directions) does not reveal **to us** *the essence of God* or the existence of God.

The created existence must first be **fully** developed.

The *human-essence* can never **fully** reveal itself, in all its intensity, through the *human-body*, because they are separate entities. One is limited, the other is not.

The created existence, though, and the Creator, God, are not separate.

The created existence is no more than the speech of God.

It requires the continued *speech* involvement of God.

Thus *the essence of God* can and will fully reveal itself through the created existence, to the created existence.

This is *The Purpose* of our creation.

Through our *development of the created existence* (when it is fully developed by our activities), the *essence of God* will reveal itself **through** and **to** our created existence.

Of course ours will no longer be the experience of a *separate existence*.

We will be one with the *essence of God*.

This is the ultimate fulfillment—revelation of *the essence of God* through the *created existence*. All relating to itself in one complete, self-relating intensity. Everything complete and perfect in this self-relationship of the *essence of God*.

Toward this purpose, and fulfillment, we were created.

The Reason

Why?

Why should God, The Essence, in His self-relating completeness as a pure potential for anything, wish to create our existence and then reveal Himself through it?

For the ultimate in self-fulfillment?

His self-relating completeness cannot be lacking in the ultimate in fulfillment, otherwise it would not be a true completeness.

Why, then, should a self-relating completeness that is omnipotent, and the pure potential for everything that is God; why should He even desire, let alone carry out, such a complicated exercise as our creation?

Yet God projects Himself through the numberless levels of *potentials*, *causes*, *sources*, *faculties*, and *systems* to that level of our creation.

For what purpose?

So that we can develop our existence. So that when we have developed our created existence, He will be able to reveal Himself to us.

This is the ultimate in fulfillment. That we, of the created existence, will recognize the true existence.

It is for our benefit.

We will be a *party* to the ultimate in fulfillment.

But **why** the desire for this creation in the first place?

I have a particularly deep desire to build a house.

I have been moving around from one dwelling to another. Now I want a home of my own. But my desire runs much deeper than this, or than any other reasoning.

It is a deep-rooted territorial desire.

I spend a number of years saving up money and dreaming up plans. Finally, after having bought some land, having consulted house magazines and architects, and having decided on the exact details of the house (even the styling of the doorknobs and the color schemes, etc.), I give orders for the house to be built.

Months pass; I go in and out on inspections, and the house is finally completed.

I move into my new home.

Surprisingly, besides the deep *satisfaction* (Nachas) that I have, things have not really changed. Life goes on quite normally.

Before I had the house I felt that I was missing something. Now that I have the house, especially when I have lived in it for a while, I do not find that I have gained anything.

It was a deep desire I had, to build the house. As if something fundamental was missing.

Yet I don't seem to have gained anything now. Although I no longer feel that I am missing that something.

If I wish to understand what it is that motivates me—in my particularly deep desire for a house, for example, I may go to a psychiatrist.

After many hours of talk, when he knows enough of my background, when I have communicated through speech all that I feel, he can help me determine (with his objectivity and knowledge) what my motivations are.

If I am not satisfied with the result, I may go to a greater psychiatrist, and relate all my feelings to him. He will listen to what I have to say, in order to get to know me, and I must talk, to help myself identify what it is I feel.

Once again, when he knows enough about me, he can help me understand what my motivations are.

He is trained and objective. I am untrained and unobjective. He can assist me in becoming more objective about myself.

If I am still not pleased or satisfied with the explanation of my motivations, I will go to a greater, and even greater, psychiatrist, until I go to the greatest.

They however, or he—the greatest psychiatrist of my time—can only help **me** identify my motivations. This he can accomplish through listening to what I say, and evaluating my motivations in the light of his knowledge and objectivity. And then he must elevate me to a greater level of objectivity.

Ultimately, if I wish to go even deeper in understanding my motivations, I can study to become **the** greatest psychiatrist myself. I must, however, be able to view **myself** with the greatest objectivity.

I suspect that I, as a human, cannot reach a very deep

level of objectivity. And this is why I need a second party. The psychiatrist.

I also suspect that I will never fully understand the depths of motivation of a territorial desire.

"Man was created in the image of God."

In order to truly understand why God **desired** to create our existence—to reach a truly objective understanding of that deep-rooted desire . . . is to be God . . .

We exist in the created reality.

We are subjective.

Only God has the ability to objectively understand His deep-rooted desires.

Only God can objectively, and therefore truthfully, understand His deep desire for creation.

EPILOGUE

Personal questions regarding the issue of purposefulness versus purposelessness often arise when one is in a "tight place" or at "high risk." Such situations occur when one is under stress, when one is depressed and has feelings of helplessness or hopelessness, when one feels isolated, when one experiences a recent loss of someone or something important (a loved one, a friend, status), or when one is ill— especially if the illness is painful, debilitating, disabling, chronic, or terminal.

According to Maimonides (*Guide of the Perplexed*), the difficulties that lead to confusion regarding the purpose of creation and life arise from two causes, the first of which is an erroneous idea of self. That is, an individual believes that the whole world exists only for his or her sake, that he or she is the center of the universe, and everything resolves around him or her. The second cause Maimonides isolates is man's ignorance of the nature of the sublunary world and about the Creator's intentions. The consequences of these two errors is doubt and confusion, which may lead many to imagine that some of God's works are trivial, others that they are purposeless, and still others that they are in vain.

During times of "high risk" one is most vulnerable and likely to attempt various dangerous alternatives. Among these are joining cults, experimenting with drugs, and attempting suicide.

Cults thrive when one is in a tight place. Today, especially among the younger generation, there appears to be a tendency to seek a savior in a guru, a mystical cult, eastern mysticism, and the like. Knowing this, cults prey upon those who are most susceptible to their influence. In particular, they target the weak. This weakness may be material, physical, mental, emotional, and/or spiritual. The strategies and tactics employed may vary from the simple to the sophisticated, the subtle to the direct, the legal to the illegal, and the ethical to the unethical. Among some of the techniques employed are direct mailings, utilization of the media, and proselytizing or soliciting at one's front door, free get-togethers where food and entertainment are provided, and sex or drugs.

Often, cults appear to offer concise, simple answers and solutions. They may even present their ideology as scripturally based. The basic claim of cults is that they can solve your problems and troubles if you follow their leader, believe in their doctrines, and do as they instruct. In actuality, they are asking individuals to give up their ability to think independently, their willingness to act, and their control over their own destinies. Stated another way, "What is implied in most of these trends is essentially a surrender of personal existence in exchange for a high measure of liberation from personal responsibility" (Berkovits 1976, p. 16).

Drugs provide a similar panacea, offering an escape from reality and from the responsibility for one's own future. This dangerous allure is present at virtually any street corner.

The ultimate destructive action that one can take is the annihilation of one's physical existence. Suicide eliminates from this existence something that is unique and that can never again be duplicated or replaced. Thus, there is an incalculable loss of potential. Not only does suicide avoid rather than solve problems, but it also sets a dangerous precedent for others. In a sense it can be said that suicide is the ultimate act of greed and selfishness.

How then, can one avoid or survive potential pitfalls? One possible course is to develop a firm, well-rounded foundation based on Torah. Ideally, such a foundation should be developing continuously throughout one's life, so that it is forever getting stronger. Those who fail to develop such a foundation may be likened to a tree whose branches are many and roots are few—the smallest wind will uproot it and blow it over. The solution is to continue to study, learn, and practice.

THE KORAN

Sura 51:55–58

55. But teach (thy Message)
    For teaching benefits
    The Believers.

56. I have only created
    Jinns and men, that
    They may serve Me.

57. No Sustenance do I require
    Of them, nor do I
    Require that they should
    Feed Me.

58. For God is He Who
    Gives (all) Sustenance,—
    Lord of Power,—
    Steadfast (for ever).

REFERENCES

Adler, F. (1975). *An Ethical Philosophy of Life*. Hicksville, NY: Regina Press.

Adler, J. (1960). *A Philosophy of Judaism*. New York: Philosophical Library.

Albo, J. (1930). Sefer Ha-Ikkarim Book of Principles, trans. I. Husik. Philadelphia: Jewish Publication Society.

Altmann, A., and Stern, S. M. (1958). *Isaac Israeli: A Neoplatonic Philosopher of the Early Tenth Century*. Oxford, England: Oxford University Press.

Ashlag, Y. (1974). Purpose of creation. In *An Entrance to the Zohar*, ed. P. S. Berg, pp. 15–18. New York: Research Center of Kabbalah.

Baal Shem Tov. The purpose of creation. In *The Hasidic Anthology*, ed. L. Newman, p. 330. Northvale, NJ: Jason Aronson.

Bahya, A. H. (1980). The Torah: a guide for life. In *Encyclopedia of Torah Thoughts*, trans. C. B. Chavel, pp. 648–655. New York: Shilo.

Belkin, S. (1958). *The Philosophy of Purpose*. New York: Yeshiva University.

ben-Horin, M. (1964–65). The purpose and meaning of Jewish existence (book review). *The Jewish Quarterly Review* 55:260–265.

Berachya (1902). Chapter 21. In *The Ethical Treatises of Berachya, Son of Rabbi Natrona: Ha-Nakdan*, trans. H. Gollancz. London: D. Nutt.

Berkovits, E. (1976). Meaning, value and person. In *Crisis and Faith*, pp. 39–47. New York: Sanhedrin Press.

Birnbaum, P. (1975). *A Book of Jewish Concepts*. New York: Hebrew Publishing Co.

Breuer, I. (1974). Man and the world. In *Concepts Of Judaism*, trans. I. Breven, pp. 135–144. Jerusalem: Israel Universities Presses.

Charles, R. H. (1913). *The Apocrypha and Pseudepigrapha of the Old Testament*. Oxford, England: Clarendon Press.

Cohen, H. (1972). The attributes of action. In *Religion of Reason*, trans. S. Kaplan, pp. 94–99. New York: Frederick Ungar.

Danby, H. (1933). *The Mishnah*. Oxford, England: Oxford University Press.

Einstein, A. (1950). *Out of My Later Years*. New York: Philosophical Library.

Elimelech (1981). Ha Azino, Likutey Shoshanim. In *The Light Beyond: Adventures in Hassidic Thought*, ed. A. Kaplan, p. 97b, 103d. New York: Maznaim.

Epstein, I. (1960). Divine purpose in creation. In *The Faith of Judaism*, pp. 229–250. New York: Soncino.

Epstein, I., ed. (1948). *The Soncino Talmud*. New York: Soncino.

Freedman, H., Simon, M., eds. (1983). *The Midrash Rabbah*. New York: Soncino.

Freud, S. (1962). *Civilization and Its Discontents*, trans. J. Strachey. New York: Norton.

Gordis, R. (1984). The truths of Genesis. *Midstream* 30:20–22.

Graetz, H. (1894). *History of the Jews*. Philadelphia: Jewish Publication Society.

Hapstein, I. H. (1981). Avodath Israel, Te Tzaveh. In *The Light Beyond: Adventures in Hassidic Thought*, ed. A. Kaplan, p. 34b. New York: Maznaim.

Hayyim, H. (1974). The purpose of life. In *The Hafetz Hayyim on the Siddur*, trans. Y. Dvorkas. New York: Feldheim.

Herberg, W. (1960). *Judaism and Modern Man*. Philadelphia: Jewish Publication Society of America.

Heschel, A. J. (1987). The people Israel. In *God in Search of Man*, pp. 420–426. Northvale, NJ: Jason Aronson.

Hirsch, S. R. (1899). The fourth letter. In *The Nineteen Letters of ben Uziel*, trans. B. Drachman, pp. 31–41. New York: Funk & Wagnalls.

Holy Scriptures (1936). New York: Hebrew Publishing Co.

Hyamson, M. (1970). *Duties of the Heart by Bachya ben Joseph ibn Paquda*. New York: Feldheim.

ibn Daud, A. (1986). The second book, introduction. *The Exalted Faith*, trans. N. Samuelson. Cranbury, NJ: Associated University Presses.

ibn Ezra, A. (1950). Yesod mora. In *Treasury of Jewish Quotations*, ed. L. Rosten, p. 249. Northvale, NJ: Jason Aronson.
—— (1987). Commentary on the Bible. In *The Judaic Tradition*, trans. N. N. Glatzer, p. 277. Northvale, NJ: Jason Aronson.
ibn Gabirol, S. *Mekkor Hayyim (The Source of Life)*, trans. Y. Fellig.
ibn Paquda, B. (1970). Second Treatise on the examination of created things and God's abounding goodness towards them, introduction. Third Treatise on the service of God, expounding various grounds for the service of God, blessed be He. In *Hovot ha-Levavot (Duties of the Heart)*, trans. M. Hyamson, pp. 125, 195-196. New York: Feldheim.
ibn Zaddick, J. (1954). Dissertation on Olam Katon: *The Microcosm*, trans. J. Haberman. New York: Columbia University Press.
Israeli, I. (1958). The book of definitions. In *Isaac Israeli: A Neoplatonic Philosopher of the Early Tenth Century*, trans. A. Altmann and S. M. Stern, pp. 23-27. Oxford, England: Oxford University Press.
Jacobs, L. (1969). *Jewish Ethics, Philosophy and Mysticism*. New York: Behrman House.
Jonah ben Abraham Gerondi (1976). Chapter 21. In *Shaarei Teshuvah: The Gates of Repentance*, trans. S. Silverstein. New York: Feldheim.
Kantor, M. (1978). *Chassidic Insights: A Guide for the Entangled*. New York: Ktav.
—— (1978). Part Two: Transition: the Purpose, the Reason. In *Chassidic Insights: A Guide for the Entangled*, pp. 59-61, 63-65. New York: Ktav.
Kaplan, A. (1979). *The Handbook of Jewish Thought*. New York: Maznaim.
—— (1981b). Part one: foundations. In *The Infinite Light: A Book About God*, pp. 7-10. New York: National Conference of Synagogue Youth.
Kaplan, M. M. (1964). *The Purpose and Meaning of Jewish Existence*. Philadelphia: Jewish Publication Society of America.
Kohler, K. (1968). *Jewish Theology: Systematically and Historically Considered*. New York: Ktav.
Landman, I., ed. (1939). *The Universal Jewish Encyclopedia*. New York: The Universal Jewish Encyclopedia.
Lazarus, M. (1901). *Ethics of Judaism*, ed. H. Szold. Philadelphia: Jewish Publication Society of America.
Leeser, I. (1867). Discourse XXI: the object of the creation. In *Discourses on The Jewish Religion*, vol. 5, pp. 338-358. Philadelphia: Sherman.
Leib, M. (1987). When it is good to deny the existence of God. In *Tales of the Hasidim: The Later Masters*, ed. M. Buber, trans. O. Marx. New York: Schocken Books.
Levi, I. (1981). Kedushath Levi, Lekh Lekha. In *The Light Beyond: Adventures in Hassidic Thought*, trans. A. Kaplan, p. 21. New York: Maznaim.

Loew, J. (1981). Netivot Olam, Derekh ha-Hayyim. In *The Jewish Mystical Tradition*, trans. B. Bokser, pp. 157–158. New York: Pilgrim Press.

Luzzatto, M. (1936). Concerning man's duty in the world. In *Mesillat Yesharim (The Path of the Upright)*, trans. M. Kaplan, pp. 18–27. Philadelphia: Jewish Publication Society.

Maimonides, M. (1904). The purpose of creation. In *The Guide of the Perplexed*, trans. M. Friedlander, pp. 272–277. London: Routledge & Kegan Paul.

Mendelssohn, M. (1975). *Moses Mendelssohn: Selections from His Writings*, ed. E. Jospe. New York: Viking.

Nachman of Braslov (1981). Likutey Moharan 18:1–2 and B39. In *The Light Beyond: Adventures in Hassidic Thought*, trans. A. Kaplan, pp. 61–63. New York: Maznaim.

Nahmonides, M. (1980). Deuteronomy 32, Ha'Azinu. In *Commentary on the Torah*, trans. C. B. Chavel, p. 364. New York: Shilo.

—— Has the Messiah come? In *The Judaic Tradition*, trans. N. Glatzer, pp. 327–329. Northvale, NJ: Jason Aronson.

Newman, L. I. (1987). *The Hasidic Anthology*. Northvale, NJ: Jason Aronson.

Nozick, R. (1981). Philosophy and the meaning of life. In *Philosophical Explanations*, pp. 586–594. Cambridge, MA: Belknap Press.

Philo (1929). *Questions and Answers on Genesis*, trans. R. Marcus. Cambridge, MA: Harvard University Press.

Rashi (1976). *The Pentateuch and Rashi's Commentary: A Linear Translation into English*, trans. A. B. Isaiah and B. Scharfman. Brooklyn, NY: S. S. & R. Publishing Co.

Rosten, L. (1988). *Leo Rosten's Treasury of Jewish Quotations*. Northvale, NJ: Jason Aronson.

Roth, C., ed. (1972). *Encyclopedia Judaica*. Jerusalem: Keter Publishing House.

Saadiah, J. (1948). *Emunot ve-Deot, The Book of Beliefs and Opinions*, trans. S. Rosenblatt. New Haven, CT: Yale University Press.

Safran, A. (1975). From existence to the void. In *The Kabbalah: Law and Mysticism in the Jewish Tradition*, trans. M. A. Pater, pp. 250–253. New York: Feldheim.

Schaff, A. (1963). The meaning of life. In *A Philosophy of Man*, pp. 55–61. New York: Dell.

Schneersohn, S. D-B. (1973). *Kuntres Uma'ayon Mibais Hashem*, trans. Z. I. Posner. Brooklyn, NY: Kehot Publication Society.

Schneersohn, Y. Y. (1986). *Chassidic Discourses*, trans. S. B. Wineberg. Brooklyn, NY: Kehot Publication Society.

Schneerson, M. M. (1972). Preface. In *Likutei Amarim Tanya*, trans. J. I. Shochet, pp. vii–viii. Brooklyn, NY: Kehot Publication Society.

—— (1979). *Letters of the Lubavitcher Rebbe*, vol. 1. Brooklyn, NY: Kehot

Publication Society.

Schulman, A. (1971). *Gateway to Judaism.* Cranbury, NJ: Associated University Presses.

Singer, I., ed. (1901). *The Jewish Encyclopedia.* New York: Funk and Wagnalls.

Spinoza, B. (1989). Including the improvement of the understanding. In *Ethics,* trans. R. H. Elwes. Buffalo, NY: Prometheus.

Steinsaltz, A. (1988). Man as the purpose of creation. In *The Long Shorter Way. Discourses on Chasidic Thought,* pp. 328–333. Northvale, NJ: Jason Aronson.

Szold, H. (1978). *The Soncino English Talmud.* New York: Soncino Press.

The Tanakh (1985). Philadelphia: Jewish Publication Society.

Twerski, A. J. (1987). Self-esteem and purpose. In *Let Us Make Man,* pp. 109–112. Brooklyn, NY: Traditional Press.

Vital, H. (1969). Etz Hayyim (Tree of Life). In *Jewish Ethics, Philosophy, and Mysticism,* trans. L. Jacobs, pp. 130–131. New York: Behrman House.

Volozhiner, H. (1988). The primary purpose of creation. In *The Torah Ethic,* ed. Z. Fendel, p. 30. New York: Hashkafh Publications.

Waton, H. (1952). *Key to the Bible.* New York: Spinoza Institute of America.

Weissman, M. (1980). *The Midrash Says Beraishis,* vol. 1. Brooklyn, NY: Benei Yakov Publications.

Wigoder, G., ed. (1977). *The New Standard Jewish Encyclopedia.* Garden City, NY: Doubleday.

Yonah ben Avraham of Gerona (1976). *Shaarei Teshuvah: The Gates of Repentance,* ed. S. Silverstein. New York: Feldheim.

Zalman, S. (1981). Tanya 36. In *The Light Beyond: Adventures in Hassidic Thought,* trans. A. Kaplan, p. 45b. New York: Maznaim.

—— (1981). Likkutei Torah. In *The Jewish Mystical Tradition,* ed. B. Bokser. New York: Pilgrim Press.

The Zohar (1934). Vol. 2 235a, Vayehi (Genesis); vol. 4 155a–b, Terumah (Exodus); vol. 4, 161a–b, Terumah (Exodus), trans. H. Sperling and M. Simon. Brooklyn, NY: Soncino.

SUGGESTED READING

Bar Hayya, A. (1969). *The Meditation of the Sad Soul*, trans. G. Wigoder. New York: Schocken Books.

Adler, F. (1913). Meaning of life. In *Life and Destiny*, pp. 3–13. London: Watts.

Efros, I. I. (1974). Theology. In *Studies in Medieval Jewish Philosophy*, pp. 67–78. New York: Columbia University Press.

Einstein, A. (1954). The meaning of life. In *Ideas and Opinions*, ed. C. Seelig et al. New York: Crown.

Fackenheim, E. (1965). Judaism and the meaning of life. *Commentary* 39:49–55.

Frankl, V. E. (1958). The search for meaning. *Saturday Review* 41:20.

—— (1959). *Man's Search for Meaning*. Boston: Beacon Press.

Gilbert, A. (1970). Meaning and purpose of Jewish survival. In *Judaism and Ethics*, ed. D. J. Silver, pp. 317–326. New York: Ktav.

Heinemann, I. (1981). The purpose of human existence as seen by Greek-Roman antiquity and the Jewish middle ages. In *Studies in Jewish Thought: An Anthology of German Jewish Scholarship*, ed. A. Jospe, pp. 115–161. Detroit: Wayne State University Press.

Heschel, A. J. (1960). The concept of man in Jewish thought. In *The Concept of Man: A Study in Comparative Philosophy*, ed. S. Radhakrishnan and P. T. Raju, pp. 108–157. Lincoln, NE: Johnsen Publishing Company.

Kaplan, A. (1983). Free will and the purpose of creation. In *The Aryeh Kaplan Reader: The Gift He Left Behind*, pp. 150–158. Brooklyn, NY: Mesorah Publications.

Katz, S. T. (1977). Man in the Bible. In *Jewish Ideas and Concepts*, pp. 99–114. New York: Schocken Books.

—— (1977). Man in talmudic literature. In *Jewish Ideas and Concepts*, pp. 115–131. New York: Schocken Books.

Lamm, N. (1964–1965). Man's position in the universe: a comparative study of the views of Saadia Gaon and Maimonides. *Jewish Quarterly Review* 55:208–234.

—— (1986). Man's position in the universe. In *Faith and Doubt*, pp. 83–106. New York: Ktav.

Meiseles, M. Man and creation. In *Judaism: Thought and Legend Anthology on Ethics and Philosophy throughout the Ages* (*Agada U-Mahashavah Ba-Yahadui*), trans. R. Schonfeld-Brand and A. Neuman, pp. 311–317.

Moses ben Nachman (Nachmonides) (1978). The law of the eternal is perfect. In *Writings and Discourses*, trans. C. B. Chavel, pp. 30–36. New York: Shilo.

Narot, J. (1978). Rabbi, have you found the meaning of life? In *The Sermons of Joseph R. Narot*. Miami, FL: Rostrum Books.

Spiro, J. (1987). Meaning. In *Contemporary Jewish Religious Thought*, ed. A. A. Cohen and P. Mendes-Flohr, pp. 565–571. New York: Scribner's.

Urbach, E. E. (1975). Man. In *The Sages—Their Concepts and Beliefs*. Jerusalem: Magnes Press/Hebrew University.

Weiss, P. (1940–1941). The meaning of existence. *Philosophy and Phenomenological Papers* 1:191–198.

Winkler, G. (1982). Purpose of life. In *The Soul of the Matter*, p. 17. New York: Judaica Press.

CREDITS

INDEX

Michael Alter received his Bachelor of Science degree from Florida State University and his Master's degree from Florida International University. He teaches American history, economics, and government at Miami Southridge Senior High School in Miami, Florida. Mr. Alter is the author of *The Science of Stretching* and *Sport Stretch*. For the past ten years he has been a member of the Havurah of South Florida, where he was inspired to study and learn, to research and finally, to write this book.